NEW PERSPECTIVES ON THE SOUTH
Charles P. Roland, General Editor

THE URBAN SOUTH

A History

LAWRENCE H. LARSEN

THE UNIVERSITY PRESS OF KENTUCKY

Copyright © 1990 by The University Press of Kentucky

Scholarly publisher for the Commonwealth,
serving Bellarmine College, Berea College, Centre
College of Kentucky, Eastern Kentucky University,
The Filson Club, Georgetown College, Kentucky
Historical Society, Kentucky State University,
Morehead State University, Murray State University,
Northern Kentucky University, Transylvania University,
University of Kentucky, University of Louisville,
and Western Kentucky University.

Editorial and Sales Offices: Lexington, Kentucky 40506-0336

Library of Congress Cataloging-in-Publication Data

Larsen, Lawrence Harold, 1931-
    The urban South : a history / Lawrence H. Larsen.
        p.   cm.—(New perspectives on the South)
    Bibliography: p.
    Includes index.
    ISBN 0-8131-0309-6
    1. Urbanization—Southern States—History.   2. Cities and towns
—Southern States—History.   I. Title.   II. Series.
HT384.U52A135   1989
307.76'0975—dc20   89-34162

This book is printed on acid-free paper meeting
the requirements of the American National Standard
for Permanence of Paper for Printed Library Materials.
∞

To DAVID

CONTENTS

[Illustrations follow page 82]

TABLES

EDITOR'S PREFACE

The South during most of its long career has been a predominantly rural area, so much so that historians have found it difficult to focus on the cities of the region. Yet the cities have been here all along; Charleston, Savannah, and New Orleans were thriving communities long before Chicago or Kansas City came into existence. Throughout the twentieth century, southern cities have been growing at a rate faster than the national urban average. But the most spectacular southern growth has come since World War II as a part of the celebrated "Sunbelt" phenomenon; this is what has finally awakened scholars to the need for studies on southern urban affairs. Today there is a substantial and growing body of work on the topic.

The author of this able volume is a veteran historian of the urban South, and he has drawn upon his broad knowledge of the subject to provide a functional explanation of the role of the region's cities. He shows that their historical development was long different in certain respects from that of cities elsewhere because the primary purpose of the southern cities was to provide service for the distinctive and expansive agricultural economy of the region. He shows also that in recent times southern cities, while retaining many features that are peculiarly southern, have grown more like other American cities as the entire southern economy and society have grown more like those of the rest of the nation.

The Urban South is an essential contribution to "New Perspectives on the South," a series designed to provide a fresh and comprehensive view of the region's history as seen in the light of the far-reaching changes of the period since World War II. Each volume is expected to be a discrete essay representing an interpretive synthesis of the best research on the subject. Twenty or more volumes are planned.

Charles P. Roland

PREFACE

The 1980 census indicated that many of the South's large cities were among the fastest growing in the nation. Urban boosters all across Dixie took heart from the statistics. Cultural and economic progress accompanied the population increases. Baltimore had supposedly experienced an "urban renaissance," Atlanta had become a "world class city," and Washington had emerged as the "capital of the free world." Still another New South seemed at hand and one with considerable substance. While only the most enthusiastic promoters accepted the premise that urbanization had become a controlling factor in southern life, it had certainly assumed a much more important role than ever before in the region. Indeed, the rapid advance of cities in the years after World War II had served to blur sectional lines. A new term, "the Sunbelt," denoted not only the South but, according to some experts, cities that extended in a great arc from Baltimore around through New Orleans and on to the Pacific Coast from San Diego to Portland.

The rapid urban changes in the South require study, as do, among other things, the roots of southern urbanization, the impact of racial factors on city building, the influence of outside forces, the impulse to continue building towns, and the relationship of urban activities in the South to those in the rest of the United States.

The urban thrust of the South is plainly not new. Throughout American history, the South has sought to construct a system of cities to meet the region's needs and almost always to do so with limited financial resources. The story of southern city building has not on all occasions been a glorious one, of course; it has involved frequent false starts and numerous setbacks. Nevertheless, and despite Jeffersonian protests against cities, the town builders of Dixie have historically forged ahead. By the end of the 1980s they had given the region urban equality with the rest of the nation.

Trillions of individual decisions made by countless men and

women contributed to the construction of cities in the American South. The historian must probe beneath the surface clutter of history, research pertinent primary and secondary evidence, identify trends, and through the use of examples and case studies create a historical synthesis. Much interesting and valuable information must inevitably be omitted, so that it becomes easy to fault the author's judgment. I should therefore emphasize that this book deals less with the question of how cities fit into the southern experience (less, for example, with the reasons why towns in the South differ from those in the North) than with the history of southern cities. I view such great epochs as the Civil War and Reconstruction in the context of their impact on urbanization. Not all occurrences in a city qualify for treatment as urban history; events do so only when they are related to the process of urbanization.

The crux of urbanization, for better or worse, is growth. A successful city, just like a person, starts as an infant, passes through adolescence, and at some point emerges as an adult. The process is sometimes compressed; the San Francisco of Gold Rush days advanced from about 800 people to more than 50,000 people within the span of a couple years. At other times matters move more slowly: the gradual rise of Washington from a hamlet to a world class metropolis is a case in point. To be regarded as cities, communities have had to cross arbitrary, bureaucratically imposed population categories evident in census definitions, which have changed over the years. The addition of certain necessary city services, such as sewerages and organized fire departments, however, helps us identify the stages of urban progress in a historical context. Urbanization is an "independent variable" without an ideological foundation. All of the places that have emerged as cities, from Moscow to New York and from Rome to New Orleans, exhibit some common experience.

Because this study is analytical, it contains, unlike old fashioned descriptive urban histories, no long lists of mayors, agonizing discussions of politics, or detailed financial statements. It also lacks a controlling theory or unique "public culture" synthesis, whether Marxist or Neo-Marxist or one associated with the New Left, the New Right, or some other function. I have tried, using traditional research methods and approaches, to draw conclusions based on evidence about the southern urban experience.

So many people helped me on this project that it is impossible to acknowledge all of them. Fredrick Marcel Spletstoser and Barbara J. Cottrell commented with great care on various aspects of the manuscript. Spletstoser's observations on southern urban history were especially valuable. I had help in a variety of forms from several of my colleagues at the University of Missouri—Kansas City, including W. Robert Brazelton, Jesse V. Clardy, Richard B. Elrod, James Stephen Falls, George D. Gale, Herman M. Hattaway, Richard D. McKinzie, and Stanley B. Parsons. Roger T. Johnson of the International Grains Program at Kansas State University discussed southern agricultural economics with me on a number of fishing trips. Other contributors included Garin Burbank, Lawrence Christensen, Patrick McLear, William Petrowski, William Pratt, and R. Christopher Schnell. James and Marian Cottrell gave me sanctuary on an island in Canada.

1

THE CONSTRUCTION
OF COLONIAL CITIES

The urbanization of the South has been not dramatic but generally mundane and rather bland. Dramatic moments involve destructive epidemics, conflagrations in wartime, and racial confrontations, none exalted or exalting. The building of the urban South saw no major battles between economic titans, no frenzied activities by thousands of land sharks and speculators racing to found towns, no great national projects involving the rapid spread of rails across the continent, no mineral rushes that created whole towns overnight, and no technological or organizational triumphs leading to industrial power on the world scene. Events of importance sometimes took decades to unfold. The history of the urban South from colonial days to the late twentieth century is basically a conventional story of development in a slow and painstaking process. Doggedly moving ahead, southern city builders, plagued by limited resources and frequently unappreciated, labored to achieve incremental growth, helped by a spurt here and there. They sought to construct an urban society compatible with their section's agrarian traditions.

It could be argued that prior to the twentieth century the South had no urban dimension. To prove such a contention we need only draw upon and manipulate traditional truisms and rationales. We might say, for example, that Baltimore, guided by the avarice of its business community, adopted and maintained Yankee values starting early in the nineteenth century. Louisville, in actuality a midwestern town unable to compete against Cincinnati and Pittsburgh for control of Ohio River trade, turned south only to further its greedy search for new markets. St. Louis, originally a southern community, switched sections. The Lion of the Valley abandoned its historic roots in order to exploit the commerce and natural resources of the upper Mississippi River valley. Washington, an aberrant city despite its southern location, found its role in the urban mosaic dictated by national considerations rather than sectional ones.

Charleston, Savannah, Richmond, Norfolk, and other old colonial towns were so closely tied to the plantation system in their formative years as to have developed without crass urban characteristics. New Orleans and Mobile, because of their French and Spanish heritages, represented special cases and were hardly places that under other circumstances would have flourished inside the Cotton Kingdom. Transportation needs, which transcended cultural values, made it necessary to create interior shipping points to help move cotton—Augusta, Columbia, Memphis, and Vicksburg, to name a few. The rising commercial and industrial metropolises of the New South, including Atlanta, Birmingham, and Chattanooga, were really "northern cities" superimposed upon Dixie by outsiders. Jacksonville, Pensacola, and other towns that prospered in Florida failed to belong at all. Indeed, the new cities of the Sunshine State resembled the Northeast more than the South in thought and spirit and starkly reflected the extent of northern penetration into the South of the Gilded Age. In short, cities in the South were out of step with the cherished agrarian concepts that shaped the region.

Unreconstructed Confederate sympathizers who denied that an urban network existed in the South did not do so from a fear of outside forces, xenophobia. Rather, such denial served a useful purpose in a section that had fallen behind the rest of the United States in the construction of cities and hence in economic, political, and social power. On the one hand, a lack of towns tended to buttress claims that the Confederacy had lost to a murderous military juggernaut created by a dominant northern urban and industrial society. On the other, urban places supposedly promoted indulgences and vices that ran counter to the pristine and much-touted values of southern agrarianism. After all, Thomas Jefferson of Virginia, one of the greatest of southern statesmen, had said, "I think our governments will remain virtuous for many centuries as long as they are chiefly agricultural; and this will be as long as there shall be vacant lands in any part of America. When they get piled upon one another in large cities, as in Europe, they will become corrupt as in Europe."[1]

Generations of southern leaders had extolled the rural character of their land, with its plantations and small farms. Of course, no one denied that cities existed in the nineteenth-century South. Indeed, the cities were there for all to see. But the view remained widely accepted that the region had little in the way of urban foundations and that the existing cities bore only a slight relationship or relevance to a nascent southern agrarian civilization that would serve as the foundation of the Confederate States of America. Certainly, the South, both antebellum and postbellum, was predominantly rural. Nevertheless, from the earliest days of settlement, southern development bore an urban physiognomy.

More than 150 years of urbanization occurred in the South before the Declaration of Independence was signed. Although the organized English settlement of the southern seaboard colonies reflected mixed motives, in the initial stages the selection of potential urban sites was of primary concern. Theoretical and practical circumstances dictated the course of action. Religious denominations stressed the need to create ordered communities. Prevailing utopian beliefs incorporated the notion that people should live in organized and compact localities. Other observers saw new colonial communities as offering the chance to reclaim a world lost by the breakup of European tribes and the decline of village life. Military considerations made it necessary to select a defensible location, preferably one on high ground. According to the conventional wisdom of some clerics, the Indians were "children of nature" placed on earth for missionaries to convert to Christianity, but others held that the aborigines were "children of the devil." There was, however, general agreement that the Spanish in Florida constituted an ever-present threat.

The first settlers needed wharves and warehouses to store and receive supplies. In addition, the crown, hoping to control trade, initially believed that centralized shipping points would facilitate the enforcement of trade regulations. Furthermore, health considerations made it desirable to select a location away from swampy ground. Finally, any progress meant expanding from an initial point: the colonists needed a base from which to explore, and eventually to settle, districts away from the coast. When the first pioneers chose a place, at the very least, they wanted a good harbor, a defensible post, a spot easily reached, and a location with ready access to the interior. The first builders of colonies gave little thought to creating communities with an urban or rural character. According to prevailing theories, rural and urban areas were "normal" and complemented each other. In fact, plans called for importing foodstuffs from England on the assumption that the colonists would be too busy with other endeavors, such as panning for gold, to cultivate crops.

British town building in the Virginia tidewater made a bad beginning. In 1585 Sir Walter Raleigh started Roanoke Colony on a sea island off the Carolina coast. The costly venture ended in total disaster; the 108 settlers, who disappeared without a trace, left behind one of the great mysteries of history. Not until early in the next century did the Virginia Company of London, a joint-stock company (an early form of corporation) operating under a royal charter, mount another major effort. In April 1607 an expedition of a hundred men sent out by the company made a landfall at Cape Henry in Chesapeake Bay. After a search that lasted a couple of weeks, the colonists selected a site for a garrison town twenty miles up the navigable James River. The spot, named Jamestown, had excellent defensive features; it was a circularly shaped piece of flat land slightly above sea level and was connected to the mainland by a narrow isthmus. The situation appeared so good that the settlers took a calculated risk, ignoring a warning in the company's instructions that they should avoid "a low or moist place because it will prove unhealthful."[2] Disaster followed; the surrounding swamps proved malarial and the drinking water brackish. Disease, coupled with Indian attacks and other misfortunes, decimated the original settlers. Furthermore, attempts to bring in adequate supplies from England or to buy food from the Indians failed miserably. During Jamestown's "starving time," numerous newcomers died shortly after arriving.

Between 1609 and 1610 the population dropped from 500 to only 60. The arrival of 150 new colonists then brought renewed hope. Governor John Smith ruled with an iron hand and put slackers to work planting corn, so that Jamestown survived. Even though it remained little more than a semimilitary trading post, overly optimistic officials, overlooking inauspicious auguries, decided to undertake an expansion program. The new settlements in the interior of Jamestown Colony included Martin's Hundred, Henrico, and Elizabeth City. In 1617 the discovery that tobacco could be grown in the colony raised hopes for future agricultural progress. Then in 1622 the Indians carried out a devastating surprise attack and destroyed or decimated most of the outlying settlements, killing the entire population of Martin's Hundred. The calamity contributed to the economic ruin of the Virginia Company of London, which had expended more than 200,000 pounds in the colony, with no return on its investment. In 1624 the British government assumed control of Jamestown and converted it into a royal colony owned entirely by the Crown. The new colony was called Virginia.

The English had little to show for their early colonization and town-building efforts. Counting the Roanoke tragedy, only 1,275 of 6,000 adventurers who went to Virginia over the years remained in the colony when the Crown took jurisdiction. At the time of the 1624 census, the two largest centers in Virginia hardly qualified as even glorified villages. Elizabeth City had 257 inhabitants and 69 houses; Jamestown had only 175 people living in 33 dwellings. The course of events was all the more frustrating in view of the efforts made by the Virginia Company of London to promote towns. The decision to found additional settlements before Jamestown had been firmly established had especially unfortunate consequences. In particular, the placement of the new towns along Virginia's main rivers at considerable distances from each other in the wilderness made a coordinated defense against the Indians virtually impossible. In the retrenchment that followed the devastation by the Indians, regulations issued in 1623 required the shipping of all exports from the colony through Jamestown. Other directives had the purpose of stimulating residential construction in Jamestown and enlarging its role as a legislative center. In a major blunder not recognized at the time, the measures failed to take into account the fact that the presence of navigable streams near the new plantations made a central shipping point unnecessary. The rise of tobacco as a profitable crop—and the basis for Virginia's eventual prosperity as a flourishing colony—contributed to the construction in the South of a rural society rather than an urban one.

Efforts continued to create towns in Virginia.[3] In 1655 the House of Burgesses, the colony's general assembly, enacted legislation calling for more communities, but nothing came of the measure, much to the frustration of Crown authorities. Because it proved impractical to ship all tobacco and other items through Jamestown, planners decided to establish additional official ports of entry on the York, Rappahannock, Potomac, and Accomac rivers. Following instructions from London, the House of Burgesses passed a town act in 1662 that provided for a tobacco levy to raise funds to build new communities at the rate of one a year. From a practical standpoint, the legislation failed. An official admitted that over a three-year period the tax netted enough money to construct only four to five dwellings. Jamestown actually experienced a further decline. In 1676 the village had only about a hundred freedmen when insurgents burned most of it to the ground during Bacon's Rebellion. The place never recovered from the blow.

Subsequent general town acts in Virginia in 1680, 1684, and 1691 provided for the creation of a number of new towns, set land prices, and gave promoters economic incentives. While the 1691 act led Williamsburg to be founded as the new colonial capital, Virginia remained almost entirely rural territory. As a contemporary observer noted, "This (i.e.) the number of Rivers, is one of the chief Reasons why they have no Towns; for every one being more solicitous for the Private Interest and Conveniency, than for a publick, they will either be for making forty towns at once, that is, two in every County, or none at all, which is the Countries Ruin."[4] Small and promising settlements did blossom at Norfolk, Portsmouth, and a few other places. Unwarranted optimism and dogged attempts to build cities persisted despite the poor record of success.

A port act passed by the House of Burgesses in 1706 supposedly offered so many benefits and privileges to town dwellers that some Crown officials, discounting all the past problems, unreasonably feared it would prove "detrimental by drawing the inhabitants off from their planting tobacco in the country to the cohabiting and setting up handicraft trades."[5] In 1710 the governor of Virginia, accepting this line of reasoning, repealed the measure by proclamation. The following year a new port bill that represented the last major legislative effort in colonial Virginia to influence town building failed in the House of Burgesses. Even though plans foundered or worked imperfectly, the attempts by Virginia leaders, mostly planters, to construct towns demonstrated their strong belief that the colony needed an urban dimension to strengthen its agrarian economy. Marketing and geographical considerations—rather than any doctrine of antiurbanism—precluded the construction of cities in colonial Virginia. The same situation prevailed in neighboring parts of the Tidewater.

The band of settlers whom Lord Baltimore had dispatched from England in 1634 to found Maryland had been ordered to establish a town. In issuing instructions, he admonished "all the Planters to build their houses in as decent and uniforme a manner as their abilities and the place will afford, and neere adjoining one to an other, and for that purpose to cause streetes to be marked out where they intend to place the towne and to oblige every man to buyld one by an other according to that rule."[6] The pioneers started a small settlement named St. Mary's on a "safe harbor" on the Potomac River near its egress into Chesapeake Bay. Maryland never experienced a "starving time," but for several years depressed tobacco prices on the world market hurt the economy. As in Virginia, most planters shipped from their own docks, and little commerce of any kind flowed through St. Mary's, which functioned only as a seat of government. In 1678 the hamlet had only thirty houses and a few small buildings. The place remained off the beaten path, and in 1695 authorities moved the capital to Annapolis. St. Mary's underwent a steady decline from its already lowly status. It served briefly as a temporary county seat and as an Anglican chapel before it disappeared entirely. There was no need for even a village in what had quickly become an out-of-the-way part of Maryland.

Over the years, Maryland officials had vigorously and overtly tried to promote urbanization. In 1668 the governor issued a proclamation designating thirteen town sites. Nothing came of the scheme because funds to build towns were unavailable from either public or private sources. The Maryland legislature, responding to pressure from the British government, which wanted to improve regulation of the tobacco trade, passed comprehensive town acts on four occasions, in 1683, in 1684, in 1686, and again in 1706. These laws, in addition to dealing with numerous housekeeping matters, specified methods of land acquisition, distribution of town lots, and town locations. The especially ambitious 1683 measure designated forty-seven town sites of 100 acres each. In keeping with Crown policy, the various towns, all on rivers or harbors, were to serve as ports of entry.

As a matter of course, plantation interests opposed city building on economic grounds, from a fear, probably with reason, that closer supervision of the tobacco trade would cost them money. Their lobbying efforts resulted in repeal or nullification of all the town acts. Only a few places founded under the various measures ever passed beyond the planning stage. Annapolis, created in 1689 under special legislation, became within five years the largest incorporated community in the colony, although it had only about forty structures. The mere passage of bills calling for towns did not mean that they were automatically created. Attempts by government planners to designate sites, especially ones that did not favor the economic desires and needs of the inhabitants, failed miserably. Even so, between 1728 and 1751, the Maryland legislature persisted in trying to promote urbanization. It passed no fewer than twenty-three special interest acts calling for towns that in the end were never built.[7] At midcentury, the Maryland and Virginia Tidewaters remained almost entirely agricultural. As long as almost all the plantations stood along the water line, there was no need for major municipalities.

The eight proprietors who in 1663 received a royal charter for a Carolina colony included cities in their grandiose plans to plant semifeudal institutions in the American wilderness. Their schemes gave them vast estates and provided for an economy based on the production of silks, wines, fruits, and oils. The political philosopher John Locke wrote part of the Carolina Fundamental Constitution of 1669, which contained provisions for a local nobility and for both white and black slavery. In planning cities, the proprietors hoped to avoid the mistakes that in their view had been made in Virginia and Maryland. Their designs called for a network of widely scattered agricultural villages, in keeping with desires for an integrated and smooth-functioning mercantile system in which they would regulate and direct economic activities.

Plans that seemed promising on paper failed in practice. People already living in the northern part of the grant welcomed and actually did business with pirates, refused to obey the proprietors' representatives, and conducted most trade through Virginia. Navigation problems caused by shoals, fog, sandbars, banks, and shallow channels made it hard for large craft to reach the tiny northern Carolina river ports. In the southern regions of Carolina, new settlers opposed the proprietors' designs almost from the moment they arrived in the colony. Political and civil strife hampered progress, economic plans failed, white slavery proved impractical, and neighboring Indians were hostile. Eventually the proprietors gave up. South Carolina became a royal colony in 1719, and North Carolina did so in 1729. North Carolina emerged as a land of small tobacco farmers served by a few tiny trading centers. Wilmington (first called Newton) on the Fear River functioned as the chief port of entry.[8]

Large rice and indigo plantations subsidized by the Crown served as the mainsprings of South Carolina's economy, while steady growth characterized the lumber, slave, naval stores, and provision trades. Commercial ties with the Caribbean and with Africa supplemented business relations with England. Coastal commerce increased in importance, and the need arose to distribute and receive goods from throughout the colony. Such conditions called for a city, and so it was no accident that South Carolina's major port, Charles Town, a small village during its adolescent years, emerged as the first magnificent jewel in the South's urban crown.

Charles Town's relatively gradual rise to prominence reflected the experience of the colony as a whole, which had a much slower rate of growth than might have been expected. The city, enjoying an excellent location on a great navigable bay seven miles from the open sea, stood on a low and flat neck of land formed by the junctures of the Ashley and Cooper rivers, both of which afforded excellent access into the interior. South Carolinians considered the tidal harbor, flanked on two sides by sea islands, among the best along the Atlantic Coast. The old Carolina proprietors, after two false starts at selecting an administrative center—nothing ever seemed to go right for them—had in 1679 designed Charles Town as the seat of government. The decision had helped touch off a building boom that saw a hundred houses constructed within a year. Thereafter the colony's numerous problems retarded progress, and Charles Town had only about a thousand residents in 1700. On top of other difficulties, Indian wars decimated the population of the interior. Undaunted, authorities predicted future progress. "The trade of this province is certainly increased of late years, there being a greater consumption yearly of most commodities imported," Governor Nathaniel Johnson reported in 1708. "And the inhabitants by a yearly addition of slaves are made the more capable of improving the produce of the colony."[9]

Charles Town advanced slowly. Its progress was vexed by a severe hurricane in 1728 and a bad fire in 1740. The storm wrecked or damaged twenty-three ships in the harbor, and the fire burned about half the town's 600 houses. The rise of South Carolina rice and indigo plantations helped Charles Town recover from both upheavals. Rice exports amounted to slightly more than 911,000 barrels in 1740, and more than 200,000 pounds of indigo crossed Charles Town docks in 1747 on the way to England. These statistics represented impressive totals. Moreover, business obtained during various wars between England and France stimulated commerce and placed Charles Town on firm financial foundations. With South Carolina's rice and indigo firmly shored up by British price supports, Charles Town's future as a trading center seemed virtually unlimited.

Even as the American Revolution drew near, Charles Town experienced its Golden Age. In 1765 the city had an estimated population of 6,000 whites and between 7,000 and 8,000 black slaves. Charles Town merchants made fortunes marketing their wares within the British Empire. Many of the elegant planters, who divided their time between their plantations and their town residences, owned hundreds of slaves and thousands of acres of land. The white population of Charles Town, a mix of English, Irish, Scots, French Huguenots, and other Europeans, was cosmopolitan and formed a society based more on wealth than on ancestry. By the time of the Revolution, Charles Town had a reputation for culture and energy. "Many will bear me witness when I say that travelers could scarcely go into any city where they could meet with a society of people more agreeable, intelligent, and hospitable than at Charles-town," an authority contended. "In point of industry the town is like a beehive, and there are none that reap not advantage more or less from the flourishing trade and commerce."[10]

Charles Town commercial interests, reluctant to lose their imperial markets and price supports, came rather late to the revolutionary movement. The merchants and planters kept control throughout the hostilities, weathered a British occupation, and were so firmly in authority at the end of the struggle that the class structure, which had been fairly fluid prior to the Revolution, solidified. As a result newcomers found it hard to advance. With the city—renamed Charleston in 1783—outside the British Empire, only time would tell whether a conservative course was the right one to take in dealing with the rapidly changing conditions. In any event the South Carolina center emerged from the Revolution as one of the largest and most significant cities in the new nation; with more than 12,000 inhabitants, Charleston dominated the urban scene in the lower South. Nevertheless, events in the Tidewater that were unrelated to the Revolution soon drastically altered economic and urban relationships in the South as a whole.

By the mideighteenth century Tidewater agriculture had already experienced a major transformation. In the tobacco fields a failure to rotate crops properly led to the exhaustion of coastal plantation lands. As tobacco cultivation moved farther and farther back into the interior and eventually onto the Piedmont, many planters found it no longer feasible to ship from their own docks. Concurrently, Virginia and Maryland officials made concentrated efforts to regulate and centralize tobacco marketing. Tobacco laws in the 1740s, specifically intended to assure quality, compelled planters to take their crops to designated inspection stations prior to overseas transport. This legislation dealt a death blow to several tobacco-exporting villages. London Town in Maryland, one of the places adversely effected by the changes, dwindled in size from forty houses in the mid-1740s to twelve in 1765. Of course, such a community, unless it found a way to alter its economic base drastically, never stood a chance of becoming a city.

Further agricultural changes came with a rise in grain production in Maryland, with wheat becoming an export crop. At the same time there was an increasing demand for goods and products from the growing number of people in Maryland and Virginia. These developments combined to create a need for cities; a few villages no longer sufficed in either colony. Norfolk, designated a town by the Virginia House of Burgesses in 1680, flourished after becoming a borough (a bureaucratic designation) in 1736. Promoters founded Alexandria on the Potomac River in 1749 on a former tobacco plantation. Two other stations, Richmond and Petersburg, showed promise. In Maryland a number of new and old places in the upper Chesapeake Bay region competed for designation as a central market. In this confused picture, Baltimore emerged as the dominant locality. Its successful promoters demonstrated the importance in town building of ample capital, logical plans, and realistic objectives—needs that would later present themselves in similar ventures all across the country.

In the beginning Baltimore appeared to have no realistic prospects, being just another Maryland town site. During its 1729 session the Maryland legislature had granted some speculators the right to settle a place initially designated as Baltimore Town on the north bank of the Patapasco River, just above the head of navigation on Chesapeake Bay. In short order, the first promoters laid out and sold sixty lots and persuaded the legislature to construct an Anglican church. Before much else happened, rival interests secured permission to establish Jones Town, located directly across a river ford from Baltimore Town. The owners of Jones Town platted twenty lots, each of which they sold for the price of 150 pounds of tobacco. Neither Baltimore Town or Jones Town grew to any extent, and a bridge erected at the ford made them virtually one locality. In 1747 the legislature, acting on a joint petition of the two hamlets, merged them into a single town called Baltimore.

In 1750 the new united community acquired a tobacco inspection station, and work started on a public wharf. Little appreciable progress followed. A census taken in 1752 showed that Baltimore had only 200 inhabitants, 25 houses, 1 church, and 2 taverns. The hamlet could afford only a single schoolmaster. The outlook was so unpromising that, according to the wisdom prevailing among local residents, the French and Indian War had curtailed western settlement and had forced people to remain near the coast, possibly keeping discouraged townsfolk from leaving Baltimore and saving the place from extinction. In any event, a band of approximately 900 French Acadians expelled from Nova Scotia by the British migrated to Baltimore but arrived virtually penniless. At this juncture, prospects suddenly brightened; an unexpected influx of money enabled Baltimore rapidly to outstrip surrounding villages and soon to surpass Annapolis as the most important trading center in Maryland.

John and Henry Stevenson, two Scotch-Irish brothers who had made fortunes in the South American guano trade, took a calculated risk by investing heavily in Baltimore. Correctly anticipating the rise of wheat growing in Maryland, they built a successful flour mill. Next they used profits from this venture and others to construct roads from Baltimore into the interior. At Baltimore, which started to grow, they erected warehouses and constructed port facilities. These activities attracted new business and also entrepreneurs, who built gristmills to exploit the increasingly flourishing grain trade. Numerous planters in eastern Maryland converted their tobacco plantations to wheat production. There followed a new round of prosperity, and Baltimore found its immediate hinterland connections enhanced. Baltimore became North America's first boom town, with thousands of newcomers arriving every year. In 1771 a surprised merchant, William Eddis, wrote from Annapolis to friends in London about Baltimore's sudden rise as a commercial center. "The commencement of a trade so lucrative to the first adventurers soon became an object of universal attention," he explained. "Persons of a commercial and enterprising spirit emigrated from all quarters to this new and promising scene of industry. . . . Baltimore became not only the most wealthy and populous town in the province, but inferior to few on this continent, either in size, number of inhabitants, or the advantages arising from a well-conducted and universal and commercial connection."[11]

Baltimore continued to prosper during the Revolution. The city's citizens, most of whom enthusiastically supported the cause of independence, furnished more than the expected quotas of men for military service, denounced suspected Loyalists, and built defenses to repulse an attack that never came. During 1777 the Continental Congress, on the run from British troops, sat in Baltimore. The confiscation of all British property in Maryland, the undertaking of successful privateering activities by locally owned vessels, and the freeing of manufacturing from colonial restraints more than compensated for the severing of the ties of empire. Baltimore shipyards, starting a business that would become important down the line, built ships for the new American navy.

As the war continued and products from overseas became scarce, several manufacturing plants opened. The new operations, all previously prohibited under old colonial regulations aimed at restricting manufacturing, included paper, slitting, linen, and woollen mills. In the course of the war, the number of people in Baltimore increased from slightly more than 6,000 to 8,000. Great physical changes ensued. According to a local historian of the city, "Market street had shot, like a Nuremburg snake out of its toy box, as far as Congress hall, with its line of low-browed, high-roofed wooded houses in disorderly array, standing forward and back, after the manner of a regiment of militia with many an interval between the files."[12] Within twenty years, Baltimore had changed from a small hamlet into a major city.

City building in the North paralleled that in the southern colonies. Natural advantages had loomed paramount in the creation of the four cities that dominated the northern urban scene by the Revolution. Two towns, Boston and Newport, were in New England. Boston, in the Massachusetts Bay Colony, founded in 1630 by members of a trading company dominated by Puritan merchants, had a splendid land-locked harbor that remained open most of the year. Although its two rivers, the Charles and the Mystic, furnished only moderately good access into the interior, New England settlements were very compact and close to the sea, so that communications by coastal schooners were relatively easy. Newport, Rhode Island, settled in 1639 by religious dissenters from Massachusetts Bay, was on an island at the foot of Narragansett Bay; most of the people in the colony lived on the bay's shores. In the middle colonies, the Dutch had laid out New Amsterdam around the Battery at the foot of Manhattan Island in 1625. Just as important as a fine harbor was the wide Hudson River, which was open to navigation by ocean shipping for a 150 miles almost straight north into the interior. In 1664, after the British occupied New Amsterdam during a trade war, it became New York. William Penn established Philadelphia at the confluence of the Delaware and Schuylkill rivers above Delaware Bay. The two streams and their tributaries functioned as magnificent water highways into eastern Pennsylvania.

In the North, unlike the South, where urban rivalries throughout the colonial period remained local in character, cities soon challenged each other and newer communities for control of marketing areas. No sharp geographical divisions or long distances delineated the boundaries between colonies. Agriculture was reasonably homogeneous; there was grain farming throughout the middle colonies and subsistence tillage in New England. The situation invited competition, with New York and Boston mercantile interests clashing along the Hudson. The two cities effectively kept Newport from gaining markets outside Rhode Island. Philadelphia and New York fought over the trade of predominantly farming regions in New Jersey. The tradition of city rivalries surfaced early and would prove tenacious.

The four largest northern colonial cities effectively controlled the region until the Revolution. Other places—New Haven in Connecticut, Albany in New York, and Marblehead in Massachusetts Bay—stayed in secondary positions and were unable to break established commercial patterns. The important towns all developed distinguishing attributes. Boston became a shipbuilding and shipowning center. Its merchants imported goods from overseas and grain from colonies outside New England. The chief exports amounted to large quantities of fish to the Mediterranean and salted pork to the Caribbean. In addition, the cultural pretensions of the Boston Puritans and a turbulent confrontational style of politics set the city apart from its major competitors. Newport, hemmed in by

Boston and New York, had no real future outside Rhode Island. Inside the colony, Newport interests had to worry about Providence's rise as an agricultural center at the north end of Narragansett Bay.

Three factors impaired New York's advance in the first half century after the British occupation: a continuation of Dutch land policies that called for large estates staffed by tenant farmers, stringent maritime and port regulations that stifled commerce, and a fur trading monopoly that wanted to slow hinterland settlement. Once New York had straightened out its pressing internal problems and had begun to produce a grain surplus for export, the city increased markedly in wealth and population. Even so, while conditions improved, disputes between tenant farmers and their landlords vexed the colony down until the Revolution. Philadelphia had relatively smooth sailing. In Pennsylvania William Penn's policies of offering free land and freedom of religion caused Philadelphia to prosper from the first. It quickly became a major grain shipping center firmly under the economic control of Quaker merchants. The same kind of entrepreneurial impulses that shaped successful urban projects in the South figured in the erection of their northern counterparts.

All the northern cities grew against a backdrop of frequent wars between England and France, coupled with clashes with the Indians. In the eighteenth century, a proximity to the war zones in the upper Ohio River valley and French possessions in Canada made hostilities a matter of immediate concern more in the North than in the South. Military activities acted as a forced draft that helped stimulate commerce. Many naval expeditions sailed against Canada from Boston, and in 1755 the British designated New York their main military headquarters for North America. On the eve of the Revolution, Philadelphia, with an estimated 40,000 people, was one of the largest provincial cities in the British Empire. New York had 25,000 inhabitants and Boston 16,000. About 11,000 persons lived in Newport. The British occupied all four cities at one time or another during hostilities. When English forces took New York in 1776, approximately 20,000 refugees temporarily fled the community. With the coming of peace in 1783, all the major northern cities looked forward to building overseas and internal markets free of the restraints imposed by British restrictions and regulations. Unprecedented opportunities seemed at hand for those willing to take the necessary risks.

Prior to the Revolution, cities throughout the colonies were all part of a cumbersome imperial system. Theoretically, under doctrines of mercantilism, the purpose of the North American colonies was to help the mother country achieve economic self-sufficiency. The Trade and Navigation acts, plus legislation restricting manufacturing, embraced the general precepts, although it cannot be said that the British necessarily followed a consistent policy. The Molasses Act of 1733, for example, was special interest legislation intended to curtail colonial trade in the Caribbean. While the British policies gave special treatment to the chief southern products (tobacco, rice, and indigo), much to the benefit of Baltimore and Charleston merchants, the whole concept and its uneven and arbitrary enforcement gave the South complaints in common with the North that helped lead to the Revolution. All the colonies had slavery, and so slavery as an issue did not divide them until after independence.

New Englanders gave little thought to tobacco subsidies, and southerners could have cared less about the Italian cod market. Regardless of these differences and others, however, shared concerns and complaints about the general thrust of English policies after 1763 united the colonial cities. The controversies between the colonists and the mother country tended to obscure the emergence of the concept of a North Atlantic community. Although the odious triangular slave and rum trade remained part of the community concept, so did other kinds of intercourse among the cities and overseas. The Revolution, by bringing together and defining diverse forces, highlighted differences and probably made regionalism in America an inevitability. Still, for reasons of tradition and precedence, the cities, north and south, continued to have many common values and goals, the roots of which stemmed from the colonial experience.[13]

Throughout the colonial period the growing cities cooperated with each other on a wide variety of concerns relating to urban services. They continued to work together to solve joint problems even during periods when relations between individual colonies were bad. As a result, different places generally took similar approaches to problem solving. Fire protection is a case in point. As might have been expected, every city sought to keep abreast of the latest firefighting and prevention techniques and sometimes solicited information from European experts. Fire safety in the closely packed colonial communities was of such serious concern that the authorities enacted legislation placing restrictions on property owners. Charlestonians, Philadelphians, and New Yorkers were all subject to rules governing the storage inside their city limits of flammable substances and explosives. Special Charles Town measures forbade cooking and other fires on ships in the harbor from

9:00 P.M. until dawn and prohibited the boiling of tar on wharves. Each householder had to have a ladder and buckets on the premises and available to firemen around the clock. Fire officials called fire-masters had the power to levy taxes for new equipment, to carry out inspections of potential fire hazards, and to blow up buildings during conflagrations to create firebreaks. In 1754 authorities upgraded Charles Town's five fire engines by equipping them with "sucking pipes" to improve their water intakes. At that time, New York had four engines.

Charles Town regulations detailed the operation of the local fire protective service. Engine managers could "enroll" whites and slaves to run the apparatus, and if the men failed to appear at a fire, could fine white firemen five pounds and give slaves thirty-nine lashes. Both whites and slaves received small hourly wages for turning out and working the engines, drilling once a month at a "publick well." Water resources never posed a problem in colonial Charles Town, but in the aftermath of a destructive fire in 1740, authorities took the first steps toward establishing an efficient and well-organized volunteer department. For several years, Charles Town had the only real fire service in the South. Then, in 1769, Baltimore moved in the direction of creating a structured firefighting company when the "Mechanical Company," aided by a general subscription of funds raised in the community, bought an engine. Everyone wanted to avoid what a governor of South Carolina called the "dreadful Consequences" of a hellish conflagration.[14]

A wide range of protective and benevolent services in Charles Town reflected the city's position as a leading colonial center. An armed watch, financed from import duties and a tavern tax, guarded Charlestonians against "Mischiefs and Insults both from ye Inhabitants and Seafaring people." Two special mounted night patrols checked on blacks found outdoors after dark. "Broils" between town toughs and visiting sailors, robberies committed by "footpads," and other felonious acts all caused problems, but of even greater concern was the ever-present possibility of a slave conspiracy or rebellion. Hence, the elaborate precautions to control the movement of blacks. But while adequate funding was on hand to watch urban slaves, it was not always available for other purposes.[15]

Because the colonial legislature refused to appropriate the necessary money to construct an adequate jail, the provost marshal in Charles Town kept prisoners in "stifling rooms" that he rented out of his own pocket. Public funds did help the city operate a workhouse, most of whose inmates were vagrants and destitute immigrants. Charitable societies, including seamen's organizations and those administered by religious orders, performed many welfare functions. Parish vestries supervised relief for the poor and assessed taxable inhabitants for the purpose. Two classes of people on welfare, the parish and the transient poor, received shelter, clothing, and medical care.[16] As in other colonial cities, regard for the public order in Charles Town extended beyond simply keeping the peace.

Commissioners in Charles Town, appointed by the legislature, managed and regulated a variety of town institutions. Charles Town, which technically never officially existed as a city, had neither a mayor nor a council. Sometimes the plans of the commissioners worked imperfectly. The commissioners of the streets, for example, found it difficult to enforce the street law of 1762 that required the licensing and numbering of certain classes of vehicles. Following the laying out of sidewalks in the late colonial period, carts and wagons frequently interfered with pedestrian traffic, openly violating ordinances. Authorities had better success, for which they were not entirely responsible, in dealing with garbage disposal. Turkey vultures, indigenous to the region, supplemented the services of other scavengers. The unpleasant and foul-smelling birds of prey performed their duties with considerable efficiency. By all accounts, Charles Town appeared a very clean city—certainly more so than its northern counterparts. Garbage, seldom collected, moldered in the thoroughfares and lanes of Boston and New York.

As for education, Charles Town did at least as well as the other colonial cities. The royal government and individuals made liberal contributions. As early as 1711 an English Anglican society established a school. Furthermore, legislative acts allowed the Charles Town commissioners to solicit gifts for educational purposes. Private education served the needs of the elite; courses of instruction emphasized the classics and the social graces. Several persons taught specialized courses in embroidery and needlework for young women. While students in the tax-financed schools paid tuition, a few children attended a free academy funded by an anonymous philanthropist.

Many urban observers felt that Charles Town did not receive a fair share of tax dollars. The South Carolina colonial assembly appointed all the important city officials, and Charles Town had only four of thirty members of the assembly. Critics claimed that the dominant planter interests deliberately kept the town in a subordinate position. Charles Town grand juries repeatedly and without success called the attention of the legislature to the "want of Public Lamps" in many streets.[17] Under the circumstances, Charles Town urban administrators, operating within the context of fiscal and governmental restraints, did a reasonably good job of caring for municipal affairs.

Health matters were of great concern in Charles Town. All the colonial cities experienced epidemics; smallpox attacked Boston on at least four occasions, and in 1741 Philadelphia suffered through a severe yellow fever outbreak. For its part, Charles Town withstood the onslaught of smallpox epidemics in 1733, 1738, and 1760; more than 700 inhabitants died in the 1760 scourge. In 1728, 1732, and 1739, yellow fever visited the community. The city's location in a swampy region virtually ensured that conditions would be unhealthy and fostered a high incidence of both endemic and epidemic disease. Various strategies were used to defend Charles Town against further depredations. An Anglican hospital was one important local institution, and public officials, concerned about preventive measures, established an isolation hospital for sick mariners and epidemic victims on a snake-infested island.

By the middle of the eighteenth century, approximately thirty physicians, many of them trained in Europe, practiced in Charles Town. John Lining, a medical doctor educated in Scotland, courageously conducted experiments on himself concerning "noninfectious epidemic diseases," which he attributed to fluctuations in rainfall.[18] Another medical practitioner, Alexander Garden, specialized in inoculating people against smallpox and improved on methods used elsewhere in the colonies. During the 1760 epidemic he inoculated between 2,400 and 2,800 people in less than two weeks. Many of the Charles Town physicians belonged to partnerships, and all owned their own apothecary shops. The pioneering smallpox vaccination and research efforts placed the city on the cutting edge of the colonial medical frontier.

From the earliest days, town planning was important in the South. The instructions written in London for the first Jamestown leaders had stated, "And seeing order is at the same price with confusion it shall be adviseably done to set your houses even and by a line, that your streets may have a good breadth, and be carried square about your market place."[19] To some extent the pioneers followed orders; the original Jamestown featured a triangular stockade, within which three straight streets formed a triangle, with a market square in the middle.

Later attempts to expand upon Jamestown's plans brought imperfect results. The plats for the various new towns envisioned by the Virginia House of Burgesses generally followed modified grid systems. Yorktown's plan called for eight short streets that crossed a main thoroughfare parallel to the York River. Marlborough, a Potomac River location that failed completely, had parallelogram-shaped blocks and lots. Tappahannock on the Rappahannock River featured a regular grid design with three different street widths. Even more elementary arrangements characterized the sites designated by the Maryland town acts. Vienna Town, Oxford, and Wye all displayed gridiron propositions. Charleston, a Maryland town founded in 1742, had a market square and other public grounds.

Although the exact layouts differed from place to place, the port cities intended for North Carolina had conventional grid designs oriented toward riverfronts. New Bern had a main road running straight back from the Cape Fear River. A wide north and south street that moved away from the river divided Edenton in half. The Carolina proprietors' "Grand Modell" for Charles Town provided a central court, subsequently given over to commercial buildings, as a focal point. As the town expanded, new additions followed along gridiron lines. Provisions for the aborted Margravate of Azilia, designated as the capital of a projected province of the same name in part of what later became Georgia, were quite elaborate. Recommendations envisioned a square city containing no fewer than four 640-acre parks. The residence of the chief public official, the Margrave, would have been on a large central plaza.[20] Such a development showed that an increasingly grandiose approach was being taken toward town planning in the colonial South.

Francis Nicholson, a talented and able colonial Crown executive, played a major role in designing new capital cities for Maryland and Virginia. Nicholson, who had seen first hand how architect and planner Christopher Wren redesigned large sections of London following the disastrous 1666 Great Fire so as to emphasize open spaces in residential districts, had definite ideas about civic design. In particular, Nicholson wanted green squares and circles, with the aim of combining buildings and landscapes to create a harmonious whole. During a short tenure as governor of Maryland, from 1690 to 1691, he supervised the planning of Annapolis. The first layout for the city featured two great circles, a large square, and several radiating streets. Nicholson envisioned "Bloomsbury Square," actually never developed, as the central ornament of a fashionable residential section. The "Public Circle," which was 500 feet in diameter, the location of the legislative building; and "Church Circle," 300 feet in diameter, remained main components of Annapolis's plan. As for the diagonal streets, a combination of a pinwheel alignment at the Public Circle and many bisecting thoroughfares created building sites that were awkwardly shaped. Although his design for Annapolis was not entirely rendered, Nicholson had a second chance.

In the late 1690s, when Nicholson served as governor of Virginia, he played a major role in planning Williamsburg. The result was a significant contribution to urban design. Duke of Gloucester Street, a mile long and ninety-nine feet wide, formed the main axis. The street ran straight east from the Capitol Square to the College of William and Mary, where it broke into three lanes in a goosefoot pattern. Midway along Duke of Gloucester Street, a market square on the south side of the thoroughfare formed an important component of the project. On the north side were the large Palace Green and the smaller Church Square. All the crossing streets had termination points situated so that houses with excellent views of the countryside could be erected. On the public squares and grounds, manicured lawns, flower gardens, wrought iron gates, and elaborately decorated fences enhanced the beauty of the design.[21] These features, taken together with the Georgian architectural styles of the day used for both public and private buildings, made Williamsburg a lovely village in the wilderness.

In 1733 James Oglethorpe's plan for Savannah in the new Georgia colony further demonstrated the extent of the attention given in the South to civic patterns. Oglethorpe, who selected the site on the Savannah River for the community, noted, "The river here forms a half-moon, along the south side of which the banks are about forty foot high, and on the top flat. . . . The plain high ground extends into the country five or six miles, and along the river side about a mile."[22] The town proper was a rectangle divided into six parts. The north and east outskirts contained 5-acre garden lots. Next came many 44-acre farms, and, after that, large 500-acre estates intended for persons willing to pay their own way to the colony. Diagonal roads furnished easy communications to all the gardens and farms. Oglethorpe created a number of political units called wards, each having forty sixty- by ninety-foot house lots. The center of each ward contained a large open square, with frontings on two sides for public buildings and commercial structures. Streets seventy-five feet wide divided the wards and lanes and provided access to the rear of all the house lots. Savannah grew slowly—it had roughly 3,000 inhabitants at the start of the Revolution—and the authorities never completely implemented the plan. The orderly and compact settlement, however, set standards that served well in ensuing years.

The Savannah design, plus those of other towns, helped to establish an urban planning tradition in the South. The response in the North was considerably different. Boston grew in a rather disorderly fashion. New York had an undistinguished design in which a grid predominated. Philadelphia had elaborate and expensive plans set aside by the Pennsylvania proprietors after land earmarked for park squares became prime commercial property. Soon grubby structures covered area that Quaker City designers had envisioned as pleasing open vistas. Savannah or Williamsburg might have suffered the same fate if they had progressed as rapidly. In its planning, Baltimore, during its first flush times, resembled Boston more than neighboring Annapolis. As real estate operators surveyed and built subdivisions, no one gave serious thought to formulating a coherent and comprehensive planning policy. In any event, even though Baltimore added little to the art of civic design, the plans of other southern cities did break new paths; examples include plans for the failed Margravate of Azilia and the moderately successful Williamsburg and Annapolis. A sense of urbanity and calculated rural beauty and symmetry gave a special flavor to the best of the southern urban designs.

Over the course of the colonial period, the towns of the South underwent major societal changes. Advocates of mercantilism, with its fixed view of the Elizabethan world, assumed an orderly class structure. So did the founders of Virginia, Maryland, and the Carolinas. From 1607 to 1776 local elites remained in control. Still, the character of the dominant groups greatly differed from that reflected in musings about the nature of society prior to the start of colonization. Individuals in positions of power were increasingly self-made men rather than foppish lords living on large landed estates. A whole new breed of city people appeared. Physicians, lawyers, and merchants gained in stature as a middle class developed. So did the owners of successful urban-centered enterprises. In Baltimore it was the usual practice for persons to live in the same place where they conducted their business. Wives and daughters often entered the marketplace to work in stores owned by husbands and parents. The old ways died hard. Shipwrights, bricklayers, pattern makers, and members of other skilled trades continued to dress differently from gentlemen with hereditary titles. "The leather apron was omnipresent among the workmen," a resident reported. "Dingy buckskin breeches, check shirts, and a red flannel jacket were their common apparel; and men and boys from the country were seen in the streets in leather breeches and aprons; they would have been deemed out of character without them."[23]

Unlike earlier generations, many of the townsmen had realistic expectations of upward mobility. Continued planter domination of affairs in the colonies and the introduction of slaves into the cities tended to obscure the rise of opportunities and of democratic strains of thought. A growing capitalist spirit translated into strong urban support for the revolutionary movement from Baltimore and Annapolis to Charles Town and Savannah.

Southerners wanted cities. The numerous general and special town acts demonstrated the seriousness of the town-building efforts. The approach taken involved state-directed planning and came close to a complete failure—no place designated as a town site under general legislation ever advanced beyond the village stage. The towns that emerged in the South were the logical consequences of settlement patterns. Entrepreneurs founded Charles Town, whose very success virtually forced the Carolina government to abandon an unpromising location and to move to the city. Further progress for Charles Town followed automatically in direct relationship to the rise of rice and indigo production in South Carolina. The Baltimore story was somewhat similar. The privately built city crushed Annapolis, despite its strong political connections, for status as the number one town in the Maryland and Virginia Tidewater. Momentum generated in Baltimore's early days continued to drive the place forward during the remainder of the colonial period. Once Charles Town and Baltimore came to control their regions, they had no need, unlike the northern towns, to compete against established competitors. Rather, Baltimore and Charles Town consolidated power with little opposition, establishing orderly precedents for later southern urbanization activities. Hinterland agricultural patterns, upon which both towns depended, had the effect of wedding urban progress to slavery. At the time, few people seemed concerned; the institution was an accepted part of life throughout the South and also throughout the North.

At the dawn of the Republic there was no real sense of separate systems of northern and southern cities. Places throughout the colonies cooperated on many matters and developed strong economic ties. No one of consequence viewed the North as taking the lead over the South in city building. Most observers assumed that the cities would continue to work together on many mutual concerns under the august aegis of the United States. A bright day seemed to lie ahead. Such was the legacy of colonial southern city building. The South had constructed towns in relationship to its needs, a characteristic that would continue to distinguish southern urbanization from that in the rest of the nation. As time would tell, despite many ups and downs, it was a method tried and true and one that would serve Dixie well.

2

THE BUILDING OF AN ANTEBELLUM SYSTEM

The early days of the new nation required the emerging cities of the South to make various adjustments. For Charleston the immediate price of independence was high because the termination of British subsidy payments for indigo and rice depressed agriculture in South Carolina. The loss of the lucrative British West Indies trade further complicated the economic picture. The closing of the Sugar Islands in the West Indies to American commerce hurt Norfolk more than it did Charleston. Norfolk, which had been literally flattened by a British naval bombardment on New Year's Day in 1776, had hardly recovered before it lost its main artery of trade. Concessions made at Savannah by the local business community in return for the early withdrawal of British occupation troops gave English merchants a temporary overseas trading monopoly. Other maritime towns— Wilmington, Richmond, and Alexandria—suffered from the consequences of hostilities. A naval blockade checked the commerce of all three places, and British soldiers burned Richmond to the ground.

Fortunately for future prospects, changing circumstances brought new opportunities outside the old Navigation Acts and the restraints on manufacturing. The merchant overseas traders of the former colonial cities could now go to any port that would receive them, as the sailing ship *Pallas* demonstrated in 1785, when it returned to Baltimore from the Orient laden with a full cargo of lucrative China goods. Three years later another Baltimore ship, the *Chesapeake,* dropped anchor in the river Ganges and opened trade with India. Other Baltimore vessels made regular runs to Bremen and attracted many German immigrants. The gradual growth of manufacturing and the start of adjustments in agriculture more than compensated for the loss of British payments.

The ratification of the Constitution, which seemingly gave the federal government the power to formulate a comprehensive trade policy, had obvious implications for the future. In the 1790s Baltimore experienced a new boom, and its population almost doubled from 13,500 to 26,500. The city enjoyed a tremendous overseas, coastal, and fisheries trade. During 1795 alone, a proud local resident claimed that a total of "109 ships, 162 brigs, 350 sloops and schooners, and 5,464 of the 'bay craft' or small coasters"[1] sailed in and out of Baltimore. Other cities, the postwar adjustment behind them, advanced steadily. Between 1790 and 1800 Charleston grew in number of inhabitants from 16,400 to 18,800. At the turn of the century, three other towns had crossed the 5,000 mark: Norfolk—6,900; Richmond—5,700; and Savannah—5,100. Although the North had two cities bigger than Baltimore in 1800, New York with 60,500 people and Philadelphia with 41,200, there was as yet no real urban lag between the two sections as defined by the Mason and Dixon Line. The United States had no large city, and only about 3 percent of the whole population of 5.3 million lived in places with 10,000 people or more; 10,000 was the traditional breaking point used by demographers until the twentieth century to distinguish between large and small cities. Indeed, as the early Republic began to take shape, the future looked very bright for both the urban and the agricultural components of the South.

In 1790, as part of a famous political deal between northern and southern interests, Congress agreed to construct a permanent U.S. capital city in the South. The undertaking was intended to stimulate southern urbanization and was, as a venture, very much in the imperfect old colonial tradition of development at locations designated by public officials. The lawmakers directed President George Washington to select the site. After due deliberation he picked a spot on the Potomac River that he had long believed to hold commercial potential. It lay just up the river from his Mount Vernon plantation, near the villages of Georgetown and Alexandria. Under Washington's personal direction and that of three commissioners appointed by Congress, one of whom was Thomas Jefferson, Pierre L'Enfant, a French-born military architect, started to plan the federal city.

By the end of 1791, Maryland and Virginia had ceded the necessary land for a District of Columbia, and Washington had used his prestige to negotiate the necessary real estate agreements with property owners in the new district. The commissioners were to oversee federal properties and arrange land sales to the general public. It was hoped that the proceeds would generate enough money to pay for government buildings, landscaping, and street paving. The procedures and objectives were akin to those followed in laying out a large subdivision. Economists predicted a rise in land values in direct relationship to the location of projected public buildings. Insiders stood to make handsome profits, so the whole operation smacked of a rather unsavory real estate venture.

L'Enfant based his plans for the city on those for Versailles, France, the site of the palace of Louis XIV. His proposals called for a regular network of rectangular streets and broad avenues, traversed by numerous squares, circles, parks, and triangles. Capitol Hill, the highest point in the District, was the centerpiece of the design. With considerable foresight, L'Enfant planned for very large blocks and avenues 160 feet wide, a provision almost unheard of in an era of very narrow streets. Indeed, his specifications placed government buildings so far apart that detractors spoke sarcastically of what they called "the city of magnificent distances."[2] Shortly after the beginning of construction, quarrels between the mercurial L'Enfant and the commissioners, who thought his ideas unrealistic and unrelated to real estate requirements, led to his dismissal.

But fears that speculators would stay away never materialized. Speculators came in droves, and their bids inflated land prices out of all proportion to the actual values. Many of the speculations failed; a development combine headed by financier Robert Morris defaulted on 6,000 lots purchased at eighty dollars apiece. At one point—a further indication of the magnitude of the collapse—the federal government gained title to an uncompleted hotel which its builders had intended to serve as a lottery prize.

Only loans of several hundred thousand dollars from the Maryland and Virginia legislatures enabled the commissioners to have the new capital city ready for partial occupancy by the federal government after the maximum ten years stipulated by Congress. Still, the District was far from a glorious governmental center. It contained only a few public buildings and small clusters of private dwellings. Swampy ground impeded travel, and the published population figure of 3,200 seemed inflated. Without continuing federal help, the place might have remained a village. Nevertheless, the strong commitment of the U.S. government to developing Washington promised to add a major city to the South.

By 1800 a coherent southern urban mosaic had emerged that consisted of two strata of cities. The first included the Atlantic coastal towns and the second the old fall-line posts that over the years had gradually expanded into towns. Small in terms of population, the locations of the second type at junction points gave them an advantage over any possible competitors. Some places of course had higher hopes and expectations than others. Along the coast, Baltimore aspired to becoming North America's greatest city. Washington's hopes were directly tied to those of the country as a whole. Alexandria and Georgetown had limited prospects. Norfolk and its satellite community, Portsmouth, continued to have vast potential. Wilmington outclassed New Bern and other points and remained the most important town in North Carolina. Charleston occupied a crucial economic position and was also the undisputed cultural center of the South. Savannah had new aggressive leaders with promising plans. The back-country towns were stepping-stones into the interior. Richmond, at the head of navigation on the James River, roughly seventy miles above Norfolk, was the emporium of the Virginia frontier. Other places, Lynchburg and Petersburg in particular, were on the verge of gaining a degree of permanency. In 1786 the South Carolina general assembly laid out Columbia at the fall line on the Congaree River, designating it the new state capital. Situated on a fertile plain by an excellent waterpower, defined as a fall of water capable of generating horsepower, Columbia had reasonably good future aspirations. Augusta, a hundred miles up the Savannah River from Savannah, was an old transportation hub founded in 1735. As southerners moved into the interior, the basis had already been established for an orderly approach to city building by either public or private means.

Richmond, 74 miles from the sea as the crow flies and 150 miles by river, was representative of the successful back-country towns. Even though the James River community was very old, most growth came after the Revolution. As early as 1609 a small exploring party from Jamestown established an outpost at the site. In the middle 1640s, the government of Virginia erected Fort Charles to protect the same settlement, challenging the Indians in their own territory. Several decades of border warfare followed—in 1659 Indian warriors won a bloody battle against a band of colonial border rangers. In 1679 William Byrd built a warehouse, and the place became known as Byrd's Warehouse until its incorporation as Richmond in 1742. A few years earlier, a member of the Byrd family had laid out three square miles of lots and streets, but few people came. In 1779 Richmond, a center of revolutionary ferment (Patrick Henry uttered his memorable "Give me liberty or give me death!" in the city), became the capital of Virginia. During 1781, when the town had about 300 houses, British raiders burned it to the ground. Real growth followed that calamity, as the settlement of the back country proceeded at a rapid rate. In the 1780s state authorities constructed a capitol based on plans that Thomas Jefferson had found in France. In 1794 a canal, which later became part of the important James River and Kanawha Canal, opened around the falls of the James River near Richmond. By the turn of the century, Richmond had achieved firm foundations as a center of both commerce and government.[3]

In 1803 the Louisiana Purchase and the subsequent acquisition of New Orleans introduced a new and unexpected element into the southern urbanization picture. The Crescent City had a past much different from that of the Atlantic ports. Jean Baptist, Sieur de Bienville, the governor of French Louisiana, founded New Orleans in 1718. Although Bienville wanted an economically successful city, he deliberately selected for defensive reasons a swampy uninviting unhealthy spot for the city, more than a hundred miles from the Gulf of Mexico. After a flood had washed away the first crude huts, military engineers surveyed streets, marked off lots, constructed buildings, raised a palisade, dug a moat, and built a levy. New Orleans grew despite the collapse in the 1720s of the "Mississippi Bubble," a financial speculative scheme in Louisiana. At the time New Orleans had 1,600 inhabitants, a volatile assemblage of soldiers, trappers, convicts, and prostitutes. The arrival from France of Capuchin and Jesuit priests, Ursuline nuns, and other respectable women led to a more stable society, but economic progress remained slow: Indian massacres and slave uprisings decimated upriver plantations and settlements and understandably complicated the building of a hinterland. New Orleans only gradually garnered an export trade. When the French lost their North American empire in 1763, about 4,000 people lived in the city.

Political changes and intrigues followed. After a brief British occupation, a Spanish governor arrived in 1766. Two years later local French merchants staged an unsuccessful revolt. Three thousand Spanish soldiers restored order and executed five of the insurgents. "I found the English in complete possession of the commerce of the colony," a new Spanish official with extraordinary powers told his superiors in 1769. "They had in this town their merchants and traders, with open stores and shops, and I can safely assert, that they pocketed nine-tenths of the money spent here."[4] He drove them out, but they soon returned and organized a large illegal trade. Following the Revolution, the Spanish closed the Mississippi River to American commerce. Plots by British, French, and American interests caused serious tensions. First French and then Philadelphia merchants held sway. In 1795 the Spanish granted the United States navigation privileges on the Mississippi River and the right of deposit at New Orleans.

A promising trade developed that appeared threatened when the Spanish retroceded Louisiana to the French. President Thomas Jefferson believed New Orleans so strategically important that the British fleet might be needed to save the United States from a new French menace. Whether his analysis was right or wrong, his 1803 purchase of all of the Louisiana Territory from Napoleon Bonaparte eliminated the danger and brought New Orleans its fourth change of government in less than half a century. When the Stars and Stripes rose over the Crescent City, it contained approximately 10,000 people. The acquisition seemed to benefit the South; almost all financial and political experts believed the Mississippi River crucial to prosperity in the United States. It followed from this interpretation that New Orleans would become a great entrepôt of commerce. If such reasoning was true, happy days lay ahead for advocates of an urban South.

At that juncture drastic changes occurred: the demands of the European textile market, the perfection of the cotton gin, and the development of strains of cotton that grew in upland regions brought about a transformation of southern agriculture. Cotton became the chief economic force in the region. Just as significantly, the new dispensation gave slavery, which some optimistic observers had predicted would die off, a new lease on life. The resurgence of slavery promised to differentiate the South further from the North, where revolutionary reforms had brought the outright or gradual abolition of the institution.

Of greater immediate import was the crisis prompted by a renewal of the Napoleonic wars. The Embargo Act of 1807 and a subsequent program of trade sanctions undertaken by the U.S. government hurt its own maritime commerce. A recovery that started in 1809 stopped with the War of 1812. During hostilities British naval squadrons blockaded American ports. In the summer of 1814 British commandoes raided Washington and burned the government buildings. Shortly afterward, the same units failed in an attack on Baltimore's approaches. Early in 1815, Andrew Jackson repulsed an English force and inflicted heavy losses in the Battle of New Orleans. On the surface the War of 1812 was simply another in a long series of disruptive events that affected city building in the South. Yet its effects were far more serious. Coupled with the shift in southern agriculture, the war gave the North, a region that had appeared in the wake of the Louisiana Purchase likely to be an increasingly isolated and decaying section, a new lease on life.

The United States made a great inward turn after the War of 1812. A set of political ideas, the American System, which envisioned a self-sufficient economy, spurred interest in possible vast markets in the New West. The defeat of the Indians east of the Mississippi River provided an opportunity for the quick settlement and exploitation of hundreds of thousands of square miles of potential farm and plantation lands. William Henry Harrison crushed the Indians of the upper Ohio River valley. On the southern frontier, Jackson overwhelmingly defeated the mighty Creek war machine at Horseshoe Bend. Even though the negotiating of fraudulent treaties and the sordid chapter of Indian removal lay ahead, there appeared to be an opportunity at hand to build a nation. Generations of European geopoliticians had long believed that whoever successfully developed the heart of North America would rise to world power. In 1815, with the coming of peace, the United States had an opportunity to test the theory.

A new chapter in the American experience was about to unfold, and a wave of optimism swept over the nation. The harbor ports that formed a great rim of cities from Maine to Louisiana sought ways to exploit the situation, even in advance of actual significant settlement. Attention centered on a number of jumping-off points into the wilderness. On the northern frontier, Albany on the Hudson River, at the eastern end of the Mohawk Valley, the so-called "water-level" route through the Appalachian Mountains, could serve as a gateway to the Great Lakes. Pittsburgh and Wheeling provided access to the upper Ohio River valley. A few frontier communities and forts already dotted the vast territory. Cleveland was on Lake Erie, and Detroit lay on the banks of the Detroit River between Lake Erie and Lake Huron. Fur traders had started factories above the confluence of the Mississippi and Ohio rivers at Kaskaskia, St. Genevieve, and Cahokia. New Orleans interests established St. Louis just below where the Missouri River flowed into the Mississippi. Cincinnati on the Ohio River showed signs of becoming an important inland commercial port. The main routes of the westward march in the South prior to the War of 1812 had been through the Cumberland Gap into Kentucky, following the National Road, or over the Smoky Mountains into Tennessee. Kentucky entered the Union in 1792 and Tennessee in 1796. Early centers in the New West were Louisville and Lexington in Kentucky, plus Knoxville and Nashville in Tennessee. These places formed a third strata of southern cities, acting as spearheads that gave the region access to large portions of the American interior.

The southern towns in the New West had typical frontier beginnings. Louisville was at the Falls of the Ohio, the only major natural obstruction between the start of the Ohio River and New Orleans. During low water it was necessary to portage around the falls. In 1778 thirteen families built a road station in the vicinity, and two years later the pioneers laid out lots, naming the place Louisville. The hamlet appeared to have little hope of survival; frequent Indian raids and epidemics killed a large number of the original settlers. In "the dark and bloody ground," Louisville gained a reputation as the "graveyard of Kentucky." Louisville had 355 people in 1800; only a good river harbor and a seasonal transshipment business kept it alive. Prospects brightened as more and more migrants moved into the Ohio River valley, and the purchase of Louisiana gave hopes to a rise in downstream traffic.

Virginians founded Lexington in 1770 at a road junction occupied for many years only by a blockhouse and three rows of cabins; bitter warfare with the Indians discouraged settlers. After 1792, Lexington started to gain in population and became the first state capital of Kentucky. In 1810 it had 4,300 people and a reputation as a cultural center with numerous debating and literary societies. Transylvania University, the only real institution of higher education west of the Appalachians, was in Lexington, a place that its fans called the "Philadelphia of the West." Knoxville, which had never had a financial boom during its early years, lost the Tennessee state capital to Nashville in 1817. Nashville stood on a bluff above the navigable Cumberland River; as early as 1710 French trappers had visited the site, situated in the middle of an Indian hunting ground. In 1780 hunters arrived from Kentucky, established a station, and engaged in the Indian trade. Nashville increased slowly to a population of 345 in 1800, as land speculation in Tennessee generated fortunes for a few pioneer families. Real growth started with the rise after 1810 of a large keel boat and barge trade. Following the War of 1812, Nashville leaders and those in the other trans-Appalachian frontier communities expected to hew out inland empires from the immense hinterlands, but circumstances over which they had no control were to end their dreams.

Shrewd moves by New York capitalists transformed the situation. In 1817—a key date in the urbanization of the United States—overlapping combinations of New York businessmen made four crucial decisions. These came during the days of sudden prosperity in New York caused by the postwar "dumping" (a technical economic term of the period) in the city by British merchants of goods destined for American markets. The movement of commodities through New York was so great that merchants found auctions a convenient way to dispose of items in their warehouses quickly. When it appeared that the British might divert shipments to other ports, New York interests persuaded the state legislature to reduce taxes on auctioned articles. As a result the goods kept coming, and postwar economic ties between New York and the United Kingdom were further cemented over the long term as a result. A second action involved plans of the Black Ball Line to run fast packet ships on regular schedules between New York and Liverpool, ultimately enabling New York to corner a large percentage of trans-Atlantic passenger traffic, plus shipments of high-duty "fine freight," which included optical instruments, machine dies, and medical compounds. Third, with strong New York backing, Governor DeWitt Clinton steered a measure through the state legislature and committed the state to the construction of the Erie Canal. The 356-mile-long waterway running from Albany to Buffalo opened over its entire length in 1825 and was profitable from the start. The results more than vindicated the men who had promoted the nation's longest canal to date and the most expensive state-financed internal improvement project. The canal received much national publicity, but a fourth development went relatively unnoticed. New York coastal schooners stopped deadheading back from southern ports. Instead, they started to carry cotton for overseas shipment out of New York.[5]

The various programs enabled New York to surge ahead toward urban greatness. Between 1810 and 1830 the population of the Empire City rose from 96,400 to 197,000, making it far and away the largest metropolis in the United States. New York's northern rivals responded as best they could. Philadelphia leaders persuaded the state of Pennsylvania to finance the Main Line, a highly unsatisfactory and unprofitable canal and railroad that ran from the city to Pittsburgh. Boston investors, by stages, built a railroad from their city to Albany, hoping to tap Erie Canal trade. Experts feared that New York, if not challenged, would monopolize western trade.

The southern coastal cities felt compelled to respond. The Erie Canal, in startling fashion, shifted settlement patterns away from the Ohio River to the Great Lakes. The National Road lost importance. It came to handle less than 200,000 tons of eastbound commodities annually at a time when the Erie Canal carried several million tons. Despite geographical and engineering problems, Baltimore interests boldly undertook to build a 400-mile-long railroad from Baltimore to Wheeling. Actual construction started in 1830, when no one knew whether tracks could even be pushed through the rugged mountains west of the Cumberland Gap. Places to the south of Baltimore carried on as best they could. Baltimore was a wealthy seafaring city with sources of credit that enabled it ultimately to spend $15 million on antebellum railroad projects. None of the other towns had the means of raising a comparable amount of money, and parochial rivalries further clouded matters. Norfolk wanted to build a railroad to the Ohio River and formulated a plan that was aborted by Richmond interests in the Virginia legislature. In retaliation, Norfolk leaders successfully opposed railroad lines and canal extensions desired by Richmond. Even so, despite their antagonism, the two cities combined to stop the internal improvement schemes of Alexandria, Lynchburg, and other cities in the Old Dominion. Curiously, Washington canal promoters had more success than the Old Dominion cities in dealing with the Virginia legislature, in the 1820s receiving money from that body and its counterpart in Maryland to dig the Chesapeake and Ohio Canal from the Potomac to the Ohio. Congress also contributed funds, sold on the idea that the project had national defense implications. The canal failed; it never progressed past the Cumberland Gap. In North Carolina, urban officials could only wish for money to undertake lavish proposals; southern officials did well when they were able to construct several local railroads. A favored promotional tactic involved linking railroad endeavors to the moving of cotton, which was much easier to sell to planter interests than visions of gigantic western commercial markets.

Charleston and Savannah had rival designs to gain Cincinnati connections. Savannah entrepreneurs conceived of a magnificent integrated sea and land transportation network. A great trunk railroad between Savannah and the Ohio River existed only on paper; money was unavailable to build it. The ocean plans had more substance. The Savannahans, with funds raised in New York, commissioned a northern shipyard to construct the steamship *Savannah*. In 1819 the innovative vessel made the first partly steam-powered trip across the Atlantic, using sails on only eight days of a twenty-two-day voyage from Savannah to Liverpool. The ship, ahead of its time, combined elements of technological success with financial failure, and so its promoters' schemes fell short. Charleston did little better. Its leaders produced a grand proposal calling for a railroad to run from the city to Cincinnati. Many urban theoreticians, particularly those with a stake in Cincinnati, predicted that the city would become the transportation and commercial center of the Ohio River valley. An important part of the Charleston railroad plan called for soliciting support from places along the projected 500- to 600-mile route. In 1836 Knoxville businessmen were first elated and then downhearted when they learned that the promoters intended the line to go straight over the mountains, at best a proposition of technologically doubtful feasibility.[6] No really detailed survey had been done; the promoters could offer only faith and a willingness to believe that a railroad could actually be built. Places along the "paper railroad" withheld financial support, as did many wealthy plantation owners in South Carolina. After the Charleston-to-Cincinnati project had died an unlamented death, Charleston's dominant groups concentrated with considerable success on constructing regional railroads designed to carry cotton. Much the same thing happened at Savannah, where the opening of Georgia cotton lands presented the community with the opportunity to hew out a profitable marketing zone. The Georgia Central Railroad between Savannah and Macon opened in 1843. More lines followed. The proliferation had the effect of challenging Charleston in its natural territory. Following false starts, promoters in both Charleston and Savannah scaled down their goals and concentrated on sound and profitable regional railroads.

The course of progress in the upper Ohio River valley thwarted southern hopes that the newly opened country would have strong ties with the South. The region quickly developed important northeastern connections; no southern railroads penetrated the area. Conversely, construction proceeded on canals in Ohio, Indiana, and Illinois designed to link up with a route between the Great Lakes and the Erie Canal. The federal government furthered the trend through the funding of various internal improvements, including Chicago harbor and river projects. Other actions worked against southern aspirations. Land sharks carried on frenzied speculation in thousands of Ohio paper villages. The Panic of 1837, in part nurtured by the unhealthy city-building activities, only temporarily checked the spiral. Well over 90 percent of the towns failed, but urban promotion together with agricultural advances resulted in many country villages and a number of "instant cities." Settlement patterns appeared chaotic. In many places several towns in close proximity to each other struggled to survive. Complicating matters was the railroads' arbitrary establishment of town sites. The communities in what became the Midwest seemed impermanent because of their hastily built structures and transient populations. The pace of settlement demonstrated that cities could be erected in a hurry. Such haste was unprecedented and ran counter to southern practices.

The more resourceful cities fought a massive economic battle for control of the Midwest. There ensued great power rearrangements that affected the sectional struggle.[7] Cincinnati and St. Louis leaders shifted their attention from the South in order to exploit opportunities present in the new midwestern markets. Cincinnati planners saw the problem in terms of the Ohio River and regarded it as a key "natural line." Nineteenth-century economic postulates held that, once established, natural lines of commerce based on geography could not be altered by either secondary or "artificial" lines. Cincinnati's conceptions led to direct confrontations with perceived rivals over markets and transportation connections. Cincinnati won. In consequence Pittsburgh capitalists abandoned attempts to establish an economic empire along the Ohio and turned their attention to ironmongering. Louisville authorities, unable to corner markets north of the Ohio, shifted their attentions to the building of railroads in Kentucky and Tennessee. The problem was that Cincinnati strategists misread the situation and failed to estimate the impact of the Erie Canal correctly. In the end they had secured prosperous Ohio River markets and constructed a large city, but they had not gained the Midwest.

St. Louis and Chicago both entertained hopes of staking out regional empires. The merchants of St. Louis, who thought in terms of natural river lines, wanted to strengthen their bonds with New Orleans by becoming the transshipment center for the produce of the upper Mississippi and Missouri valleys. It was more profitable to operate small steamboats above St. Louis than below it. By 1850 the city, the biggest in the North American interior, held 77,900 people, but success proved elusive. The metropolis of the Mississippi, the erstwhile "Lion of the Valley" and "Memphis of the American Nile," found its hopes dashed by Chicago, a new city on Lake Michigan.

Chicago, incorporated in 1834, after a slow start complicated by the Panic of 1837, achieved a well-deserved reputation as the "Wonder City of the West." Its cunning and able commercial managers rejected the ascendancy of natural lines. They viewed first roads and canals and then railroads as weapons of conquest. Highways constructed by Chicago interests extended into grain-growing areas in Illinois and Indiana. These roads, together with a reputation for honest dealing, helped Chicago businessmen garner a large percentage of the emerging midwestern grain trade. A canal running from Chicago to the Mississippi River took trade away from St. Louis. None of these actions helped the South; no matter what city won the Midwest, the section promised to be a separate one with strong ties to the Northeast. New realities had drastically changed the methods and goals of city making above the Mason and Dixon Line but not below it.

Southerners doggedly pushed ahead with the construction of cities along traditional lines. There was no grand design. It was simply that an increasingly insular plantation society did not require large numbers of cities, nor could it afford the kind of destructive rivalries that occurred in the early Midwest. A fourth stratum of cities, of which New Orleans was the most important, appeared along the Gulf Coast. Another old French town, Mobile, became increasingly significant as cotton culture spread into Alabama and Mississippi. The former Spanish Florida centers of Pensacola, Tampa, and Key West were small communities off main transportation lines. None of these three places entertained serious hopes of quick development. The best hope for rapid urban progress rested in a fifth stratum of cities—inland river ports and railroad centers intended to facilitate the cotton trade. As these cities advanced, they had the potential of providing lucrative markets for the older localities that ringed them. At the same time they furnished a possible way for the South to acquire impressive urban components that would more than counterbalance the loss of the Midwest. The carefully constructed southern network would contrast starkly with the helter-skelter pattern of midwestern city building.

The most important emerging southern interior towns were new cities, products of the aftermath of the War of 1812. Speculators established some, state authorities others. Advances in steamboat and railroad technology assumed considerable importance and compressed into a few years events that would once have taken decades. Steamboats made possible the regular movement of goods and produce on the South's great rivers. The Western and Atlantic Railroad, which in the 1840s opened up northern Georgia, was one of many short lines that contributed to city building. Chattanooga, Tennessee, and Atlanta, Georgia, both started as railroad centers. Atlanta, designated by the state legislature in 1836 as a junction point, was a classic railroad town originally named Terminus. In 1828 the governor of Georgia authorized the establishment of Columbus as a trading post at the head of navigation on the Chattahoochee River. Columbus soon became a river port, from which steamboats carried cotton down the Chattahoochee and Apalachicola rivers to the Gulf. Macon, in central Georgia on the Ocmulgee River, was a hamlet until the arrival of the Georgia Central Railroad in 1843.

Vicksburg, platted by speculators in 1819, eclipsed Natchez, its older rival, to become the chief Mississippi River shipping point for central Mississippi. Wagons, pulled by six to eight yoke of oxen, hauled cotton into Vicksburg for transfer downriver to New Orleans. In 1821 speculators founded Little Rock on the Arkansas River at a ferry crossing used by travelers on the Arkansas and Great Southwest Trail. The town was at a geographic breaking point between a vast alluvial plan to the east and rough highlands to the west. Montgomery, incorporated in 1819 when the Alabama legislature combined three villages into one, soon became an Alabama River port. In the late 1830s, adding another transportation dimension, it obtained railroad connections. The Mississippi River city of Memphis, founded in 1819 after the federal government forced the Chickasaws to relinquish western Tennessee, increased rapidly in population following the establishment of cotton plantations in its immediate three-state region.[8] By midcentury, the urbanization activities had helped to create an integrated communication system. Cotton gathered at Macon moved from there to a portal, say at Augusta, and then on to Charleston for ocean shipment.

Despite their predominantly commercial roles, the antebellum southern cities displayed much in the way of natural beauty. Richmond stood on two undulating plateaus divided by a small valley. Columbia and Augusta had heavily forested rolling hills; Lexington lay in the heart of the lush Kentucky bluegrass country. Rich natural vegetation gave New Orleans and Mobile a semitropical appearance. Atlanta, near the foothills of the Smoky Mountains, featured a multitude of hills and valleys. Montgomery, Memphis, and Little Rock all stood on river bluffs. Vicksburg perched on a neck of land high above the Mississippi. New Orleans and Mobile alone featured much in the way of elaborate planning. Bienville sanctioned a design for New Orleans that had a square, the *place d'armes*, as a focal point. An orderly plan that he devised for Mobile called for a modified grid with a church square. Most of the newer places, including Macon, Montgomery, and Columbia, had gridiron designs. A grid sometimes caused unexpected problems. The Memphis grid went up and down hills that might more appropriately have received different treatment. Chattanooga's city fathers laid out their town as if it had been on flat land rather than in the mountains. Fortunately, throughout the urban South lush foliage obscured the more unsatisfactory aspects of designs. Moreover, some cities sponsored tree planting programs along principal streets and in designated parks and squares.[9]

Southern cities impressed visitors. In 1829, Basil Hall, an English sea captain, identified the fundamental quality that made Charleston a place set apart. "What gives Charleston its peculiar character, . . . " he concluded, "is the verandah, or piazza, which embraces most of the houses on their southern side. . . . Except in the busy, commercial parts of the town, where building ground is too precious to be so employed, the houses are surrounded by a garden, crowded with shrubs and flowers of all kinds, shaded by double and treble rows of orange trees; each establishment being generally encircled by hedges of a deep green, covered over with the most brilliant show imaginable of large white roses, fully as broad as my hand. . . . I was much struck with the sort of tropical aspect which belonged more to the port of Charleston than to any other I saw in America."[10]

Anne Royall, a well-known American travel writer who toured Washington during John Quincy Adams's administration, found the adolescent nation's capital "scattered over a vast surface," but dominated by "enormous" buildings. She wrote, "These edifices; the elevated site of the city; its undulating surface, partially covered with very handsome buildings; the majestic Potomac, with its ponderous bridge, and glistening sails; the eastern branch with its lordly ships; swelling hills which surround the city; the spacious squares and streets, and avenues, adorned with rows of flourishing trees, and all this visible at once; it is not the power of imagination to conceive a scene so replete with every species of beauty."[11] Monumental buildings, white sails, red roses, and shaded gardens all left lasting images in the minds of visitors to the Atlantic southern coastal cities.

No town left a deeper impression than New Orleans. Prior to the Civil War the city was undeniably the cosmopolitan center of the "Old South." In the 1840s a northern sightseer, Joseph Ingraham, a prominent Episcopalian clergyman and religious author, concluded that New Orleans had all the characteristics necessary to make it a great city. He used the city market as a literary device to make a central point. To him, it was a "House of Representatives," where "delegates" from every family studied the interests of their "constituents" through judicious negotiations for products. "If the market at New Orleans represents that city, so truly does New Orleans represent every other city and nation upon the earth," he claimed. "I know of none where is congregated so great a variety of human species, of every language and colour. . . . Persians, Turks, Lascars, Maltese. . . . If a painting could affect the sense of hearing as well as that of sight, this market multitude would afford the artist an inimitable original for the representation upon his canvas of the 'confusion of tongues.' "[12] Who could doubt, after reading those words, that New Orleans was a very special place? Indeed, Ingraham coined the epithet Crescent City.

The city builders of the Old South saw progress in terms more of growth than of furthering southern urban distinctiveness. A strong spirit of enterprise existed in the southern cities. In all of them, merchant organizations played commanding roles in formulating and advancing economic policies. Elected officials either came from the business community or reflected its interests. Greater degrees of democracy in city government failed to have much impact on changing the character or goals of local administrations. As in the North, a strain of boosterism accompanied the rise of cities. "Baltimore," an enthusiast proclaimed, "possesses in its locality . . . advantages surpassing those of any city in the world."[13] A Memphian assured potential northeastern investors, "The plan and local situation of Memphis is such as to authorize the expectation that it is destined to become a populous city." J.W. Grayson, a Louisville promoter, discounting reports that his town was unhealthy, said that it "must, under the guidance of science and wise legislation, become, if it is not already, one of the healthiest cities in the world."[14]

The cotton city of Mobile had a very aggressive community dominated by merchants from the United Kingdom and the American North, almost all of whom arrived in the 1820s and 1830s. Banker and businessman Thaddeus Sanford, a Connecticut Yankee, edited the *Mobile Register*, which championed community betterment. Two other leaders, cotton merchants William John Ledyard from New York and Jonathan Emanuel from England, were civic activists. Ambitious newcomers, just as in many other cities throughout the country, found that money brought quick entry into leadership positions. The elite turned over frequently; family background had little significance. Several leaders acquired a stake in the community by buying real estate. A resident claimed in the 1830s, "No one gets rich who does not embark in speculation in real estate, which has turned into gold in the hands of all who have touched it."[15] Although some entrepreneurs played politics, the majority exercised control through civic and business organizations. In general, the leadership worked together to create a community consensus on municipal concerns and commercial priorities, but affairs did not always run smoothly. Bad management caused the Mobile city government to default on its debts, and attempts to broaden the economic base proved elusive. To reverse a feared stagnation, business leaders put their best face forward. They called for railroads, direct trade with Europe, and manufacturing. A business directory proclaimed in 1850, "A new era of prosperity is beginning to dawn and a bright prospect to the Mobilian is in full view."[16]

J.D.B. DeBow, a strong proponent of southern progress, had predicted much the same thing for the South in 1846 when he wrote about the possible consequences of a splendid urban future: "The growth of the various cities which scatter themselves throughout the valley of the Ohio and Mississippi rivers, has been so rapid and extraordinary. . . . If the West continues its rapid progress for the next fifty years unabated, and the same proportion of population at the expiration of that period reside in cities, it has been computed by an intelligent writer, that there will be at least twenty cities westward of the Alleghany mountains with a population of half a million of human beings each. If such a thought as this does not awake in our bosoms true conceptions of the greatness of our country, we know not what will."[17] The linking of northern and southern urban prospects highlighted an important fact: urbanization continued, as it had in the colonial period, to cut across the emerging sectional boundaries.

The newer southern cities, with minor regional variations, greatly resembled those in the Northeast and Midwest. In downtown areas, eclectic two- and three-story brick rectangular structures lined the streets. Some places had ordinances that prohibited the construction of wooden buildings in congested districts. An occasional building in the Federal, Georgian, or classical style, usually a public hall, church, or bank, broke the monotony of the commercial landscape. As elsewhere in the nation, entrepreneurs considered first-class hotels, theaters, and railroad stations symbols of prosperity and progress. Tax money frequently helped to pay for such places. Advocates appealed to civic pride in gaining support for projects, just as they did for gas systems, street improvements, and other urban services.

Residential architecture in the upper South, except for row houses patterned after those in Baltimore, differed little from that in the lower Midwest. One- and two-story box-shaped single-family dwellings predominated, many of balloon-frame construction. In the lower South, open galleries and verandahs placed to take greatest advantage of cooling breezes were in order, as were high ceilings designed to help the air circulate better. Few columned mansions graced the southern cities; the wealthy usually resided in brick two-story houses set near the street on narrow lots. Many slaves lived in small shacks behind their owners' homes. Utilitarian rather than romantic considerations dictated southern architectural forms. Antebellum southern urban dwellers made no conscious attempt to define a strikingly different mode of architectural expression.

Cities all over the South continued to build upon past accomplishments in urban services and to provide new ones as conditions warranted. As might have been expected, the citizens who paid the most taxes—downtown commercial interests and residents in the solid residential districts—received the best services. Because property owners paid all or part of the cost of street improvements, the quality varied markedly from one part of town to another. According to Mobile's amended charter of 1843, for instance, "the mayor, aldermen and common councilmen shall have a proper regard to the appropriation of the same to the improvement of the different wards of the said city, in proportion to the amount of taxes paid by each ward."[18] A questionable assumption held that expenditures in the better parts of town would spill over and eventually rebound to the advantage of the entire community.

Towns traditionally adopted services pioneered in other places. Gas for lighting purposes served as a case in point. In 1818, Baltimore, using public appropriations, constructed a gas works, and other cities followed suit. In the 1830s a private concern obtained franchises to erect gas works in both New Orleans and Mobile. Louisville and Washington gained gas companies during the 1840s. By that time gas lighting had become a prestige item. A writer for the *Lynchburg Virginian* claimed, "The mere fact that a town is lit with gas is an assurance to a stranger that there are intelligent enterprising, and thrifty people. . . . It is a passport to public confidence and respect, a card to be admitted into the family of well-regulated cities."[19]

The biggest customers of the gas service companies were public street lighting departments. Street maintenance constituted major drains on urban treasuries. Cities sometimes levied special taxes in order to improve the streets; Alexandria charged property owners from $1.25 to $1.30 per foot of frontage to pave a main thoroughfare. Street cleaning continued to be treated in a casual manner. A few places relied, with little success, on abutters, whose responsibility it was to sweep in front of their property. Baltimore had alleys and lanes that no one ever cleaned, while municipal herds of pig helped to keep other streets clear of garbage. Norfolk authorities experimented by using domestic cows to eat vegetable matter that accumulated along the waterfront.

Performance in other areas of civic responsibility varied. Education received lackluster support; New Orleans, Baltimore, and Louisville did not even have public schools until the 1820s. Support for a public system in Mobile came from town leaders who believed that compulsory education would instill in poor whites a sense of public order. Authorities, in keeping with the latest northeastern reform trends, placed an emphasis on the practical three R's at the expense of the classics. Conversely, Charleston and Richmond pioneered in establishing almshouses for the poor in an effort to clear the streets of beggars. With a measure of success, southern cities accepted considerable civic responsibilities, all of which added to growing tax burdens. Even so, as in colonial days, most charitable functions remained in private hands. In championing the private approach, the *Mobile Advertiser* put forward a widely held position: "Private charity speaks of a philanthropic heart—such gifts are the off-spring of genuine benevolence. Men may be found who would vote away public funds for charitable purposes, who would not give a dime from their own pockets to clothe the naked or feed the starving—hence we think that the liberal private donations and tender of personal services made by our citizens, reflect much more credit upon the city, than had twice the amount voted by the corporate authorities."[20] During an 1853 outbreak of yellow fever a local organization called the "Can't Get Away Club" cared for almost 2,000 patients. Benevolent groups, including the Protestant Orphan Asylum Society and the Mobile Port Society, also ministered to the needs of the less fortunate in Mobile society. In Mobile and elsewhere a groping toward more comprehensive social services characterized urban solutions to problems.

Protective organizations ranged from poor to adequate. Boards of health, even though badly underfunded, gradually acquired greater control over sanitary concerns. New Orleans, Baltimore, and Washington maintained public hospitals and infirmaries. The New Orleans Charity Hospital dated from the eighteenth century. Both Baltimore and New Orleans had extensive smallpox vaccination programs. During nonepidemic periods, health authorities in southern cities performed valuable services by gathering data on local sanitary conditions and making nuisance inspections. Police services differed markedly from place to place. Both Louisville and Lexington employed salaried policemen, New Orleans officers had a reputation for being corrupt, and newspaper accounts claimed that the Charleston police slept on duty and frequented grog shops. The English "police idea," which called for regimented uniformed police officers with clearly designated duties, very slowly reached the South. In antebellum days, only Baltimore had a highly organized professional police force. Although the greater number of arrests throughout the urban South were for drunkenness and assault and battery, by the 1850s burglaries had increased to the point where some observers feared a crime wave. In a few cities businessmen set up their own private police units, and some municipalities responded by hiring more night watchmen, so that they appeared to be taking action.

Fire protection remained an even more casual function; no city operated an all-professional force. Volunteer departments, furnished by city governments with engine houses and equipment, guarded against fires. Ordinances excusing members from other civic duties had the aim of encouraging enrollment in the fire companies. At one point Charleston had twenty volunteer units and Richmond seven. Some companies developed dual functions as both fire units and political clubs, so that it was difficult to replace or change them even after they had outlived their usefulness. Pressure for water systems to fight fires led to the building of extensive waterworks in a number of places, including municipal facilities in Richmond, Savannah, and Nashville.[21] A slow upgrading was a major feature of protective activities in the southern cities.

Disorders, fires, and epidemics added to the perils of city life in the South. Baltimore gained a justifiable national reputation as a town prone to violence. August 1835 saw a severe riot following the failure of the Bank of Maryland, and in 1839 only the calling out of a regiment of city guards prevented a nunnery from being plundered. The day after the 1840 presidential election, toughs attacked the offices of the *Baltimore Patriot* and injured several people. In 1847 and 1848 rival fire companies engaged in a number of brawls, while an election riot disturbed the peace in October 1848. Baltimore was not the only center of urban violence. French Creoles and American newcomers fought on numerous occasions in New Orleans; ethnic strife swept over Louisville in midcentury. Keelboat men who frequented Nashville were notorious for lawlessness. Drunken sailors frequently went out of their way to pick street fights in Mobile.[22]

Almost every place claimed to have had a "Great Fire." In 1815 flames consumed 400 houses in Petersburg. Augusta underwent a trial by fire in 1829 when a conflagration gutted between 400 and 500 buildings and accounted for $1 million in damages. A blaze that destroyed Louisville's commercial district in 1840 sparked a statewide movement for better fire protection in Kentucky.[23] Epidemics occurred with depressing regularity. In 1822 a a scourge of yellow fever threatened to depopulate Louisville. New Orleans, known as the "wet grave," experienced almost annual epidemics. Between 1810 and 1837 alone there were fifteen yellow fever outbreaks. In 1839 yellow fever killed more than 1,300, and another 1,800 perished after contracting the disease in 1841. A sixth of the population of Memphis expired from yellow fever in 1828.[24] During 1832 a national cholera pandemic affected the South. In September 1832, 125 of 500 inmates at the Baltimore almshouse perished from cholera. Even under the best of circumstances, a dark shroud of calamity hung over the cities of the South.

The troubles that Savannah encountered in 1820 were comparable to those of other cities. On the night of January 11, 1820, a fire that started in a livery stable raged out of control, fanned by high northeast winds. The city's half dozen fire companies, supported by hastily organized bucket brigades, failed to check the flames. Two explosions of illegally stored gunpowder helped spread the conflagration. Before the blaze had spent its fury and died the following afternoon, 463 buildings lay in smoking ruins, and between 3,000 and 4,000 people were homeless. The distaster almost entirely wiped out the business section of Savannah. "The town presents a most wretched picture," an eyewitness to the disaster wrote. "There is not a hardware store, Saddler's shop, Apothecary's shop, or scarcely a dry goods store left."[25]

No sooner had the city started a slow recovery from the $5 million holocaust—relief donations came from all over America—when yellow fever struck Savannah. Heavy spring and summer rains filled many cellars in the burnt district, creating excellent breeding places for mosquitoes. At first, authorities denied that an epidemic was in progress. The mayor said that "one . . . section . . . has been rather unusually unhealthy . . . ,but the disease . . . is confined principally to strangers and people of intemperate, dissolute habits . . . and is no more than the ordinary bilious fever of the climate."[26] Such sophistry failed to stop the epidemic. In September the mayor, in the very same prepared statement in which he said that yellow fever was not present in Savannah, advised all those who could do so to flee the city. More than 6,000 of the 7,500 residents took his advice, but before the malignancy ended with the coming of an October frost, about 700 inhabitants had perished. The twin blows of the fire and the fever badly hurt Savannah. Despite the elaborate plans of its business leaders, Savannah failed to grow during the remainder of the decade. Its plight served as a grim reminder of the effects that disasters could have on a city at a crucial moment. Only the steady expansion of cotton production in the lower South and the exploitation of the West Indies lumber trade enabled Savannah to resume its advance.

The trend toward making cotton the fabric of the southern economy continued throughout the antebellum period. Cotton production rose from 40 million pounds in 1834 to 457 million pounds in 1844. By midcentury the amount had increased to nearly a billion pounds. The Cotton Kingdom contained the seeds of its own destruction. A reliance on slave labor and on foreign markets automatically set the South apart from the rest of the country without isolating the region. The special protection that the cotton system required for survival helped ignite an unwanted sectional conflict.

Balancing free and slave states became a national policy. The American System lost its attraction for southerners, who heartily disapproved of high tariffs designed to build up northeastern manufacturing and to fund internal improvement projects. The South Carolina Nullification Crisis and the subsequent Compromise of 1833 signaled the inherent danger; a tariff controversy over technical issues held the potential for altering the course of Union.

The move toward states' rights reflected a desire to preserve and protect a system that was actually relatively new. When the abolitionist movement started in the 1830s, southern agrarian leaders reacted by trying to construct a closed society inside the South and by framing elaborate arguments designed to defend the rights of minorities within and outside the halls of Congress. Statesman John C. Calhoun called slavery a "basic good," southern postmasters pulled abolitionist tracts from the mails, and free black seamen were not allowed ashore in some southern ports. Such actions further hurt the emerging urban South, in part because the developing sectional creed posed a grave threat to the traditional openness and cooperation between the nation's cities.

Routine commercial intercourse, taken for granted over the decades, became suspect in the eyes of southern nationalists, who made impassioned speeches about the threat posed by alleged northern dominance of the South. "We rise from between sheets made in Northern looms," a southerner said in 1850, "and pillows of Northern feathers, to wash in basins made in the North, dry our beards on Northern towels, and dress ourselves in garments made in Northern looms; we eat from Northern plates and dishes; our rooms are swept with Northern brooms; our gardens are dug with Northern spades and our bread kneaded in trays or dishes of Northern wood or tin; and the very wood which feeds our fires is cut with Northern axes, helved with hickory brought from Connecticut or New York; and when we die our bodies are wrapped in shrouds manufactured in New England, put in coffins made in the North."[27] It followed from such reasoning that the South should build a manufacturing base to meet sectional needs. As events had already proved, this good was much more easily discussed than accomplished.

Supporters of southern industry had to swim against an agrarian tide. Slave labor was very costly; skilled white labor was not readily available. A few states had laws making business incorporation difficult. As cotton interests became more and more entrenched, some agrarians found industry inherently evil and debilitating, especially when compared with the supposedly more noble pursuit of farming. Most experts, while concerned about the impact of manufacturing on society, rejected such an extremist position. Paternalistic experiments carried out in New England mill towns, notably Lawrence and Lowell in Massachusetts, had positive results; the use of closely supervised women operatives hired for specific tours of duty had checked the possible growth of a militant proletariat.

In the South, the Piedmont, with its numerous excellent sources of waterpower, had articulate proponents of manufacturing. As early as 1828 the North Carolina legislature proclaimed that the "hand of nature" dictated the rise of industry in the Tar Heel State. William Gregg was one of the leading supporters of an industrial South. His model cotton mill at Graniteville, South Carolina, attempted to prove that Piedmont facilities could effectively compete with those in New England. A South Carolina editor claimed that the use of slave labor would automatically lead to industrial success, but Gregg disagreed and asserted that adequate capitalization represented the key element. One expert contended that underfinanced factories, which he called "cheap factories," would be self-defeating, while an Alabama creditor said cotton mill owners were "public benefactors" who would provide jobs for poor whites and render the South independent of outside influence. No massive amounts of capital were forthcoming, however. Southern money remained tied up in slaves and plantations; northern funds flowed in other directions.[28] Manufacturing that started in Dixie was primarily consumer oriented, geared to the production of wooden containers, furniture products, leather goods, and hardware.[29] These were the very kinds of products that impassioned orators claimed placed the South under northern domination.

The extensive use of slave labor made the southern cities an important cog in the Peculiar Institution. Because of low wage levels, chronic shortages of white day laborers plagued the southern cities. In antebellum days the South attracted only a small percentage of the hundreds of thousands of immigrants who came to America. Considerable numbers of Irish and German aliens did settle in New Orleans, Louisville, and Baltimore. Still, in numerous places both foreign-born and native white workers found it difficult to compete with slave labor. Even though the number of slaves in Baltimore dropped from 4,400 in 1820 to 2,900 in 1850, most cities registered increases in that thirty-year span, as indicated by Table 1.

Vast numbers of urban slaves toiled as domestic servants. Still, human chattels could be found in almost all other lines of employment. At Richmond they made up the majority of the workers in the tobacco and iron industries. In 1850 the New Orleans Levee Steam Cotton Press owned 104 slaves; a Mobile owner trained a

Table 1. Number of Slaves in Selected Southern Cities, 1820 and
          1850

| | Slaves | | Increase | |
City	1820	1850	Number	Percent
Baltimore	4,357	2,946	−1,411	−32
Charleston	12,652	19,532	6,880	54
Louisville	1,031	5,432	4,401	426
Mobile	836	6,803	5,967	714
New Orleans	7,355	17,011	9,656	131
Norfolk	3,261	4,295	1,034	32
Richmond	4,387	9,927	5,540	126
Savannah	3,075	6,231	3,156	103
Washington	1,945	2,113	168	9

slave to examine cotton grades. Slaves worked as stevedores in several ports. At railroad and river junctions they performed the transshipment work. Under a hiring-out system, masters signed contracts for their slaves' services or allowed them to negotiate their own work agreements in exchange for a percentage of the pay. This loosening of traditional restraints was linked with the fluid and complex labor requirements of urban areas. The hiring out of slaves made it possible to deal with short-term employment needs.[30]

Alarmists contended that city life undermined the Peculiar Institution. In 1835 a Louisville editor aroused fears that urban slaves had stopped regarding themselves as being in bondage and contended that they became "insolent, intractable, and in many instances wholly worthless."[31] The perception that urban slaves failed to mind their masters helped to spawn fears of slave rebellions; Denmark Vesey's alleged 1822 plot in Charleston colored white thinking. Some suspicious people called the actual number of urban slaves much greater than had been indicated by official statistics. Supposedly, masters cheated on the number of slaves they owned to avoid municipal head taxes. In addition, large groups of runaways were said to lurk in back alleys and outskirts. Growing populations of free Negroes were a special worry. A Mobile editor, concerned about racial competition on the job, declared, "There are now among us free negroes whom the law proscribes holding situations which scores of young white men among us would be glad to get."[32] The number of free Negroes in major southern cities generally increased between 1820 and 1850, as shown by Table 2. Although the proportion of whites generally rose faster than that of blacks, several

Table 2. Number of Free Negroes in Selected Southern Cities, 1820 and 1850

City	Free Negroes		Increase	
	1820	1850	Number	Percent
Baltimore	10,326	25,442	15,116	831
Charleston	1,475	3,441	1,966	133
Louisville	93	1,538	1,445	1,553
Mobile	183	715	532	291
New Orleans	6,237	9,905	3,668	59
Norfolk	599	956	357	60
Richmond	1,235	2,369	1,134	92
Savannah	582	686	104	18
Washington	1,696	8,158	6,462	381

southern cities took steps to reduce their slave populations. In the 1850s Savannah cut its black inhabitants from 14,700 to 7,700; the number of slaves in Charleston dropped from 19,500 to 14,000. In spite of such measures, no major downward movement occurred in the number of either slave or free Negro urban dwellers.

In the first fifty years of the nineteenth century, southerners proceeded with the task of constructing an urban network, one increasingly designed to serve the demands of the plantation economy. By 1850 the South had thirteen places with a population of more than 10,000.

Baltimore	169,000	Savannah	15,300
New Orleans	116,400	Norfolk	14,300
Louisville	43,200	Petersburg	14,000
Charleston	43,000	Wheeling	11,400
Washington	40,000	Augusta	10,200
Richmond	27,600	Nashville	10,200
Mobile	20,500		

Dixie contained two of six "Great Cities" in the United States—in nineteenth-century demographic terms, metropolises of 100,000 or more. The Atlantic and Gulf Coast towns formed the backbone of the urban South. Baltimore was the biggest place in the section; in the whole country only New York, which had 515,500 persons, was larger. Washington and Charleston both ranked among the top twenty American cities. Savannah and Norfolk continued to show progress. Mobile was a major center. New Orleans was the nation's fifth city in size. The important Piedmont towns were Richmond, Petersburg, Wheeling, and Augusta. In the old New West, Louisville

Table 3. Population of Five Southern Interior Cities, 1840 and 1850

City	1840	1850
Memphis	–	8,841
Montgomery	2,171	8,728
Macon	3,927	5,720
Atlanta	–	2,752
Little Rock	–	1,967

and Nashville continued to rise in importance. Between 1840 and 1850 Baltimore gained 66,700 inhabitants, Louisville 22,000, Washington 16,600, and Charleston 13,700.

Equally impressive was the population growth during the forties of some of the newer interior cities, as shown in Table 3. Montgomery grew by 6,500 and Macon by 1,800. Memphis, Atlanta, and Little Rock all rose after 1840. Yet actual figures for frontier cities meant little, because, given the right circumstances, midwestern experience suggested that they would be capable of spectacular population increases. During the 1840s Chicago mushroomed from 4,500 people to 30,000 and Milwaukee from 1,700 to 20,100. Potential was what counted, and southern nationalists could only hope that places like Atlanta and Chattanooga had the right stuff from which cities were made.

Throughout the period after the War of 1812, the South found itself increasingly falling behind the rest of the nation in the building of new cities; the implications for the American economy as a whole were serious. The rise of the port of New York upset the slow and orderly approach being taken to city building in the South, where activity was conducted within the contours of established norms. The cities on the southern Atlantic seaboard failed to secure communication links of the type necessary to challenge the Empire City. The emerging Midwest lined up with the Northeast; Cincinnati and St. Louis, despite their ties to the South, switched allegiance, primarily for monetary reasons. Southerners' careful way of building strata of cities designed to serve the needs of a cotton economy accentuated a growing gulf between the sections.

3

THE RAVAGES OF CIVIL WAR AND RECONSTRUCTION

Southern city builders entered the 1850s on an optimistic note. The Compromise of 1850 gave rise to hopes for an end to the sectional crisis, and a general renewal of ties with the North seemed in the offing. The growing gap in purpose and scope between the southern and the northern urban systems continued to pose problems. Even so, none of the points of difference seemed insurmountable, especially if the new southern interior cities grew rapidly and the old coastal centers expanded their commercial functions. As it was, the differences between the sections had not poisoned economic relationships. New York merchants continued to enjoy amicable commercial arrangements with their counterparts in Charleston, Mobile, and New Orleans. Furthermore, a common feeling of urbanity served to unite American city people. Charleston gentility and hospitality were legendary, and the cosmopolitan traditions of New Orleans reflected the nation's growing cultural diversity.

Few responsible observers realized that a terrible trial of pestilence, sword, fire, and humiliation lay ahead for Dixie. Frightful epidemics would decimate whole cities, invading armies would destroy entire urban districts, and a victor's peace would humble a proud people. By the end of Civil War and Reconstruction, the goal of southern leaders would be not how to overcome the North's commercial advantage but rather how to regain something approaching equal status within the Union. The thoughtful arguments framed in antebellum times by southern statesmen about how best to protect the South's position paled by way of comparison.

Southern commercial conventions held between 1837 and 1859 had attempted to set economic policies for Dixie. The conventions were a natural consequence of the growing paranoia and sense of isolation that swept across the South after William Lloyd Garrison commenced publication of the *Liberator* in 1831. Garrison's call for the immediate abolition of slavery without compensation to slave owners sharpened sectional variances and placed the South on the defensive. The delegates at the conventions represented a cross section of southern life. Luminaries in attendance at one time or another included statesman John C. Calhoun, manufacturer William Gregg, and editor J.D.B. DeBow. Some of the meetings attracted as many as a thousand people, and the proceedings received wide notice throughout the South.

Three distinct periods characterized the convention movement. The first, which featured several assemblies held from 1837 to 1839 in either Charleston or Augusta, dealt with the threat to the South posed by the rapidly increasing wealth and power of the North. Representatives paid special attention to the rise of New York and its overseas trade. In the 1840s a second sequence of conventions in New Orleans and Memphis concentrated on formulating a southern railroad strategy designed to unify the eastern and western parts of the South. During the 1850s the third set of meetings considered a range of issues related to southern nationalism. The gatherings fell increasingly under the control of "Fire Eaters" intent on using the sessions as justification for promoting secession as a practical means of countering increasing northern economic incursions into the South.

The conventions, over the years, first recognized problems, then established goals, and finally expressed a general sense of frustration with the course of national events that eventually led to the creation of the Confederate States of America. Gloom and doom characterized the early meetings. The call for the 1837 convention issued by the business community of Athens, Georgia, reflected the situation. It stated: "A crisis has arrived in the commercial affairs of the South and Southeast; a crisis the most favorable that has occurred since the formation of the American Government to attempt a new organization of our commercial relations with Europe. We ought to be our own importers and exporters, for the very best reason, that we furnish nearly all the articles of export in the great staples of cotton, rice and tobacco. This is a singular advantage for any people to enjoy. Yet, with all this in our favor by nature, we employ the merchants of the Northern cities as our agents in this business."[1] New York imported six times the amount of its exports; all the southern states put together imported only one-fourth of theirs. None of the early conventions came up with a specific way of altering foreign trade patterns to encourage direct trade between the South and Europe. The conclusion was that the state of things was unnatural and that it should not continue. There was a growing recognition that commercial penetration by outside forces had social and political implications that menaced the peculiar nature of southern society.

Calhoun hoped that the second wave of conclaves in the 1840s would overcome parochial political prejudices and lead to a spirit of cooperation between the eastern and western southern states. He regarded the Mississippi River and its tributaries as an inland sea with the capacity to bridge the growing gap between the Atlantic and Gulf ports. Calhoun wanted large and comprehensive internal improvement projects designed to connect the lower Mississippi valley with the South Atlantic cities. He envisioned an immense network of railroads and canals. Here was a vision of southern nationalism at its best. As a matter of record, Calhoun's proposals were star crossed. Even such a distinguished southerner was unable to stop the spirited entrepreneurial rivalries among cities in the South.

New Orleans railroad plans aimed at helping the city's position at the expense of its competitors. In 1852, at a commercial convention in the Crescent City, banker and railroad promoter James Robb of New Orleans received a thunderous ovation from a partisan hometown audience when he proclaimed, "Our fate and interest are blended with those of the Great West. . . . We have only to increase the facilities of getting here, when the people of the West will look naturally to New Orleans as the center of the arts, of fashion, and of ideas, as the people of France do to Paris."[2] Such an insular brand of boosterism—so much a part of the American experience—spelled the decline of the convention movement when it should have been approaching full bloom as an instrument for sectional cooperation.

The last convention, a grim affair, seemed to follow naturally from the failure of the earlier gatherings to solve the South's commercial problems. The sessions became the sounding board for politicians who contended that the South was subservient to the North. An 1858 article in *DeBow's Review* speculated on how the delegates would travel to a Montgomery convention: "They will start in some stage or railroad coach made in the North; an engine of Northern manufacture will take their train or boat along; at every meal they will sit down in Yankee chairs, to a Yankee table, spread with Yankee cloth. With a Yankee spoon they will take from dishes sugar, salt, and coffee which have paid tribute to Yankee trade, and with

Yankee knives and forks they will put into their mouths the only thing Southern they will get on the trip."[3]

The statement was an apt prologue to the Montgomery gathering. Those in attendance, instead of searching for harmonious themes, wasted time in acrimonious debates over such peripheral issues as the possible revival of the foreign slave trade. No one quarreled about either the existence of slavery or the vitality of the cotton economy. By then the loyalty issue had so crystallized across the South that northern-born merchants who had lived in Mobile for thirty years and who supported slavery found themselves under attack. Men of moderation across Dixie found their motives questioned. Over the years the primary contribution of the conventions was to prompt inquiries about the needs of the southern economy. By illustrating the inability of the South to compete on equal terms with the North, the meetings actually furnished a rationale for southern nationalism and hence secession.

All the conventions stressed the need for a great commercial city in the South that could compete with New York. A general consensus held that the South could at best only afford one gigantic metropolis. Unfortunately, the recognition of a condition did not automatically lead to a solution, because the problems associated with building such a place went deeper than nationalistic theory. No matter how desirable it might have been for southerners to unite and concentrate their resources on creating a city to rival New York, the section's urban leaders proved unwilling to sacrifice their own ambitions on the altar of southern nationalism. Charleston and Savannah continued to contend for the cotton trade; Mobile and New Orleans worked against each other in constructing railroads. The Piedmont towns, from Virginia through Georgia, vied for northern capital to build cotton mills. As elsewhere in the country, a strong spirit of urban rivalry held sway. No one wanted to help a competitor get ahead.

Hinton Rowan Helper, a brilliant and alienated native of North Carolina, created a national sensation in 1857 when he claimed in his widely read polemical book *The Impending Crisis of the South: How to Meet It* that the slavocracy's manipulation of the economy blocked the emergence of a magnificent southern commercial city. He said that the actions of a selfish few allowed northern interests to drain $120 million annually from the South. As a direct consequence southern money had gone toward building New York, Philadelphia, Boston, and Cincinnati at the expense of Norfolk, Beaufort, Charleston, and Savannah. Commenting on what would have resulted if the dollars had stayed in the South, he wrote, "How much greater would be the number and length of our railroads, canals, turnpikes, and telegraphs. How much greater would be the extent and diversity of our manufactures. . . . How many more clippers and steamboats would we have sailing on the ocean, how vastly more reputable would we be abroad, how infinitely more respectable, progressive, and happy, would we be at home." Concluding with an impassioned plea for urbanization, he declared, "Almost invariably do we find the bulk of floating funds, the best talent, and the most vigorous energies of a nation concentrated in its chief cities; and does not this concentration of wealth, energy, and talent, conduce, in an extraordinary degree, to the growth and prosperity of the nation? Unquestionably. Wealth develops wealth, energy develops energy, talent develops talent. What, then, must be the condition of those countries which do not possess the means or faculties of centralizing their material forces, their energies, and their talents? Are they not destined to occupy an inferior rank among the nations of the earth? Let the South answer."[4]

Actually no plot fermented, although it was true that the plantation economy had failed to generate the tremendous amount of surplus capital necessary to build great cities quickly. Especially in formulating the transportation strategies necessary to gain control of vast marketing areas, southern urban leaders had to operate within severe fiscal restraints that left little margin for error.

New Orleans, which tried very hard to become the great metropolis of the Mississippi valley, served as a prime example.[5] The refinement of boilers made it possible for steamboats to go upriver against strong currents and added a new dimension to the city's commercial possibilities. In the 1820s, members of the French, Spanish, and American business communities gazed with pleasure on the "forest of masts" that lined the levee. The general prosperity that accompanied the presidential administration of Andrew Jackson helped New Orleans; exports and imports rose from $26 million in 1831 to $54 million in 1835. Regional cotton and sugar planters borrowed vast sums of money in New Orleans and became increasingly dependent upon the city's financial institutions. At that juncture the Panic of 1837 severely affected the banks of New Orleans; a gigantic $72 million in uncollectable mortgages caused all except a few of the houses to fail.

The unhappy situation served as a stark indication of the Crescent City's vulnerability to outside forces. After several down years prosperity returned, and the amount of grain brought downriver for transshipment at New Orleans increased, despite difficulties caused by huge drayage costs, poor docking facilities, and spoilage. During the Mexican War, New Orleans was a principal military staging base, and the unprecedented business generated tended to hide deficiencies. In means of distributing goods the city compared unfavorably with Atlantic coast ports. As a result New Orleans was a poor importing center, and shipping rates were high. A detailed 1858 analysis indicated that a loaded 700-ton vessel sailing from Charleston to Liverpool could expect a profit of $2,054.01. The same ship sailing from New Orleans to Liverpool would have earned only $552.96. To make matters worse, the construction of railroads from the Northeast to the Midwest, augmenting water links, threatened to deal a death blow to natural lines of communication. Consequently, the New Orleans business community reexamined its objectives and realized to its dismay that the bulk of Midwest trade was permanently lost. Technology had turned against the Crescent City; the iron horse rather than the steamboat reigned supreme in America.

New Orleans gradually adopted a railroad strategy. Grandiose proposals called for the quick obtaining of Pacific coast connections. One aborted scheme called for a complicated link that involved both sea and land and meant building a railroad in Mexico across the Isthmus of Tehuantepec. A railroad actually started in the direction of California failed after less than two miles of tracks had been laid. More limited and realistic railroad proposals aimed at securing regional hinterlands and feeding the Mississippi River trade. Robb made the plans, DeBow handled the publicity, and Judah P. Benjamin, a wealthy plantation owner and political leader, provided a measure of respectability. Robb's New Orleans, Jackson and Great Northern Railway, 206 miles long, ran to Canton, Mississippi, where it joined other lines and consolidated the "Black Belt" cotton trade for New Orleans. Another road, the publicly aided New Orleans, Opelousas and Great Northern Railway, thrust west eighty miles from the New Orleans suburb of Algiers to Brashear on Berwick Bay, making Texas connections via the Morgan Line of steamers. The road, very difficult and expensive to build through snake- and alligator-infested swamps, was a limited success. The "sugar region" trade that it brought to New Orleans would have come anyway.

Because New Orleans's program worked imperfectly, critics found fault. Even so, while mistakes abounded and goals overreached, the men involved in New Orleans's railroad planning made their decisions within an objective framework that took into account the declining role of the Mississippi River. They therefore concentrated on a strategy of consolidating their own markets in the lower Mississippi River valley. Although this course of action was far from what extremists like Helper or the Fire Eaters wanted, consolidation represented the best option available.

Throughout the 1850s, railroad considerations constituted a primary element in southern economic thinking. Jefferson Davis emerged as a leading communication theorist. Within the South, he wanted an elaborate east-to-west system. Within a broader framework, he envisioned a "Pacific Railroad" running from Memphis to California, but the fires of sectional conflict dashed his plans, although he did succeed in helping Mobile interests obtain a federal land grant for the Mobile and Ohio Railroad. When it was completed, just prior to the Civil War, from Mobile to Columbus, Kentucky, on the Ohio River, the 472-mile-long railroad was the longest in the South and the cornerstone of Mobile's overland transportation strategy. As early as 1852 an official for the Mobile and Ohio Railroad made a speech in which he bragged about all the trade that the line would supposedly take away from the Crescent City.

Louisville was another place with growing southern railroad ambitions. After Cincinnati thwarted the plans of Louisville's leaders to build trunk railroads in Ohio and Indiana, they turned south, first constructing local roads in Kentucky and Tennessee. Of greater significance was the Louisville and Nashville Railroad, owned jointly by Louisville and Nashville capitalists. The road, which by the end of the 1850s had a trunk line that ran between Louisville and Nashville, held tremendous potential as a route into the center of the lower South. Baltimore had already made important progress in railroading. The Baltimore and Ohio Railroad, finally completed to Wheeling in 1853, soon gained through connections to St. Louis. As a result the Monumental City became the only southern Atlantic coastal city to penetrate the Midwest successfully, no mean feat in the American railroad battles of the mid-nineteenth century.

Some southerners hoped in vain that railroads would overcome sectional differences. In February 1861 William Burwell, a Virginia economist, anticipated that a "series of trade zones" centered in Chicago, Cincinnati, Louisville, Memphis, and New Orleans would "become principal depots for the collection and exportation of the trade along the Ohio and Mississippi valley, as well as for the importation and distribution of merchandise."[6] Southern nationalists, who abhorred such thinking, never found an effective way—beyond championing tracks in the South with a different gauge from those in the North—of preventing railroads from overcoming sectional boundaries.

Throughout the 1850s yellow fever continued to pose a threat

to southern city people that on occasion overshadowed the growing
sectional conflict. Victims died a swift and painful death. A minister
who had lived through numerous New Orleans epidemics wrote,
"Often I have met and shook hands with some blooming, handsome
young man today, and in a few hours afterwards I have been called
to see him in the black vomit, with profuse hemorrhages from the
mouth, nose, ears, eyes, and even the toes; the eyes prominent,
glistening, yellow, and staring; the face discolored with orange color
and dusty red. The physiognomy of the yellow fever corpse is usually
sad, sullen, and perturbed; the countenance dark, mottled, livid,
swollen, and stained with blood and black vomit; the veins of the
face and the whole body become distended, and look as if they were
going to burst."[7]

In 1855 yellow fever swept through Norfolk, killing 2,000 people, including the mayor and other leading citizens. A stunned sur-
vivor wrote, "But for the occasional appearance of an idle white
vagabond, sauntering along the wharf, gazing wistfully into the
water, we should have imagined ourselves wandering amid the ruins
of a lost city."[8] The Norfolk epidemic would have qualified as one
of the worst disasters of its kind if it had not been for an even more
terrible one that had struck New Orleans two years earlier.

In 1853 a general yellow fever outbreak engulfed the lower Mississippi valley. New Orleans had been virtually free of the disease
since the death of 2,000 people in a 1847 pestilence. The absence of
yellow jack had caused unrealistic optimism in medical circles. In
November 1852 the editors of the *New Orleans Medical and Sur-
gical Journal* claimed that soon the scourge would be "among the
diseases that have passed and gone; and the students of medicine
will seek only in the record of the past, to learn its history—its
symptoms and its treatment." They cited the effectiveness of a
swamp-draining program designed to remove "miasmatic influences."[9]

A favored theory held that swamp gas caused disease, but many
local residents were not so sure. In any event, sanitary laxities
abounded. Stagnant water stood in vacant lots, the streets were filthy
and muddy, and no technological means existed for the systematic
flushing of street gutters and canals. The unsanitary conditions
caused little concern among local officials, who refused to appropriate the funds required for sanitation because they were unwilling
to admit to having been wrong. One of New Orleans's medical authorities actually advanced the theory that large amounts of filth
and offal in the streets retarded the formation of a yellow fever
atmosphere. Such sophistry did not stop outsiders from calling the

Crescent City "a pesthole," "the wet grave," and "the city that time forgot."[10]

The 1853 New Orleans epidemic started slowly and then swept like an angel of death over the stricken city. The first victim expired in late May, and others followed. In the beginning the newspapers ignored the outbreak, but on June 10 an observer reported an "unquestionable case" of a child who turned yellow and threw up an "unmistakable, old fashioned, coffee-grounds black vomit."[11] By mid-July, when deaths averaged more than sixty a day, epidemic conditions could no longer be ignored. The press slowly acknowledged the danger of the moment.

A crisis followed in New Orleans, as desperate and perplexed medical men, grasping at straws to contain the outbreak, ordered the killing of all stray dogs and the quarantining of the slaughterhouse district. During the first week of August the fever, which raged with special vehemence in German residential sections, carried away 947 victims. A report told of seventy-one bodies at one cemetery "piled on the ground, swollen and bursting their coffins, and enveloped in swarms of flies."[12] A total of 228 sufferers went to their graves on August 8, and on August 21 officials recorded 269 interments. Death carts went door to door searching for victims, and grave diggers were hard to find, even at the high wage of five dollars a day. Four hundred cannon shots and the burning of tar failed to purify the air.

New Orleans sanitary workers, particularly those associated with the Howard Association, performed heroic service throughout a horrible summer in which rain fell almost every day. The affliction decimated nearby towns. A dispatch dated September 7 from little Thibodauxville on the Great Northern Railway lamented, "Stores closed; town abandoned; 151 cases of fever; 22 deaths; postmaster absent; clerks all down with the fever."[13] Before the epidemic ran its course in late fall as many as 11,000 may have perished in New Orleans, and more than 5,000 died of yellow fever in the next two summers in and around the city. A local sanitary commission established to combat yellow fever recommended improvements in the sewerage and an inquiry into the value of quarantine regulations. In the end very little was done; no one knew for sure what caused yellow fever.

The growing sectional emergency muted concerns about potential epidemic conditions. Pressing national problems occupied center stage. The troubles that followed the enactment of the Kansas-Nebraska Act in 1854 starkly illustrated the inability of the federal government to solve the problem of the extension of slavery into the territories. With the collapse of the Compromise of 1850, a host of sectional issues defied resolution. The Panic of 1857 hit the Northeast especially hard, but world cotton prices remained high. According to many southern Fire Eaters, the South's good fortune demonstrated the superiority of an emerging southern civilization. The premise required selective judgments; in 1857 alone at New Orleans fifty-eight mercantile houses failed, and trade declined by $36 million. A large upward swing in New Orleans during the three years prior to 1860 served to cloud affairs further.

During the economic crisis, New York came in for violent attack as the embodiment of all southern grievances against the North. "New York," declared an editorial in the *Vicksburg Daily Whig* on the eve of the Civil War, "like a mighty queen of commerce, sits proudly upon her island throne sparkling in jewels, and waving an undisputed commercial spectre over the South. By means of her railroads and navigable streams, she sends out her long arms to the extreme South; and with avidity rarely equalled, grasps our gains and transfers them to herself—taxing us at every step and depleting us as extensively as possible without destroying us."[14] Such bombast ignored the belief among northern extremists that New York, by virtue of its long-standing trade ties, had southern tendencies. Right down until the eve of secession, relations between northern and southern cities continued to cut across political boundaries.

The Confederate States of America started with a shattered urban network. At the outset three of the largest cities in the South remained in Union hands. Federal troops secured Washington, which had 61,000 people, before the start of hostilities. In May 1861, Union soldiers moved into Baltimore (212,400), and President Abraham Lincoln soon suspended habeas corpus in the city for the remainder of the war. These actions followed clashes between Massachusetts troops passing through the Monumental City and local pro-Confederate elements. Louisville (68,000) yielded to Union troops without military opposition, as did Kentucky's other important cities: Lexington (9,300), Covington (16,500), and Newport (10,000). Both Covington and Newport were right across the Ohio River from Cincinnati. The northern actions removed any immediate threat to Cincinnati, a possibility much feared by Queen City residents, and secured valuable jumping-off points into the C.S.A. St. Louis nearly came under Confederate control at least temporarily, but a quick military response by U.S. forces prevented Missouri secessionists from seizing the city. Without much fanfare, the Union gained a tremendous strategic military and economic advantage over its Confederate adversary.

One could hardly imagine a more inauspicious beginning for the Confederacy. Only six cities, as opposed to thirty-nine such cities in the North, had as many as 20,000 people.

New Orleans	168,700
Charleston	40,500
Richmond	37,900
Mobile	29,300
Memphis	22,600
Savannah	22,300

New Orleans was the only metropolis in the entire new nation. The second biggest municipality, Charleston, actually declined in population by 2,500 between 1850 and 1860. Six other Confederate cities had more that 10,000 inhabitants.

Petersburg	18,300
Nashville	17,000
Norfolk	14,600
Wheeling	14,100
Alexandria	12,700
Augusta	12,500

The Confederacy lost Alexandria, and Wheeling in the first hours of hostilities. Five other significant Condererate towns had under 10,000 residents according to the 1860 census.

Montgomery	9,800
Wilmington	9,600
Atlanta	9,500
Columbia	9,100
Vicksburg	4,600

When slaves were subtracted, the Confederate cities looked even smaller. There were 13,900 human chattels in Charleston, 13,400 in New Orleans, 11,700 in Richmond, 7,700 in Savannah, and 7,600 in Mobile. Nor did the C.S.A. gain many urbanities by persuading the western state of Texas to join; the Lone Star's largest cities were San Antonio and Galveston, which had respective populations of 8,200 and 7,300. If the goal of the Fire Eaters was the creation of a true agrarian nation, they had come close to success.

In an age in which cities increasingly stood for wealth and power, the Confederacy had to contend with the loss or disruption of the upper half of the carefully built southern urban mosaic. The Louisville and Nashville Railroad closed north of Nashville, Atlanta no longer functioned as a shipping point for cotton sent north via Chattanooga, and Memphis lost an important downriver trade in midwestern products. The closure of the Mississippi River especially hurt New Orleans. Along the Atlantic seaboard, Savannah, Charleston, Wilmington, and Norfolk saw the suspension of northeastern trade nurtured since colonial days. In addition, the cities lost all the advantages associated with membership in the Union, not the least of which had been large expenditures for railroad aid and various internal improvement projects. Some places entertained hopes that increased cotton shipments would more than compensate for any short-term losses. Wishful thinkers believed that North American trade would return to normal once northerners had accepted southern independence. Richmond leaders, touting the potential of their city, gained what they regarded as a considerable plum in June 1861 when it was designated the Confederate capital, but the northern determination to prosecute the war to a conclusion dashed any last hopes that the acquisition of the Confederate government could be used as a means of realizing an urban advantage.

The North won by wrecking the South's means of waging war. Union strategists never officially adopted Winfield Scott's Anaconda plan, which called for constricting the South through a naval blockade and dividing it in two by taking the Mississippi River. The actual northern assault on the South proved much more comprehensive. By the summer of 1863, combined land and sea actions had opened the Mississippi River. A gradual tightening of a northern naval blockade virtually drove Confederate commerce from the high seas. The capture of Fort Pulaski in January 1865 near the mouth of the Cape Fear River virtually closed the port of Wilmington and effectually ended most significant blockade running. Meanwhile, in the fall of 1864 William Sherman took Atlanta, began his famous march to the sea, and occupied Savannah at the end of December. He then moved north through the Carolinas and on into Virginia, while Ulysses S. Grant tied down Robert E. Lee's forces at the approaches to Richmond. Lee's surrender on April 9, 1865, marked the end of the Confederacy. The experiment in nation building below the Mason and Dixon Line had ended in complete failure.

Four years of Civil War brought hard times to Dixie's cities. There was despair and frustration inside New Orleans when the great ships of the Union navy, after running the forts at the mouths of the Mississippi, anchored off the Crescent City and forced it to surrender under the threat of naval bombardment. When the Federals laid siege to Vicksburg, the inhabitants were obliged to live in caves and eat rats prior to their glorious surrender. A military band serenaded Sherman with Italian opera music as he watched his soldiers burn Atlanta. Federal fighting men, running amuck, burned and pillaged in Columbia. Admiral David Farragut was lashed to the mooring of his flagship, the *Hartford,* as it and other Federal ships swept into Mobile Bay.

Union troops sang "The Battle Hymn of the Republic" as they tramped through otherwise empty streets in occupied Charleston. Sleek black-hulled blockade runners loaded cotton at the Wilmington waterfront. Units of the Confederate army put the torch to Richmond's commercial districts during their withdrawal in early April 1865 so that military stores could not fall into Union hands. The flames brought to an end the city's hopes of becoming the great center of the C.S.A. The flickering embers were a reminder of the vast quantities of blood and treasure expended to protect and defend the failed experiment of southern nationalism.

During the Civil War, southern towns, north and south, enjoyed shifting fortunes. None of the places beyond the Confederate orbit sustained any appreciable war damage. Louisville flourished throughout hostilities as a staging base for northern operations; the Louisville and Nashville Railroad carried tremendous amounts of military traffic. At Baltimore, a bottleneck caused by a gap between railroads running into the city from the Northeast and on to the Potomac front generated a tremendous transshipment business. In addition, Baltimore contractors made money building military fortifications. The Baltimore and Ohio Railroad tried to remain neutral without success; with shifts in the fortunes of combat, both sides used the line and on occasion tore it up. Washington rose in power and prestige as the conflict progressed. Alexandria, which suffered a serious blow when Union authorities confiscated stacks of rails intended for a regional railroad, served as a major Union hospital center. Norfolk, which had yet to recover fully from the 1855 yellow fever epidemic, lost almost all its trade during the northern occupation. After its fall, Memphis was a center of illicit trade between the North and South until Union officials clamped down. Nashville, occupied by both Union and Confederate forces, was at different moments a storehouse for both sides.

From the fall of New Orleans to the tightening of the blockade, Wilmington, Charleston, Savannah, and Mobile garnered a large cotton trade. Augusta, hardly scarred by war, enjoyed considerable economic good fortune as both a munitions and convalescence center. Atlanta, its population temporarily doubled by refugees, did very well until its destruction.[15] Several places, among them Atlanta and Richmond, experienced large temporary increases in population. In the end, the realities of the fighting and the great issues involved came home to all the Confederate cities, including those that experienced little or no physical damage. Even places outside the Confederacy sustained more injury than was known at the time; the struggle ruined traditional hinterlands, ushering in a long period of agricultural depression.

After the war, southern cities that had remained outside the Confederacy tried as best they could to emphasis their ties to Dixie. Going a step further, a Louisville editor claimed—while taking a slap at northern merchants—that his town played a humanitarian role in the stricken South. He wrote in the *Louisville Journal* in 1867, "First: since the close of the war, our merchants have acted toward those of the South in a spirit of truest magnanimity. . . . This generous example has scarcely had one imitator in the opulent cities of Cincinnati, Philadelphia, New York, or Boston, whose merchants have enjoyed and grown fat on the custom of the South in years past. Second: In time of direst adversity the Southern people never appealed to our citizens in vain. Louisville was for six or eight months the great central storehouse from which the famished thousands in Alabama, Mississippi, Georgia, and the other States were fed." He omitted to say that Louisville business interests made tremendous amounts of money supplying the Union army.[16]

The occupation governments varied in severity. One of the harshest was that imposed in New Orleans under the rule of controversial Massachusetts general and politician Benjamin Butler, whom diarist Mary Boykin Chesnut called a "hideous cross-eyed beast."[17] Butler incurred ill will with inconsistent, sensational, and eccentric decisions. In keeping with his contention that civil government was subordinate to the whim of military officers, he arrested prominent citizens, suppressed newspapers, seized property, and ordered Episcopal clergymen to include in their morning prayers words of praise "for the President of the United States and all in civil authority." In a notorious affront, he said that any southern white female who insulted a Union soldier should "be regarded and held liable to be treated as a woman of the town plying her avocation."[18] Even his well-publicized sanitary program to clean up New Orleans, based on his contention that the city's condition threatened the health of northern troops, came in for attack. Local leaders considered it unnecessary and an insult to their town. Butler was an extreme case. Nathaniel Banks, his successor in New Orleans, ran a much less pugnacious administration.

The more successful military administrations were rather benign. John W. Geary, a former territorial governor of Kansas, the head of the Savannah military government, won the praise of the mayor and other leading citizens for his evenhanded rule, as did the evenhanded Union officials who ran Augusta following its occupation. In Tennessee, Andrew Johnson, appointed military governor by Lincoln, had set an important precedent by leaving the city governments almost entirely in place. During the ensuing period of Military Reconstruction in the South, military commanders, Freedmen's Bureau commissioners, and other radical regime officials often tried to interfere with mayors and councils. In Tennessee the governor took over the police departments in Chattanooga, Memphis, and Nashville.[19] Even so, traditions of local control were so strong in America that the state Reconstruction governments had little direct impact on the art of urban administration.

Social regulation of newly freed blacks became an important concern of white civil governments. While blacks served as mayors and aldermen in the Reconstruction South, they never controlled an important city for any length of time.[20] In Wilmington, whites gerrymandered the city so that each black ward had twice as many voters as a corresponding white one. The odious black codes, which provided for a wide variety of segregated facilities and institutions, never went into full operation because of the enactment of the Civil Rights Act of 1866. Urban race relations, rather casual in the past, became strained at the municipal level. In Memphis white mobs burned black districts and murdered innocent blacks in broad daylight simply to reassert white supremacy. Despite such odious actions, there were some instances of racial accommodation. During the Reconstruction period in New Orleans, authorities succeeded in desegregating the schools and public transportation.

Conditions in Baton Rouge, Louisiana, typified more moderate white racial attitudes. In the course of 1865, blacks swarmed into the city and became a majority, to the alarm of white officials, who established a night patrol and strengthened the police department. The editor of the *Baton Rouge Advocate,* expressing the views of many whites, said that he longed for a return to the day when even minor offenses, such as blacks' use of insulting language, were "settled with a dose of fifteen or twenty lashes." Reestablishing authority over blacks became a goal of whites. By April 1867, at the start of Military Reconstruction in East Baton Rouge Parish, civil authorities already had racial matters in hand. The Baton Rouge municipality had taken the lead in dealing with the "darkies."[21] In Baton Rouge and elsewhere, well in advance of a legal system of segregation, the precedent had been firmly established of using civic authority to keep blacks in a subordinate position.

Railroads were crucial to the recovery of the southern urban system. During the conflict the Confederate government converted the few southern rail and iron shops to ordnance production. Confederate troops demolished tracks to prevent their use by Union forces; Sherman's "bummers" ruined thousands of miles of lines. The war saw the destruction of more than half the railroad tracks in the South. Estimates of the damage ran as high as $28 million. At the start of Reconstruction, southern interests still owned most of the afflicted system. The return by the federal government of 3,000 miles of railroads to the private owners and the sale on liberal terms of $11 million in military railroad equipment were of considerable help. State aid, much of it tinged with the corruption of carpetbag rule, aided a few lines, but the majority of roads they rebuilt as best they could without any outside help. Within five years after the war, all except a few insignificant rural lines had resumed operation. Still, through the 1870s freight rates in the South were twice as high as those in other parts of the country, and during the decade southern routes built only 4,000 of 35,000 miles of railroads constructed in the United States. In the aftermath of the Panic of 1873, half the railroads in the South either went into receivership or defaulted.

A movement of northern railroad interests into the South added a new and important element. Many carpetbag owners, little more than small-time pirates, went under, doused by a sea of red ink. The powerful Pennsylvania Railroad was another matter; its Southern Railway Security Company gained control of eleven trunk lines and many other lines before becoming overextended and folding in 1875. The Atlantic Coast Line and what ultimately became the Southern Railway system evolved from various reorganizations and mergers. Other outsiders ventured South. Collis P. Huntington of California gained control of the Chesapeake and Ohio Railroad; the Illinois Central Railroad acquired a New Orleans trunk connection. Both the Louisville and Nashville Railroad and the Baltimore and Ohio Railroad fell under the domination of northern capitalists.[22] It afforded little solace to know that the trend toward railroad consolidation was nationwide in scope. To unreconstructed Confederates, outside ownership, even if it resulted in better service, was another indication that the postwar South was unable to chart its own destiny. The carefully built regional system of antebellum short lines designed to move cotton no longer existed.

Southerners lacked the resources to restore their cities rapidly. Columbia, for instance, still showed the scars of war more than a decade and a half after Sherman's troops had passed through. In 1879 New York reporters who toured Dixie found Mobile "dilapidated and hopeless," Norfolk "asleep by her magnificent harbor," and life in Savannah and Wilmington "at a standstill." They agreed that, "tried by Northern standards, there are only a few cities between the Potomac and the Rio Grande that can be said to be growing and prospering."[23] The depression that followed the Panic of 1873 bore down hard on Dixie, as the national economy remained flat until the end of the 1870s.

During the Civil War decade, five of the Confederate states underwent a decline in industrial production. In 1880 only three states in the entire South—Maryland, Kentucky, and Virginia—ranked in the top twenty of the thirty-eight states in manufacturing. Equally distressing were the consequences of the collapse of the plantation economy. The production of all major crops languished. Not until 1879 did the number of cotton bales produced surpass 1859 totals. Fluctuations in cotton prices and changed marketing arrangements contributed to a bleak picture. A giant potential post-war expansion of the cotton market, predicted by experts who made the mistake of discounting the importance of the opening of new sources of supply in Egypt and India, failed to occur.[24] The emerging sharecrop and crop lien systems threatened to keep both white and black farmers in permanent poverty. None of these developments furthered the creation of prosperous urban hinterlands—so many forces buffeted southern cities that the urban network remained in disarray throughout Reconstruction.

During the 1870s still another round of terrible epidemics added dimension to the plight of the urban South. In September 1873, right at the start of the national depression, yellow fever, cholera, and smallpox struck Memphis simultaneously. Out of 7,000 people felled by yellow fever, 2,000 died. Of 1,000 cholera victims, 276 perished. Smallpox raged among the black population. More than half the 40,000 inhabitants temporarily fled town. Next, in 1878 a massive yellow fever outbreak afflicted the lower Mississippi River valley. In Memphis, a quarantine did not prevent 19,500 persons from leaving. Of those forced to stay, 17,600 contracted yellow fever. In all, 5,200 succumbed to the dreaded disease. New Orleans was almost as hard hit; the official death toll reached 4,046. These disasters, compounded by another yellow jack scourge in Memphis the following year that claimed 500 victims, spurred reform efforts.[25]

Memphis and New Orleans responded differently. Memphis authorities accepted the results of an investigation by a new federal agency, the National Board of Health, which attributed the city's troubles to poor sanitary facilities. Memphis had virtually no sewers outside the business district, and filth from open gutters accumulated in adjacent bayous. Memphis adopted and carried through on a sewerage plan proposed by George Waring, Jr., a prominent member of the National Board of Health. Waring, a "noncontagionist" who rejected the "germ theory" of disease, steadfastly argued that "sewer gas" and other odors caused disease. Because he believed that lethal vapors accumulated in large outlet sewers, he called for "separate systems" of sewers for ground runoff, household wastes, and human excreta. His fellow board members claimed that Memphis would soon "become one of the healthiest cities in the valley of the Mississippi."[26] They did not mention the fact that the cause of yellow fever remained a mystery.

As for New Orleans, Dr. Samuel Choppin, president of the Louisiana board of health, remarked, "Undoubtedly the most impressive lesson of the great epidemic of 1878, to the people of this city, was the importance of improving its sanitary condition."[27] The continued drain on the Crescent City's population, plus the demands by northern health experts that it be placed under a permanent quarantine, led to concerted efforts at reform. The Auxiliary Sanitary Association, a new organization that was primarily privately financed, directed a massive cleanup campaign. Potential business losses rather than human costs brought about the first tentative steps in a locally supported program of sanitary reform. Concern about health matters constituted another problem with which southern urban leaders had to contend in rebuilding the section's urban components.

During a period of defeat and humiliation for Dixie, articulate spokesmen came forward to promulgate a creed designed to allow the South to regain its place in the Union quickly. Right after the war, J.D.B. DeBow, reiterating a view he had enunciated prior to hostilities, wrote, "*We have got to go to manufacturing to save ourselves. We have got to go to it to obtain an increase in population. Workmen go to furnaces, mines, and factories—they go where labor is brought.*"[28] In the 1870s agitation for an urban and industrial South intensified. By the end of the decade the New South creed had emerged.

Several of the leaders of the movement were journalists, including Henry Watterson of the *Louisville Courier-Journal*, Richard Edmonds of the *Baltimore Manufacturers' Record*, and, above all, Henry Grady of the *Atlanta Constitution*. They called for welcoming northern capital to build up southern society. North of the Mason and Dixon Line they told potential northern investors what they wanted to hear, that the Civil War changed attitudes and that white southerners regarded northerners as brothers under a single flag. The South was said to offer unparalleled opportunities for those willing to take advantage of them. Race was supposedly no longer an issue. Speaking of blacks, Grady wrote, "The love we feel for that race you cannot measure nor comprehend."[29] Conversely, the New South advocates had little trouble convincing southerners that they had been ruthlessly exploited by generations of northerners. Now they predicted that an influx of northern money would enable the South to achieve independence by acquiring new factories and transportation systems without having to pay for them. Everyone had something to gain from the changed conditions.

The concept of the New South moved its spokesmen to extravagant praise. Grady conjured up visions of a harmonious, stable, and prosperous South. He said, "I see a South the home of fifty million people; her cities vast hives of industry; her country-sides the treasures from which their resources are drawn; her streams vocal with whirring spindles; her valleys tranquil in the white and gold of the harvest . . . ,sunshine everywhere and all the time, and night falling on her gently as wings of the unseen dove."[30] Edmonds, extolling the Southland, proclaimed, "The more we contemplate these advantages and contrast them with those of all other countries, the more deeply will we be impressed with the unquestionable truth that here in this glorious land, 'Creation's Garden Spot,' is to be the richest and greatest country upon which the sun ever shone."[31] Watterson bluntly stated, "The South, having had its bellyful of blood, has gotten a taste of money, and it is too busy trying to make more of it to quarrel with anybody."[32] Glory awaited all who wanted to help the South attain its destiny.

The men of the New South creed talked much differently about the race issue before southern audiences from the way they spoke in addressing northerners. "But the supremacy of the white race in the South must be maintained forever, and the domination of the negro race resisted at all hazards, because the white race is the superior race," Grady declared before a group of white supremacists. "This is the declaration of no new truth; it has abided forever in the marrow of our bones and shall run forever in the blood that feeds Anglo-Saxon hearts."[33] Edmonds, who wrote movingly about the "progressive evolution" of blacks "from the darkness of slavery into the fullness of freedom," accepted the concept of white racial superiority. He claimed that the economic plans of "white men" would be realized by using the "strong muscles of industrious negroes."[34] Watterson, a bitter opponent of the Ku Klux Klan, thought that freedmen needed the protection of their former owners. In print he actually called blacks "barbarians" and "ignorant and degraded" people hardly removed from African jungles.[35] Here was a difficulty with the New South creed. A New South resembling that extolled by Grady, Watterson, Edmonds, and their colleagues necessitated changing and moderating the racial attitudes of the region and its leaders. Until attitudes altered, Dixie would remain apart from the rest of America.

The men of the New South creed came forward at a dark moment to paint pictures of castles in the sky that uplifted the spirits of their fellow southerners. Even those who rejected their call for northern capital were moved by their visions of a restored South. The New South spokesmen did not dwell on failure. Rather, they talked of the wonderful days that lay ahead. They were keepers of the faith—honorable heirs to southerners' ambivalence regarding the kind of cities they wanted. Keeping the dream of progress alive was of special concern as Reconstruction drew to a close and a new chapter in the life of the South was about to unfold. In no small measure, the course of urban development would decide the fate of Dixie over the next several decades.

4

THE ADVENT OF THE NEW SOUTH

The purveyors of the New South creed claimed that a combination of southern managers and northern money had the capacity to develop cities quickly. After all, Chicago, not even incorporated until 1834, had made dramatic progress. Its population grew from 30,000 in 1850 to 503,200 in 1880, making it the fourth largest city in the nation and the fastest growing place in the world. There seemed no reason why well-established southern cities, some with roots stretching back into the colonial period, could not grow in similar fashion. Nevertheless, while Henry Grady and other New South leaders talked in broad sectional terms, they actually sought to promote their own cities at the expense of rival communities.

Even though the concept of the New South received widespread support, it never constituted a coordinated movement with clearly stated objectives. Working at cross-purposes was not necessarily counterproductive; urban rivalry had been a constant theme in the American experience. The South's largest problem was an age-old one—it did not have the resources to develop an urban network on the same scale as that in other parts of the nation. The men of the New South creed, like J.D.B. DeBow in earlier times, talked around the situation, substituting rhetoric for specific programs. Southern cities attracted some outside capital, but to northern investors the South remained a sideshow. More concretely, urban promoters in Dixie were unable to overcome the realities of the depressed state of agriculture in the South. A subservient relationship to outside banking interests further complicated matters. Dixie's cities grew in the 1880s, although far from the extent predicted by New South advocates. In a decade that proved crucial in shaping the American

Table 4. National and Southern Places Compared by Size and Place, 1880

Population Size	Number of Places		Percent in South
	Nation	South	
Places over 4,000	580	63	13
Places over 10,000	227	30	13
Places over 20,000	99	17	17
Places over 100,000	20	4	20

urban mosaic for many years to come, the South fared poorly. Consequently, many people became reconciled to the dismal reality that there was no way that the region could quickly regain a position of distinction in the American Union.

The 1880 census, which surveyed the nation at a crucial crossover point as an older rural society gave way to a new industrial one, raised important questions about southern urban prospects. At that date, when the South consisted of all the states of the old Confederacy except Texas, plus Maryland, Kentucky, and the District of Columbia, the census data showed a serious erosion of the section's urban status in the United States. Between 1870 and 1880, cities with more than 10,000 inhabitants increased in the country as a whole from 165 to 227 but only from 26 to 30 in the South. Other 1880 demographic statistics also reflect the South's urban plight, as illustrated by Table 4. The figures, which show Dixie lagging far behind the rest of the nation, reflected developments outside the South—the building of a great railroad network, the exploitation of mineral and timber resources, the growth of medium-sized industrial and agricultural centers, and the consolidation of markets by regional metropolises. Considering the depressed conditions that followed the Panic of 1873, progress seemed amazing. Advocates of the New South creed were right to extol the region's potential. Unfortunately, possible investors not only worried about their welcome but weighed their chances of making more money elsewhere. With profits in the range cattle industry said to average more than 40 percent per annum and speculative mining stocks seeming to offer unlimited returns, few plungers expressed more than a passing interest in the South.

In 1880 the best product the South had to market was an urban network of thirty cities with more than 10,000 people (see Table 5), an important demographic crossing point in the Gilded Age. The old Atlantic coastal towns had histories that reflected faded glories and

Table 5. Southern Cities over 10,000 in 1880

City	Total Population	City	Total Population
Alabama		Maryland	
Mobile	29,132	Baltimore	332,213
Montgomery	16,713	Cumberland	10,693
Arkansas		Mississippi	
Little Rock	13,138	Vicksburg	18,814
Dist. of Columbia		North Carolina	
Georgetown	12,578	Wilmington	17,350
Washington	147,293		
Georgia		South Carolina	
Atlanta	37,409	Charleston	49,984
Augusta	21,891	Columbia	10,036
Columbus	10,123		
Macon	12,749	Tennessee	
Savannah	30,709	Chattanooga	12,892
		Memphis	33,592
Kentucky		Nashville	43,350
Covington	29,720		
Lexington	16,656	Virginia	
Louisville	123,758	Alexandria	13,659
Newport	20,433	Lynchburg	15,959
		Norfolk	21,966
Louisiana		Petersburg	21,056
New Orleans	216,090	Portsmouth	11,390
		Richmond	63,600

renewed hopes. Baltimore remained the South's largest commercial and industrial city. Since the Civil War, Washington had more than doubled in size, primarily because of the growth of the federal government. Washington simply overwhelmed the nearby communities of Georgetown and Alexandria. Norfolk's prospects seemed bright; in 1880, as often in its history, prosperity seemed just around the corner. Neighboring Portsmouth remained a satellite city. Wilmington faced the age-old problem of trying to develop a hinterland. Charleston continued to experience a genteel decline in status; Savannah had aggressive leaders and few resources. In the old Virginia back country, Richmond was the largest city, while Lynchburg and Petersburg had emerged as factory centers. In South Carolina, Columbia hoped to recover from the war by attracting industry to its impressive Congaree River waterpower. Augusta, long a major transportation hub, appeared on the verge of acquiring an important manufacturing dimension. The largest cities in the old New West were Louisville and Nashville, as they had been from the earliest days of settlement. Cumberland, Maryland, one of the first settlements on the western side of the Appalachians, was a railroad division point. Lexington had been eclipsed by Louisville; Covington and Newport had grown because of their proximity to Cincinnati. Along the Gulf coast, Mobile continued to function as a significant cotton-shipping port and railroad terminal. The metropolis of the lower South remained New Orleans. Although the Crescent City had failed to fulfill the predictions that it would be the greatest city in North America, it continued to function as one of the nation's most important ports. Some of the places on the edges of the South appeared old and beaten down; others continued to have fairly good prospects.

The hopes of the postwar South rested with the central river and railroad cities, most of which had just started to grow in the years immediately before the war. In 1880 these places, ravaged by the vicissitudes of hostilities and hurt by the destruction of the old agricultural system, remained virtual frontier communities, whose prospects required evaluation according to different standards from those used for the older and more established southern cities. Two of the new towns, Columbus and Macon, wanted to expand their roles as cotton-processing centers. Vicksburg progressed slowly; Little Rock was the only place of importance in an underdeveloped area. Chattanooga and Montgomery intended to grow as industrial centers. Memphis had been hurt by terrible epidemics. Atlanta, after making a swift recovery from the Civil War, looked ahead to achieving metropolitan status. The odds were long against building an urban empire from this group of cities, but optimistic entrepreneurs believed the southern interior towns had chances as promising as those of their counterparts in the golden West. In 1880 Los Angeles had only 11,200 people, San Diego 2,600, and Seattle 3,500. Opportunities to build cities persisted in the United States.

The band of men who promoted a South of cities and industry emphasized the supposed opportunities in what one of their number praised as "the coming El Dorado of American adventure." Henry Grady claimed in 1884 that the South had surpassed the trans-Mississippi West as a land of opportunity. "The time will come," he said, "when there will be an amendment to the shibboleth, 'Westward the hand of empire holds its sway.' "[1] Unfortunately, actual conditions in Dixie were somewhat unpromising. The South entered the 1880s with an agricultural system unsuited to the needs of a free market; land barons and country merchants presided over a fragmented economy in which sharecropping and crop liens stifled individual enterprise. The dominant agricultural groups were sympathetic to the needs of the commercial interests that had long charted affairs in the cities. After all, the country and town combinations had marketing ties stretching back to antebellum days. Unfortunately a desire to improve conditions was not enough to bring about significant changes. The traditionally limited functions of almost all of the southern towns precluded any rapid advances.

As previously noted, the section had cities geared to the needs of a plantation economy based upon King Cotton. In the wake of Reconstruction, the postwar southern leaders had little to sell potential outside investors except dreams. For better or worse, cities could make the South more like the rest of the nation. They functioned as a common denominator that overrode sectional considerations, but there seemed little necessity for more of them in the South. For the moment the main task was to shore up the existing urban network. Under the circumstances, even that task was not going to be easy. Of course, the men of the New South creed could not admit that the South had little need for more cities; they had to put their best foot forward and claim, as Grady did in 1886 in a speech before northeastern businessmen, "Somehow or other we have caught the sunshine in the bricks and mortar of our homes, and have builded therein one ignoble prejudice or memory."[2]

Grady preached his doctrines of a changed South during an urban boom in America, for the 1880s saw the completion of the basic elements in the nation's urban network. Many established places added large numbers of inhabitants. During the decade Chicago grew by more than 500,000 people and New York by 250,000. On the edge of the Great Plains, Kansas City and Omaha emerged as regional metropolises, fueled by huge amounts of outside capital, as the rapid settlement of the central plains led to countless opportunities in agribusiness. Even greater riches awaited on the Pacific coast. San Francisco was a dynamic and flourishing city. One of the largest land booms of the nineteenth century was under way in Los Angeles, where thousands of speculators threw money to the wind; some lots changed hands several times in a single day. In the Pacific Northwest, the arrival of eastern rails touched off a spiral of land speculation. Tacoma, Seattle, and Everett vied with one another for control of the Puget Sound region. A spirit of progress was abroad from Maine to California. Under the auspices of a series of overtly probusiness presidential administrations, the country appeared about to become an urban and industrial society.

The continual rise of New York had followed almost naturally; the city's business community had emerged stronger than ever from the Panic of 1873. In a period marked by the consolidation of wealth, the money power was centralized as never before in the Empire City. Great investment banking houses benefited from a wave of mergers and stock transactions that made trusts and monopolies an integral part of economic life. In many ways, the worst fears of antebellum southern statesmen had materialized, but with the South in an inferior position and agrarianism vanquished, little could be done to check the concentration of wealth in New York. The attacks on Wall Street by Populist orators in Kansas and Nebraska had a familiar sound; the message had been heard before south of the Mason and Dixon Line.

Of course, any attempt to obtain outside capital on a vast scale meant going hat in hand to New York banking interests, because no one else had access to the sums of money necessary to direct the course of national development. Thus when Grady and others asked investors to come south, they were in effect promoting New York domination, a historic turn of events in Dixie. For understandable reasons, supporters of the New South creed, when speaking inside their section, glossed over the need for New York capital and instead emphasized that southern whites had taken the lead in rebuilding their defeated land.

The extent to which southern communities could integrate into a nation of cities was of vital significance for the section's future. As an urban society cut sharply across old sectional barriers, economic integration was only one aspect of a larger whole. If cities in the South differed radically in character from those elsewhere, they might not fit in, and the New South creed would die at birth. If it did, the section might find itself permanently reduced to colonial status. Therefore, the social statistics of southern cities took on new importance. Numbers and percentages concerning a wide variety of subjects, ranging from the incidence of immigrants to school attendance, registered the state of urban progress in the South by showing what southern cities were like and where they stood in relation to the rest of America.

Between 1870 and 1880 the population of the United States rose from 36.6 million to 50.2 million, an increase of 26 percent. In 1880 there were 14.2 million southerners, accounting for 28 percent of the people in the country. In character Dixie's population differed sharply from that elsewhere. Of the nation's 6.6 million blacks, 6 million, or 83 percent, lived in the South. Conversely, the South contained only 306,000 of the country's 6.7 million foreign born, for a total of 5 percent. These figures alone set the South apart. Of all southerners, 39 percent were black and 2 percent foreign born. No southern state had a foreign-born population of more than 10 percent. In the rest of the United States, fewer than 1 percent of the people were black and 19 percent foreign born. Southern leaders, ignoring the presence of blacks, liked to claim that the section's population was homogeneous, a statement which failed to reflect conditions accurately.

The demographic profiles of the thirty southern cities with more than 10,000 people in 1880 did not fit into any neat category. A total of 1.4 million inhabitants, 10 percent of the southern population, lived in such places. These municipalities differed from the South as a whole in that blacks accounted for 31 percent of the urban populace and foreign born for 13 percent. Indeed, 61 percent of all immigrants in the South lived in the thirty cities, compared with only 8 percent of the blacks. Oppressive legislation made it hard for black sharecroppers to leave the land. Cities had attracted most of the foreigners who settled in the South since before the Civil War. Yet in ethnic composition the South's cities were unlike their counterparts throughout the rest of the United States. Most of the 197 cities of more than 10,000 outside the South had insignificant numbers of blacks, and roughly 30 percent of their populations were foreign born. Being white supremacists, none of the New South supporters emphasized the racial mix in southern cities, although they had no choice except to recognize that the future of the South rested upon the shoulders of city people.

Absolute numbers provided another way of considering the populations of southern cities. In 1880 fifteen of the thirty largest cities had more than 10,000 blacks.[3] The most were the 57,000 in New Orleans, the 53,700 in Baltimore, and the 48,400 in Washington. Only three northern cities had more than 10,000 blacks: Philadelphia (31,700), St. Louis (22,300), and New York (20,000). As for foreign-born, thirty-nine places in the nation had more than 10,000 immigrants. The South had but four of those communities: Baltimore (56,100), New Orleans (41,200), Louisville (23,200), and Washington (14,200). While the numbers represented large concentrations of people, they hardly compared to the totals in the seven American cities with more than 100,000 immigrants, which included 593,500 alone in the New York-Brooklyn area. The fewest immigrants in the southern cities were 294 in Columbus and 338 in Columbia; the lowest black totals were 315 in Newport and 391 in Cumberland. Obviously, in these demographic respects southern cities differed from the rest of urban America.

In 1880 a total of 146,000 of the 182,000 foreign born in the thirty municipalities of 10,000 or more in the South lived in the eight largest cities of the section.[4] The greatest number of foreign born in the eight cities, people who had come from Germany, Ireland, and Great Britain, accounted for 80 percent of the urban immigrants. Baltimore had the most British-born residents, or about 3,000. The only other cities with more than a thousand were New Orleans, Washington, and Louisville; in spite of claims that the South personified the best of Anglo-Saxon civilization, the region's cities had attracted few Englishmen. The majority of Irish immigrants lived in the North, where between 15 and 20 percent of the inhabitants of New York, Boston, and Chicago were from the Old Sod. Seventeen places outside the South had more than 10,000 Irish immigrants. Even so, there were considerable congregations in Dixie: 14,200 in Baltimore and 11,700 in New Orleans. Although the Midwest contained more than half the Germans in the nation, Baltimore had 34,100, or 10 percent of all the people in the Monumental City. In addition, the 13,900 Germans in New Orleans and 13,500 in Louisville represented large totals by comparison with many other places in the nation.

New Orleans continued to have a reputation as a cosmopolitan city. It had 6,900 French-born residents, more than any city except New York, which had 9,900. With 2,000 Italians, New Orleans had proportionally the most people of that nationality in the country. Native resentment of them was indicated in official Louisiana state documents, which called them "Dagos," and by the 1891 lynching of Italians in New Orleans. Overall, the increasing number of immigrants in the large southern cities had the subtle effect of gradually changing their character and making them more like localities outside the section.

The 1880 statistics indicated that both black and white populations of the eight largest southern cities had been born close to home. A total of 90 percent of the people in Richmond were born in Virginia; 89 percent of all Charlestonians were from South Carolina. Their own states had contributed between 70 and 80 percent of the populations of Atlanta, Nashville, Baltimore, and New Orleans. Some 74 percent of all Washingtonians were from the District of Columbia, Maryland, or Virginia. Louisville, even though right across the Ohio River from Indiana, still counted 67 percent of its inhabitants as Kentucky natives. None of the other fifty largest cities in the country had such provincial population characteristics. Moreover, only two Dixie cities had more than a thousand persons who had been born more than one southern state away. More interesting were the statistics for migrants from outside the South, which showed that only the four metropolises contained more than a thousand northerners. Baltimore, for example, had 7,000 Pennsylvanians and 3,000 New Yorkers. More typical figures were the 24 Wisconsinites in Atlanta, the 86 Rhode Islanders in Atlanta, and the 3 Nebraskans in Nashville.

The New South advocates used religion to buttress their creed. Grady claimed, "The South is American and religious," asserting that "God-fearing people" supported the "old fashion" by according equal honor to God and the U.S. Constitution.[5] In 1890 the U.S. census office took what officials claimed was the nation's first scientifically conducted religious enumeration. It indicated that the 17 southern cities of the 124 cities in the nation with populations of more than 25,000 had many religious organizations, numerous houses of worship, much valuable property, and substantial membership counts. Of special significance were the figure for church members as a percentage of total population; there was a marked difference between rural and urban areas. The national average for urban communicants was 38 percent; the percentage for the United States as a whole stood at 45 percent. Only three of the southern cities had lower percentages of communicants than the nation as a whole. Membership statistics, of course, were far from exact as measurements. Still, the totals reflected the strong strain of religiosity in the late nineteenth-century urban South.

In 1890 totals for the seventeen largest southern cities reflected the diversity of religion in America. In eight cities, Roman Catholics accounted for 10 percent or more of the total population and in three cities for more than 20 percent: New Orleans (28 percent), Covington (27 percent), and Louisville (21 percent). The totals for Protestant groups followed sectional trends. Regular Baptists accounted for more than 10 percent of the city dwellers in the seventeen cities. Six places were between 5 and 10 percent Southern Methodist. Colored Methodists made up 30 percent of Mobile and 12 percent of Charleston residents. The biggest percentages of Methodist Episcopals were the 6 percent in Charleston, of Episcopalians the 5 percent in Mobile, and of Southern Presbyterians the 3 percent in Mobile. Of the people in nine of the towns, 1 to 4 percent had a Jewish affiliation; the largest number was 3,500 in Baltimore. In addition to the main-line denominations, a variety of Pentecostal and other groups contributed to the richness of southern urban religion.[6] The reality was far different from the propaganda used to further secular causes.

In the course of Reconstruction, officials sought to rekindle interest in education. A basic problem was that hardly any money was available. In the 1870s, Georgia, Alabama, and South Carolina all temporarily closed their public school systems. In 1880 school statistics for the thirty largest southern cities told a depressing story. Only the four largest cities spent more than $100,000 during the year, while thirteen towns expended less than $30,000. Generally, student-teacher ratios in the city schools were at least 60 to 1. For blacks the ratio was frequently as high as 100 to 1. Inadequate facilities made the situation bleaker. Many schoolhouses were poorly maintained converted sheds or private homes. Overcrowding was a frequent problem. Atlanta authorities tried to alleviate matters by giving white students priority over blacks; Savannah officials instituted an automatic promotion policy. The courses of instruction minimized so-called frills. Mobile students studied basics: orthography, reading, writing, grammar, geography, and arithmetic. Few places had foreign language, music, or physical education programs. The educational system challenged only a small number of students. Not surprisingly, daily attendance, poor everywhere, was usually under 50 percent.[7]

Developments in urban higher education in 1880 appeared much more promising, even though many of the leading institutions had few students, few faculty members, and few books. Enrollments varied from 524 at Baltimore City College to 15 at Washington's Howard University. The libraries of several institutions contained fewer than 2,000 volumes. The Johns Hopkins University, the most prestigious in the South, had 159 students, 33 faculty members, and 9,000 library books.[8] Southern higher education represented an important sectional asset, but a few small, elitist institutions exerted disproportionate influence. With their predominantly classical curricula, they appeared bastions of conservative thought rather than breeding grounds for change.

A growing sense of urbanity continued to characterize the southern cities at the dawn of the early metropolitan era. While business interests continued to dominate affairs and obvious ethnic, racial, sexual, and class differences remained, the gradual emergence of a small middle class and of a shared set of values among city people gave rise to a distinctive urban culture. The city, both individualistic and communal, forced people to share experiences. Even reclusive urbanites had to venture forth to shop with others in department and specialty stores. Daily newspapers carried a wide range of materials on all aspects of life in the city and concentrated on business, human interest, disaster, crime, and political topics.

Other shared experiences served to set city folk apart from their country brethren. Horse racing at Churchill Downs, Pimlico, and other great tracks attracted thousands of spectators. The theater was a uniquely urban phenomenon. All towns had their "red light" entertainment districts; none was so well known as the French Quarter and Storyville in New Orleans. Stylish restaurants and ornate taverns were peculiar to the urban scene. Cities stimulated the fine arts to such an extent that most music, painting, and literature was born in an urban setting. Although the city had the capacity to bring out the worst in human beings, it could also bring out the best. The passage of time threw the urban cultural trends of the Gilded Age into high relief. Reformer Frederic C. Howe concluded, "The modern city marks an epoch in our civilization. Through it, a new society has been created. Life in all its relations has been altered. A new civilization has been born, a civilization whose identity with the past is one of historical continuity only. We but dimly appreciate the full import of this fact. And yet, it is more significant, possibly more pregnant for the future than any previous political or social change."[9]

The great currents of industrialism that transformed the United States almost missed the South. In 1880 the backbone of manufacturing in the South lay in sixteen cities that ranked among the hundred largest in the United States. The only places in the top twenty in value of products were Baltimore (eight) and Louisville (seventeen). The total value of products for the sixteen cities amounted to about $200 million. More than half were in Baltimore ($78.4 million) and Louisville ($25.4 million). By comparison, the value of products for the three largest American industrial centers alone exceeded $1 billion.

Capitalization figures were of considerable interest in determining the state of southern industrial progress. Of the $130 million invested in southern manufacturing, $100 million was in the sixteen largest municipalities. The only southern cities with an industrial capitalization of more than $9 million were Baltimore ($36.6 million) and Louisville ($21.8 million). Statistics for other towns indicated a pattern of many small and undercapitalized firms. New Orleans claimed 915 manufacturing establishments valued at $8.6 million. Atlanta's 196 factories had a capitalization of $2.5 million. Agribusiness was the major sectional industrial pursuit. In Baltimore more than $8 million was invested in flour milling, fertilizer processing, tobacco making, and meat packing. Richmond had five flour mills valued at $1.2 million. Capital in Augusta's six cotton mills amounted to $1.4 million.

The South lacked heavy industry. The only concentrations of

machine shops and foundries, basic to the operation of an industrial economy, were $6 million worth of establishments in New Orleans, Richmond, Baltimore, and Louisville. Covington, Newport, and Baltimore each had iron and steel mills with a total value of $3 million.[10] Rapid change seemed possible, as evidenced by developments in the heart of the coal and iron district in Alabama. New iron furnaces at Birmingham, not even founded until 1871, prompted rapid growth. Unfortunately, a whole series of Birminghams would have been needed to build an industrial empire in the South. Without a dramatic rise in the South's industrial capitalization, there seemed no quick way for the section to gain parity on a national level.

The actual task of driving Dixie ahead fell to urban business leaders all across the South, many of whom thought in much broader terms than simply a single city. Some of the most masterful capitalists in the South were from the North. Henry Morrison Flagler of Cleveland, Ohio, a former Rockefeller partner, played a major role in opening up Florida and William D. ("Pig Iron") Kelley of Pennsylvania was instrumental in building up the Alabama iron and steel industry. The greatest native southern industrialist was James Buchanan Duke of Durham, North Carolina, who turned a small tobacco company founded by his father into one of the largest trusts of the period, the American Tobacco Company. He took advantage of technological breakthroughs in cigarette production, and he achieved success through a combination of ability, comparative freedom from government regulation, and methods that his competitors considered ruthless. The South had many businessmen of stature ready to take the risks necessary to achieve success. The leaders of the Wilmington firm of Alexander Sprunt and Son used innovative methods to transform the overseas cotton-exporting business. They engaged in considerable experimentation and endured hardships that would have deterred lesser risk takers. E.H. Summers built the New Orleans cotton firm of Hillford, Summers and Company into a major enterprise. In Columbus, a locally owned cotton mill, the Columbus Manufacturing Company, employed hundreds of women and children. More than 2,000 operators worked in Petersburg's eight cotton manufacturies.[11]

Depressed agricultural conditions tended to vitiate many of the manufacturing advances. The sorry state of southern farming and the continued dependence on outside capital precluded the spectacular gains envisioned by the proponents of the New South creed. Although all the southern states had probusiness governments, it was simply not enough for Dixie's entrepreneurs to master what Grady called "the great commercial chessboard."[12]

Little help came from southern urban governments. The Gilded Age, generally an unhappy period for American city halls, witnessed much graft and corruption. One of the worse scandals occurred in Washington. Alexander Shepherd, a Ulysses S. Grant appointee, was accused of distributing lavish patronage and construction contracts. He once reported to a congressional committee expenditures for a project of $6.6 million when actual costs amounted to $18.9 million. Before leaving for Mexico, Shepherd left behind a significant legacy. Upon completion of physical renovations that he supported, Washington emerged as one of the country's most beautiful and livable cities.[13] Unfortunately, few other places had the resources to follow the standards set in Washington.

Statistics for 1880 indicated that almost all the South's largest towns were in poor financial shape. The high costs associated with Reconstruction and a concurrent reluctance on the part of municipal authorities to assess property at its true valuation and to establish adequate tax bases were partly responsible. The state of Dixie's economy made the taxes far harder to bear than in the more prosperous portions of urban America. Outstanding bonded debts added to the tax burdens in the cities of the South. The District of Columbia's debt, the nation's largest, amounted to $21.7 million. Baltimore's $20.2 million debt and those of New Orleans and Louisville, $15.3 million and $8.1 million respectively, were also discouraging.[14] Twelve other southern cities had bonded debts of more than $1 million. Outstanding bonded debts reflected the need to fund floating debts and to refund old debts. At least nineteen cities had yet to pay off bonds issued for railroads or other transportation schemes. As cities broadened their functions, urban leaders had to resort to bond issues to stay afloat. There was no way communities in the South could finance large, necessary, and expensive projects, such as sewerages and waterworks, without increasing their bonded indebtedness. In many cases, however, faced with health and sanitation crises, they had no choice but to do so, hoping that user fees collected over several decades would eventually pay off the bonds.

It remained a major goal of southern city fathers to improve the quality of life. Several of the park systems in the South predated a national City Beautiful movement that caught the interest of the general public in the 1850s with the planning of Central Park in New York. By 1880 Savannah's committee on parks had spent $20,000 to improve parks, twenty-three of which were 1-acre squares at intersections that in some cases had been part of James Oglethorpe's original plan. The city of Charleston owned 33 acres of public grounds and intended to acquire an additional 20 acres. The

Battery at the harbor's edge featured tree-shaded walks and benches. In Atlanta, the 5-acre City Hall Park was the centerpiece of the city's 312-acre park system. Macon's Central City Park had a total space of 720 acres. Donated to the municipality by the state and designed by a former Macon mayor, it contained a large stand of trees, a racetrack, and a fairgrounds building. Of New Orleans's 660 acres of public squares, the most famous was the original main square. Renamed Jackson Square, its distinguishing attribute was an imposing equestrian statue of Andrew Jackson.[15]

Baltimore and Washington had the South's largest park systems. The Monumental City had many park squares with statues of famous people. After the Civil War, Frederick Law Olmsted, considered the leading American park designer, planned Baltimore's 693-acre Druid Park. An imposing stone gateway served as the main entrance. Visitors could savor the park's various attractions by driving over twenty miles of winding roads. Druid Lake, actually a water reservoir, featured a fountain that sent a jet of water a hundred feet into the air. Nearby, herds of deer and flocks of sheep ranged over the grassy hillside. In Washington, great improvements included the upgrading and extension of the park system. Pierre L'Enfant's plan had set aside numerous desirable locations for parks and for public and government buildings. Some property was sold or given away; the rest, amounting to 513 acres, remained in federal hands. Much of the land served as the grounds for government buildings, including the Capitol and the White House. Manicured lawns, beautiful flower gardens, and winding walks added to the beauty of Washington, as did the numerous squares and circles that graced different parts of the city. Outlying intersections contained unimproved spaces designated as triangular reservations. Numerous opportunities existed to honor American heroes, at the same time further enhancing the beauty of Washington. The redesigned city, from the elaborate Capitol grounds planned by Olmsted to the smallest circle, represented an important manifestation of the national City Beautiful movement.[16] Parks enhanced the beauty of metropolises in Gilded Age America: Fairmont in Philadelphia, Belle Isle in Detroit, and Golden Gate in San Francisco. None assumed the monumental quality of those in Baltimore or the historical character of those in the District of Columbia.

Spokesmen of the New South creed ignored the housekeeping side of city building. Who, after all, could get excited about street surfaces when the paramount task was to provide the philosophical foundations for a South of cities? But someone had to fill the potholes and make decisions concerning public safety, or a city could

Above, an 1838 view of Baltimore, the "Monumental City." The Battle Monument afforded an example of beautification and ornamentation in the antebellum urban South. Below, Louisville's bustling Main Street in 1846. Lined with three- and four-story commercial buildings, it was typical of pre-Civil War urban America and had little in the way of distinctive southernness.

All illustrations are from the National Archives.

Above, Key West, ca. 1856, already displayed the attributes of urbanization, especially the "forests of masts" associated with American ports of the period. Below, Georgetown, D.C., in this 1862 Mathew Brady photograph, had the appearance of a closely packed urban center. Note the empty Chesapeake and Ohio Canal in the foreground.

Mathew Brady's photographs of the ruins of a railroad roundhouse in Atlanta in 1864 (above) and of destroyed buildings in Richmond in 1865 (below) provide stark evidence of the destruction wrought by the Civil War on the urban South.

Above, an 1865 view of Charleston's Bay Street shows the kind of street conditions that all urban Americans of the Reconstruction era (not just those in the South) had to cope with every day. Below, this view of bridge construction across the Ohio between Newport and Cincinnati, taken in 1870, demonstrates the growing suburban character of Newport and its sister city, Covington. In all but name the two Kentucky cities had lost much of their southern identity.

Two differing views of Washington, D.C.—above, a lithograph of "Newspaper Row" in 1874; below, a photo of marshes on the Anacosta River in 1882—are indicative of the blending of urban and rural conditions characteristic of much of Gilded Age urban America.

Above, an August 1881 photo of weather-beaten wharfs between Piety and Desire streets in New Orleans illustrates the slow pace of economic recovery in the post-Civil War urban South. Below, beautification efforts characteristic of the nineteenth-century South are half hidden in this Charleston city park as citizens camp out in the aftermath of the earthquake that struck the city on August 31, 1886.

Above, Pennsylvania Avenue in Washington, looking toward the Capitol, was by 1915 a major thoroughfare. Throughout much of its history, Washington has remained a metropolis of national stature. Below, in 1921 the littered alley entrance to a Baltimore garment factory emphasized the problems associated with the rise of industry in the South.

Right, crude oil stills, rundown tanks, and "cat crackers" at the Baton Rouge Esso refinery in 1945 graphically show the rise of the petrochemical industry in Louisiana.

Below, the famous "March on Washington for Jobs and Freedom" of August 28, 1963, was a dramatic event that helped lay the groundwork for the Civil Rights Act of 1964.

not function. In their newspapers, the New South editors urged that local services be improved, commented vigorously on conditions they felt needed attention, and took sides on questions of public concern. Without codifying their actions, the men of the New South used their pages to further important aspects of city building. They realized that knowledge and experience in urban problem solving and decision making were necessary for successful urbanization. Cities in the South, as elsewhere in the nation, shared certain concerns regarding urban services; in this area southern urban antecedents crossed sectional barriers. Urban authorities had to cope with many consequental and often vexing tasks. The methods and priorities varied markedly, even within a single community. There was little, however, in the way of radical experimentation. No place wanted to appear backward, so the tendency was to take a safe course and to work within established norms. In any event, the ways in which emerging communities handled their first large-scale urban and social services problems indicated their relative maturity and responsibility as well as the expense that city fathers and citizens were willing to incur for civic improvements.

Street maintenance was a constant source of frustration. No one knew what surfaces were best. Authorities found cobblestones noisy under traffic conditions, difficult to clean, and hard to replace. Granite and sandstone blocks were noisy and expensive; wood, cheap and easily installed, wore out quickly and became permeated with horse urine and axle grease; seashells cracked on impact, creating a surface much like broken glass; asphalt, still in the experimental stage, melted under the rays of a hot sun; and broken stone and gravel, inexpensive and readily available, proved hard to maintain.[17] Many city governments were content to throw gravel on the main thoroughfares and simply concentrate on keeping the streets passable. Lack of resources made it impossible to tend all the streets. Even in Washington, which had the highest level of urban services in the South, 96 miles of 230 miles of streets remained unimproved. More startling were the figures for New Orleans, where 472 miles of 566 miles of street surfaces had no pavement. Similar conditions prevailed elsewhere. Charleston had 36 miles of dirt streets in a total of 54 miles; only 3 miles in 100 miles of lanes in Atlanta had a surface.[18]

Paving substances varied greatly in cost, quality, and availability from city to city. In 1880 the price of cobblestone by the square yard was 60 cents in Alexandria, 36 cents in Norfolk, and $2.25 in New Orleans. Broken stone sold for 70 cents per square yard in Covington and $1.50 in Memphis. Repair costs added to civic burdens. Some cities used the method employed in Macon, where the chain gang serviced the roads at an estimated cost of $5,000 annually.[19]

Sidewalks were subject to much less wear and tear than the streets. In the commercial districts they were usually made of fairly permanent substances. The downtowns of Louisville, Alexandria, and Augusta all had brick sidewalks. Lynchburg's were of gneiss stone.[20] Walks in the residential sections of southern cities were almost always wood planks or dirt paths running along drainage ditches because high costs made other materials impractical.

It was difficult to clean streets when horses represented the primary form of transportation. In a single working day of eight hours, a thousand horses deposited about five hundred gallons of urine and ten tons of dung in the streets. Cities had roughly one horse for every four persons.[21] Constant travel theoretically merged street dirt with gravel and the dirt of unsurfaced streets, but in fact thoroughfares became quagmires under heavy horse traffic, unless there was adequate drainage, which there seldom was. Street-cleaning methods, results, and expenditures differed across the urban South. Lexington and Memphis required householders to sweep in front of their dwellings before pickups by private crews. Authorities in Alexandria, Norfolk, Covington, and Macon arranged to have public ways swept only when it seemed necessary. Columbia's sanitation budget was so small that available manpower scrubbed open surface drains. Atlanta's force did much of its cleaning in the commercial parts of town. Working within such per annum budgets as $810 in Alexandria, $15,000 in Savannah, and $105,800 in New Orleans, officials fought a losing battle to keep the streets clean. A wide number of uses were found for the street sweepings. Street departments in Baltimore, Richmond, and Charleston sold high-grade manure for fertilizer and dumped the rest onto low-lying lots. Columbia ordinances simply called for depositing the dirt outside town. Memphis owned a special boat that carried street matter downriver for unloading.[22] Unhappily, practical economic considerations frequently overrode the need for better health and sanitation.

The need to remove dead animals was another problem. Horse carcasses were sometimes abandoned to rot in the streets. The dead bodies of cats and dogs were sometimes discarded in the streets or left in vacant lots. Southern cities found ways to dispose of the carcasses as a matter of necessity rather than from any desire to assume responsibility and usually did so as cheaply as possible. The quality of the work varied greatly. Baltimore spent $3,500 annually to remove deceased beasts to local bone-dust factories. Washington contractors hauled away 6,415 animal remains in 1880 for use in what an official vaguely called "various ways." An Alexandria regulation required owners to bury any creature larger than a domestic cat beyond the city limits. Charleston attempted a cooperative arrangement; the municipal scavenger collected and dumped small dead beasts into a nearby swamp, and local farmers carried away decayed horses, mules, and cows for grinding into fertilizer. The town contractor in Mobile charged owners ninety-five cents a head to ship approximately 800 animal bodies a year to a fertilizer plant downwind from town.[23] Whether by public or private means, people throughout the urban South needed to improve methods of disposing of dead animals. It was small consolation that similar circumstances prevailed in other parts of the country.

In 1880, garbage and ash disposal added to the cost of urban services in southern cities. Householders routinely mixed the two substances. Every city of importance had public garbage collectors, with the exception of Covington, which hired a private contractor. Crews throughout the South removed refuse on regular schedules, from daily to twice weekly. Practices differed, depending on the community. In Baltimore the drivers of garbage wagons blew a horn at intervals to warn patrons to have their garbage ready for collection. Even if individuals followed instructions, serious health menaces frequently resulted from haphazard disposal practices. Once the garbage wagon passed, few people cared about the fate of its contents. In some places, including Washington, large amounts of garbage went uncollected. A health officer in the District of Columbia admitted in an 1880 report that decayed offal accumulated throughout his jurisdiction in alleys, yards, vacant lots, and cellars. With the daily addition of putrefying animal waste, potato parings, eggshells, dishwater, and other refuse, the resulting concoction emitted foul odors and noxious gases, especially on hot steamy days. Residents of Washington and elsewhere frequently complained about poor service and piles of street garbage, but to the despair of reformers, there was little interest in increasing appropriations by raising taxes.[24] The "garbage question" remained unanswered in America during the Gilded Age.

Inefficient disposal of sewage caused increasing concern among southern sanitary experts. In a period of growing fears about a possible connection between a lack of sewers and high urban death rates, only a few southern cities had anything resembling sewer systems. Others had sanitary arrangements that were little better than nothing. At Lexington, where no new lines had been constructed for several years, a few limestone sewers eighteen inches square emptied into the sluggish Elkhorn Creek. Augusta relied on old sewers once used exclusively for drainage. The inadequate sewers that served Macon discharged into a swamp outside the city limits. Montgomery had unventilated brick and wooden mains, none of which flushed very well. Baltimore had twelve miles of storm sewers but no system designed to carry away regular sewage. Tidal waters caused such serious difficulties at the outlets on the river front that the city remained without sewers until the early twentieth century.[25]

Because New Orleans had a very high water table, almost all sewage passed through open drainage gutters and canals. Throughout the Gilded Age, New Orleans had no underground sewers, a lack that contributed to the community's serious health hazards. Memphis was the only southern city with a comprehensive sewer system.[26] Elsewhere large quantities of excreta ran into porous privy vaults rather than into sewers. Liquid household wastes—the runoff from laundries and kitchens—ran into gutters, backyards, or cesspools. No town had effective regulations regarding the disposal of industrial wastes. In the absence of adequate systems of sewerage, crucial sanitary issues remained unresolved.

In 1880, in keeping with national norms, many southern cities had waterworks. In the previous twenty years, the number in the country had increased from 200 to 500. Although the general trend was in the direction of public ownership, several southern cities lacked municipal works. In fact, neither Portsmouth nor Lexington had waterworks. Even a small system cost more than $100,000 to construct. Memphis had a private works valued at $650,000, and one at Montgomery cost $130,000. Both of the waterworks used machines to pump water, as did a new concern in Charleston that brought up water from artesian wells a thousand feet deep. Chattanooga's Lookout Water Company, organized in 1866, pumped Tennessee River water through twelve miles of lines. A few municipalities had publicly operated works. Norfolk spent $500,000 on a pumping station that moved half a million gallons of water daily through twenty-five miles of lines. At New Orleans, the waterworks had a checkered history. In 1869 the city bought an old private works, only to sell it again in 1878 to the New Orleans Water Works Company. The facility, which had an estimated worth of $1.3 million, pumped untreated Mississippi River water directly through seventy-one miles of pipes.[27] No one worried much about purification, and the quality of drinking water steadily deteriorated as the Gilded Age progressed. Sewage and industrial waste polluted watering grounds so badly that by the second decade of the twentieth century, the water in almost all places needed chemical treatment to make it reasonably safe for human use. The best policy to follow was to boil water prior to drinking it.

Public transportation underwent major changes in the Gilded Age. Privately owned horse railroads became important symbols of urban progress even if they provided inadequate service. Petersburg, Portsmouth, Columbia, Macon, Lexington, and Montgomery had no lines, but most southern cities did. Firms built street railroads in several places in the years immediately after the war. Charleston's and Augusta's opened in 1866, Atlanta's in 1869, and Norfolk's in 1870.

As might have been expected, the metropolitan centers had the largest horse railroads, and a city often had more than one route. In 1880 Washington had five different horse railroads, with a total length of close to thirty-one miles. They all charged the standard national fare of five cents a ride. Horse railroads in Louisville carried more than 8 million passengers annually. The fifty miles of tracks required the services of 323 men to operate 173 cars pulled by 726 horses and mules. One hundred and forty miles of horse railroads, which attracted 24 million riders yearly, serviced New Orleans. To run this large transit system there were 373 cars, 1,641 horses and mules, and 671 employees.

In smaller places, the horse railroads frequently ran for only a couple of miles down a single street. Sometimes the roads ended at a pleasure ground or amusement park owned by the traction company. Lynchburg's two-mile line had 6 cars pulled by 12 horses and 12 mules. Eight men operated the single-track line. The horse railroad in Norfolk had 4 miles of track. Charleston's line, 21 miles long and using 57 cars, 125 horses, and 89 employees, hauled 1.5 million passengers yearly. The horse railroads of Augusta, running over 4.5 miles of track, employed 37 men, who used 7 cars and 34 horses to carry more than 377,300 passengers annually. The horse railroads in the southern cities afforded another indication of increasing urbanization.[28]

Omnibuses, large cumbersome vehicles with a standard capacity of about forty riders, augmented horse railroads in many places. Those in Washington ran between depots and hotels. In Richmond and Savannah they served hotels, railroad stations, and steamboat landings. Atlanta, despite its size, had none.[29] In many localities, given the fixed routes of horse railroads and the nature of the omnibus service, private conveyances, horseback, or walking remained the easiest way of getting around.

Southern municipalities assumed primary responsibility for internal security and stressed law and order at the expense of other forms of protection. In 1880 health services were very weak in all except a few places. Generally, the mayor and council did little more than appoint a board of health. These organizations, usually but not always including a physician, met infrequently except during epidemics and had insufficient resources to undertake meaningful protective programs. The boards in Lexington, Covington, and Newport did not even have regular budgets. Members of Atlanta's five-man body received salaries of $100 a year to make recommendations to the city council. Columbia had a twelve-person advisory board that included only two physicians; the chief health agency in Montgomery was a branch of the state board of health. Chattanooga's board had a twelve-month budget of approximately $500, and during an epidemic the board could spend as much as an additional $250. It had no authority to quarantine infected areas, but like most boards it could wield emergency powers in a crisis. Forward progress frequently came only in the wake of catastrophe. In 1879, for instance, Memphis obtained an independent board with broad sanitation responsibilities. In its first year the board spent $35,000 on a wide variety of activities that related to the health of the city, with expenditures alone for street cleaning and garbage removal amounting to $20,000.[30] Almost all of the rest of the money went to fill in old cesspools and privy vaults. Health authorities in cities fortunate enough to have remained relatively free of epidemics were unable to convince elected officials of the need to give high priority to health services. For practical political reasons, many officials did not want to hurt their chances for reelection by implying that their city had a health problem.

By 1880 nearly all the cities in the South had professional fire departments. An exception was the relatively new center of Chattanooga, which continued to depend on volunteers divided into three companies of 102 men. Departmental expenses for 1879 amounted to $5,400; losses in eight fires reached $15,500. As long as a system worked, there seemed to be no compelling reason to change it. Professional departments were not usually formed until a disastrous fire had discredited the volunteers or until firefighting had become more complicated and the era of the bucket brigade and volunteers had ended. Several of the professional departments in the South were impressive from a statistical standpoint. Petersburg's force of thirty-three full-time firemen had at its disposal six hose reels, one hook-and-ladder truck, and 1,500 feet of what authorities called "good hose." During 1879 the department responded to thirty-one alarms, only three of which were false. Fire losses amounted to $110,000, while the cost of running the department for the year was $9,200.

Charleston's fourteen steamer and three truck companies relied on 11,200 feet of hose; the department's budget amounted to $26,000. The funding required to run a first-rate department increased markedly as a city expanded in population. The need for rapid response usually meant that a single central station was insufficient. Louisville's department had many line companies, funded by a twelve-month budget of $108,500. The Baltimore force had a $175,000 annual budget, and the chief engineer, who received a salary of $2,000 a year, supervised the daily activities of 208 firemen. During 1880 the Baltimore Fire Department answered 343 alarms, and fire damage for the period, amounting to $580,300, was mainly caused by two large blazes.[31]

Firemen ran considerable risks in exchange for few benefits and privileges. Even with the move toward professionalization, there remained a reluctance to regard firemen as full-time employees because the old volunteer tradition died hard. Still, firefighters were generally held in high esteem by the public. The mayor of Louisville observed, "Our firemen, as they always have been, are active and fearless in discharge of their duties."[32]

Civic authorities put much effort and money into building police departments. In all cases, the law officers were under civilian control. Usually, the mayor had the power to appoint the chief, subject to confirmation by the city council. Under a variation of this method, a police board had selection powers. In actual practice, the authorities left day-by-day administration to high-ranking police administrators, maintaining jurisdiction over budgetary matters. In 1880 relatively large annual salaries paid to top law enforcement officials—they were the highest paid public officials in the South—demonstrated the importance attached to police work. The superintendent of the metropolitan police in Washington made $2,610, the chief of police in New Orleans $3,480, and the marshal of the Baltimore force $2,500. The heads of the police departments in Montgomery, Augusta, Chattanooga, and Macon received salaries of about $1,000. Southern police chiefs had wages comparable to and in many cases better than their counterparts in other parts of the country. The superintendent of the large Chicago department made $3,780; chiefs in medium-sized Peoria, Fond du Lac, and Oshkosh were compensated at rates ranging from $650 to $1,000.[33]

The annual salaries and duties of men in the lower ranks reflected the financial resources available for remuneration of public employees in southern cities. Patrolmen seldom made as much as the national annual average of about $900; those in Chattanooga, Augusta, and Macon received $600 and those in Savannah $720.

Police departments in the South required officers to wear modified standard blue metropolitan uniforms and to carry specified accouterments. In accordance with national standards, the men had to purchase their own uniforms and equipment. Beats and duty hours were long and hard; the lawmen in many southern cities worked twelve hours daily, the national average. Norfolk peace keepers patrolled twenty-six miles of streets and lanes and performed their duties on schedules of six hours on and twelve off. Macon officers toiled twelve hours on and twelve hours off as they tried to protect 116 miles of thoroughfares.[34] Police everywhere, while devoting their primary efforts to protecting prime business property and residential properties, kept high crime districts under close surveillance. But the value of having police officers walk long hours on the beat provided more the semblance of a deterrent than an actual service that stopped crime in the streets.

Southern city dwellers tolerated heavier expenditures for police departments than for other urban services. In 1880 Baltimore spent $590,000 and Washington $302,000 for police protection. Some smaller cities had impressive funding levels. Charleston's budget was $68,600, Memphis's $35,000, and Augusta's $30,000.[35] Expenditures were generally higher in the South than elsewhere; fear of what some white editors called the "black brute" continued to permeate southern life. "A single day rarely passes that a case of lynching is not flashed over the wires and the cause is almost the same in each instance, the rape of a white woman or child by a big, burly negro," the *Nashville Banner* noted on May 16, 1881. "It is rape and hang. As often as it is done, that often will a devil swing off into eternity." A decade later, the editor of the Louisiana *Alexandria Town Talk* wrote that "whenever a negro or a white man rapes a woman that man dies. It is understood by both races that a proven case of rape means death."[36] Such inflammatory statements, repeated all across the South, added to white racial fears and furthered a law-and-order syndrome. Of course, popular opinion notwithstanding, rape did not constitute the primary reason for the lynching of blacks.

Blacks accounted for a high proportion of all arrests. Some white leaders used the police as a means of harassing blacks to keep them aware of their place in society. Nashville policemen made regular weekend sweeps in which they automatically arrested on suspicion all blacks whom they encountered. Authorities held the blacks for a few days and then released them without formal charges or a trial. During the short incarceration, they performed roadwork or other menial tasks.[37] The relationship between law enforcement and the perceived needs of the white majority in regard to the omnipresent race question was never officially admitted, nor was much written about it in annual reports.

The cities of the New South continued to experience the same service and protective problems prevalent in the Old South. The only real difference was that the questions had increased in magnitude as a consequence of growth. Just as before the war, not enough money was available to give a high level of support to a wide range of civil endeavors. Moreover, public safety took precedence over health and fire protection. As in other ways, the legacy of the Peculiar Institution continued to be a significant factor in determining policy in cities. Lurking beneath talk of law and order was the fear of black violence; institutionalized forms of protection from blacks helped deplete already hard-pressed city treasures.

None of the South's thirty largest communities in 1880—with the possible exception of debt-ridden Washington—had the public or private means to furnish residents with uniformly high levels of service. Thus Baltimore had a large waterworks but no comprehensive sewerage. New Orleans expended more money on sidewalk repair and extensions than on drainage ditches designed to carry away kitchen slops and household wastes. Lynchburg, with a horse railroad, had few paved streets. Richmond was better at disposing of dead animals than at removing garbage. To a greater or lesser extent, all the cities tried to set priorities, always influenced by politics and immediate needs. The same considerations influenced policy in other sections of the country, but in the South the burden of a depressed economy and race complicated matters. Attempts by southern city leaders to deal with considerations ranging from sewerage to a harsh racial policy on law and order were further indications of tentative progress toward an urban society.

Throughout the 1880s southern urban promoters sought to convey the impression that great advances were being made. A Birmingham resident, catching what he considered the spirit of events, wrote, "Why, men would come in at four o'clock in the morning and begin making trades before breakfast. Property changed hands four and five times a day. . . . Men went crazy two hours after getting here. . . . A brand-new sensation was born every day." This description, characteristic of claims made all over America about the wonders occurring in cities of the Gilded Age, contained a grain of truth. Birmingham was a "boom town" and the showcase of the New South. Boomers claimed that riches lay for the taking throughout Dixie. Middleboro, Kentucky, was expected soon to reach metropolitan proportions, fueled by what the *Baltimore Manufacturers'*

Record claimed was "fully $10,000,000" in English investment capital.[38]

Other promotional projects were the subject of similar exaggerated claims. The organizers of Cardiff, Tennessee, predicted amazing success for their "paper city," located in what their promotional literature called the "Richest and Most Inexhaustible Coal and Iron Region in the South." Richard Edmonds in his book *The South's Redemption from Poverty to Prosperity*, published in 1890, contended that unnamed New England capitalists planned to pour several million dollars into a gigantic industrial complex at Fort Payne, Alabama. Real estate companies in dozens of southern towns worked to attract funds, spawning a land boom that brought in some northern currency. The peak years came between 1887 and 1890, when promoters gambled sums that were considerable by southern standards on new town sites touted as potential industrial complexes.[39] True believers thought the millennium at hand. Henry Grady wrote in *The New South*, "The promise of her great destiny, written in her fields, her quarries, her mines, her forests, and her rivers, is no longer blurred or indistinct, and the world draws near to read."[40]

Actually, prosperity was spotty. Much of the money went into ironworks in Alabama, lumber operations in Louisiana and Arkansas, and land booms in Florida. Enthusiastic promotional froth about huge investments in Cardiff and Middlesboro held no truth. It became increasingly clear that southern prosperity paled when compared with that of the rest of the country. The real action was in the West and in the great timber stands of the upper Midwest. For every dollar poured in the South, a thousand more went toward opening up and cutting down the North Woods of Wisconsin, Michigan, and Minnesota. In the 1880s, on the banks of the Missouri and Kansas rivers in Kansas City, land worth more than $88 million changed hands in a single year during a boom. Great booms in southern California transformed Los Angeles and San Diego from unimportant country towns into regional centers. Between 1880 and 1890 the population of Los Angeles grew from 11,200 to 50,400 and that of San Diego from 2,600 to 16,200. In the Northwest, around Puget Sound, the arrival of rails from the East touched off a flurry of speculative activity. During the 1880s, Seattle's population leaped from 3,500 to 42,800; Tacoma had 1,100 residents at the start of the decade and 34,900 at the end. Such growth was what the southern cities, particularly the newer ones in the interior, needed. But the South failed to rise as the New South soothsayers had predicted.

The 1890 census made for very depressing reading in many quarters south of the Mason and Dixon Line—in the 1880s the South actually lost ground. During a decade of rapid urbanization, the number of places in the United States with populations of more than 2,500, which the census considered the breaking point between rural and urban territory, increased from 939 to 1,348. At the end of the 1880s only 192 of those communities were in the South. Other urban statistics presented an even gloomier picture. From 1880 to 1890, when the number of places in the United States with populations of more than 10,000 rose from 227 to 354, an increase of 127, the South added only 18 such cities. Numerous American cities experienced rapid growth, with a total of 117 places adding more than 10,000 inhabitants. Only 16 of these were in the South.

Of special interest were the large population increases enjoyed by a number of medium-sized midwestern industrial cities. For instance, from 1880 to 1890, Grand Rapids gained 28,300 people, Peoria 11,800, Toledo 31,300, and Youngstown 17,800. None of these communities achieved metropolitan status, but they became manufacturing towns of the kind the men of the New South wanted for their section. Like significant numbers of people, industry moved from east to west rather than from north to south. In the twelve states treated by the census as part of the north-central division, the number of cities with populations of more than 8,000 rose from 95 in 1880 to 152 in 1890. No comparable growth occurred in the South. The number of places with more than 8,000 inhabitants increased from 35 to 44. According to census experts, there was a rough correlation between industrial and urban expansion. With regard to the situation in the South, a census official stated, "The industries of these states are mainly agricultural, and while manufactures and mining are making some progress they are still in their infancy. . . . In certain of these states that proportion of urban population is still trifling; thus in Mississippi it constitutes but 2.64, in North Carolina but 3.87 and Arkansas but 4.89 per cent of the total population."[41]

The census estimated in 1890 that capital invested in American industry amounted to $6.5 billion, more than double the figure of ten years earlier. Total investments in the South reached $585 million, against $2 billion in the north-central division alone. In 1890 only the southern states of Maryland (fourteenth) and Kentucky (sixteenth) ranked in the leading twenty American manufacturing states in gross value of products. The money invested in southern manufacturing had increased markedly, up from $234 million in 1880. In an era of almost no inflation, this increase was impressive. Manufacturing capital in Georgia rose from $11 million to $57 million, in Alabama from $11 million to $46 million. Yet these gains

seemed small by national standards; industrial investments outside
the South rose by more than $3.5 billion. Manufacturing capitali-
zation in the state of New York grew from $500 million to $1.3
billion. The additional $800 million added to New York's capital
base was more than the total worth of all Dixie's industries.[42] The
"industrial revolution" in the North generated so much money so
quickly that the South could not catch up.

Only a few bright spots broke an otherwise depressing picture
in the urban South. The capitalization of manufacturing in Baltimore
soared from $38.6 million to $92.8 million. New Orleans ($26.3
million), Washington ($28.9 million), and Louisville ($36.1 million)
all had fairly substantial capital bases upon which to build in the
future. These figures seemed small, however, by comparison with
Chicago's total of $359.7 million. In all, seventeen southern cities
ranked among the top 100 cities in aggregate capital. Richmond's
capitalization more than doubled during the 1880s, increasing from
$6.9 million to $16.8 million. In the same span the midwestern city
of Columbus, Ohio, which had a heavy industrial base comparable
to that of Richmond, enjoyed an increase in capital investment of
from $5.4 million to $16.2 million. Except for Richmond and the
South's four largest manufacturing areas, no city in the region had
more than $10 million invested in manufacturing. Industry in the
Piedmont remained in an early stage, although there had been some
gains.

The highly publicized new interior manufacturing centers experienced disappointingly little progress. Chattanooga did not even
rank among the top 100 industrial cities. Atlanta had $9.5 million
and Memphis $9.4 million in manufacturing capitalization in 1890.
These increases were more than 300 percent, but so were those of
many northern industrial centers. By contrast, the capital invested
in Peoria plants jumped from $4.2 million to $15.1 million, and
Peoria was only a cog in the midwestern manufacturing empire.
Birmingham had yet to fulfill its promise. In 1890 the aggregate for
all industries was $4.6 million and for iron and steel $1.6 million.
Racine, Wisconsin, just another rising midwestern mill town with
5,000 fewer people than Birmingham, reported $11.2 million in
manufacturing capital. In Pittsburgh $48.2 million in an industrial
capitalization of $108.4 million was in iron and steel.[43] Clearly, the
magnificently conceived attempt to raise the South to the level of
the North had failed; the predictions of Grady and his colleagues
turned sour.

The unrealistic expectations of the men of the New South creed
obscured urban accomplishments in Dixie during the Gilded Age.

Building on foundations laid as far back as the colonial period, the South continued to construct cities in relation to the needs of the society. A depressed agricultural society did not require burgeoning towns. The developments that occurred represented a necessary urban consolidation accompanied by limited progress. The old and new cities modernized many of their urban and social services. Cities could be built and peopled with great speed; the Oklahoma land rush cities of Guthrie and Oklahoma City, from scratch, acquired populations of more than 10,000 between dawn and dusk in 1889. The southern cities, poised to expand, bided their time until the South could rise again.

5

HOLDING THE LINE

During the 1890s the South stopped overtly trying to compete with the North and turned inward. Widespread opposition developed to any policy that sought accommodation with the new northern industrial order, although the goals of the leaders of the New South movement were not necessarily rejected en masse. After all, shortly after his untimely death in 1889, Grady came to rank as one of the South's fallen heroes. Moreover, Henry Watterson continued to gain stature as a sectional leader, and Richard Edmonds's *Baltimore Manufactures' Record* remained the South's foremost commercial publication. Rather, the change in emphasis related directly to the realities of sectional relations. Of particular significance was the growing perception that the North had lost interest in trying to influence the course of southern events.

The South underwent a period of retrenchment based on the recognition that there was continuity in southern history. Back in the 1850s the delegates active in the commercial convention movement had reached the conclusion that the South could not compete with the North on its own terms; they concluded that a unique southern civilization should take its own distinctive path. Forty years later, following the Civil War, the Reconstruction period, and the abortion of the New South concept, a new generation of southern leaders, for somewhat different reasons, reached essentially the same conclusions. In the 1850s the main reason for retrenchment was economic. No one gave much thought to racial problems because they were mainly handled by the institution of human slavery. During the 1890s the top priority involved retaining the supremacy of the white race. The result was legislation, including the Louisiana separate car act, sustained in 1896 by the U.S. Supreme Court in *Plessy* v. *Ferguson*. In the aftermath of that controversial decision, state legislatures throughout the South enacted whole bodies of laws that created a highly structured segregation system based on the separate but equal doctrine. In 1898, the U.S. Supreme Court in *Williams* v. *Mississippi* accepted the "Mississippi Plan," which called for the disfranchisement of black voters.

During both the 1850s and the 1890s the North cared little about the development of an autonomous South. Few northerners had paid much attention to the full ramifications of the convention movement until it was too late. And no great outcry in the North arose to oppose the trend in the South toward white racial domination, although the Jim Crow laws regulated race relations more completely and along the same lines as the discredited black codes of the immediate post-Civil War era. Northern attitudes contrasted sharply with those of 1861. The circumstances had changed—there was no Abraham Lincoln, and the Peculiar Institution was long dead. The rise of industry and the exploitation of previously virgin areas had drastically changed northern priorities.

Agricultural discontent served as another indication of the South's growing isolationism. Supporters of the Populist movement opposed the New South approach to solving economic problems; they wanted to eradicate rather than encourage what they perceived as outside domination of southern economic institutions. Although it usually went unrecognized, a direct connection existed between the agrarian revolt and the South's historic inability to erect a great mercantile and banking center able to control credit, all the while offering farmers low interest rates, bargain prices, and other inducements. The leaders of the agrarian movement would have been perfectly at home at one of the prewar commercial conventions. Indeed, the Civil War represented but an interlude in the quest of southern agrarians for more equitable commercial arrangements.

During the 1870s large numbers of distressed farmers in the South had joined the Patrons of Husbandry. About a thousand local chapters sprang up, but beyond performing the task of educating farmers about the need for joint political action, the southern Grange had little impact on affairs. The movement also spawned internal disharmony, which New South spokesmen ignored in their propaganda about investment opportunities. In the 1880s the Grange gave way to a series of state-level alliances of farmers and to local groups called agricultural wheels. A large number of the members were tenant farmers and sharecroppers united in opposition to land barons. This combination gave rise to the Southern Alliance and also to schemes for the cooperative marketing of farm products. By the 1890s, business opposition and insufficient capital had doomed these plans, causing a reappraisal of goals and objectives that led to the subsequent entry of the Southern Alliance into the political arena. Rejecting overtures for a great national Populist party, some Alliance supporters formed populist organizations that often allied with the Republican party. Most leaders, however, worked through the southern Democratic party, a bulwark of white supremacy. The Alliance, which initially claimed to have considerable black support, declined in importance after agrarian Democrat William Jennings Bryan lost the 1896 presidential election. The bitter realities of abject poverty and racial strife took their toll from Dixie's inhabitants. As long as the rural South remained depressed and divided, the promise of southern life envisioned by the architects of the New South remained an impossible dream. The failed agrarian crusade was not an aberration but another frustrating episode in the South's economic inability to build cities that could have freed the section from outside domination.

In the final analysis, southern urbanites responded negatively to the agrarian efforts, despite urban and rural interdependence. The prospect of black and white farmers' banding together in a community of interest to achieve specific political ends frightened many urban dwellers. The antiurbanism that culminated in Bryan's campaign pointed up divergent urban and rural interests. City people did not want to pay more than absolutely necessary for their food products; rural folk felt gouged by urban businessmen at just about every conceivable level. Interest rates and shipping rates were causes of continual friction. On the other hand, few southern businessmen listened seriously to the proposals put forward by the Southern Alliance. Nor did they formulate significant counterproposals. Of course, more was involved than simply the protection of vested interests. Everyone agreed that a southern agricultural depression had started long before the Panic of 1893. The failure of the rural South to recover from the Civil War assured the section of what its nationalists considered colonial status within an industrialized United States. Yet the traditionally cautious nature of southern city building also meant that, because of the South's consistent lack of investment capital, there was by and large an unwillingness to take risks. Of course, the men of the New South creed described a section in which business leaders were alert to change. Although this scenario may have been accurate in a few places, notably the rebuilt city of Atlanta and newly industrialized Birmingham, it did not extend to the urban South as a whole. City building continued to take its course, proceeding along customary conservative channels.

In 1890 the South contained forty-eight cities of more than

10,000, as indicated by Table 6. The thirty cities that had formed the backbone of the southern urban network in 1880 all experienced population gains during the following ten years. Eight of the towns enjoyed increases in excess of the national average of 56.5 percent for all the people in the country living in urban territory. Atlanta grew by 75.18 percent and Chattanooga by 125.72 percent. Six of the southern towns were among the forty largest places in the United States. Baltimore was the nation's seventh largest city. New Orleans ranked twelfth, Washington fourteenth, and Louisville twentieth. All told, the South's four largest cities continued to be the section's only true metropolises. Richmond, in the thirty-fourth position, and Nashville, in the thirty-eighth, were urban centers of respectable size although they fell short of metropolitan status. The precarious state of the southern economy precluded the building of instant cities.

The 1890 population statistics for the thirty largest 1880 towns further reflected the continued gradual evolution of the southern urban system. In an age in which many potential investors based their decisions in part on urban growth rates, census returns had considerable economic ramifications. Within this context, several old towns were just not growing very fast. Baltimore had 434,000 people and Washington 230,400. Savannah, which had 43,200 residents, continued to gain on Charleston, a city of 55,000. Norfolk, which had 34,900 people, was the principal port and the second largest city in Virginia. A population of 20,000 cemented Wilmington's hold as North Carolina's number one port. Alexandria, Georgetown, and Portsmouth were unimportant in the larger scheme of urbanization matters. Along the Piedmont, Richmond's 81,400 persons made it the largest fall-line city. Neither Petersburg nor Lynchburg improved upon their positions in Virginia. Columbia remained the second largest city in South Carolina. Augusta enhanced its industrial base. Louisville, a city of 161,000 inhabitants, moved ahead as a regional banking, transportation, and commercial center. Lexington continued to lose ground to Louisville. Covington and Newport, glorified suburbs of Cincinnati, along with Cumberland, were for all practical purposes no longer in the southern urban network. Nashville, with 76,200 people, continued to be central Tennessee's major center. New Orleans, despite a sluggish 12 percent rate of increase, had 242,000 residents and remained the leading city of the lower South. Mobile, throughout its history in the shadow of New Orleans, had hardly grown since antebellum days. For the most part, long-established urban relationships remained unchanged.

Mixed growth rates during the 1880s in the interior of Dixie did

Table 6. Population Trends in 48 Southern Cities, 1880–1890

City	Population		Increase	
	1880	1890	Number	Percent
Alabama				
Birmingham	3,086	26,178	23,092	748
Mobile	29,132	31,076	1,944	7
Montgomery	16,713	21,883	5,170	31
Arkansas				
Fort Smith	3,099	11,311	8,212	265
Little Rock	13,138	25,874	12,736	97
Dist. of Columbia				
Georgetown	12,578	14,046	1,468	12
Washington	177,624	230,392	52,768	30
Florida				
Jacksonville	7,650	17,201	9,551	125
Key West	9,890	18,080	8,190	83
Pensacola	6,845	11,750	4,905	72
Georgia				
Atlanta	37,409	65,533	28,124	75
Augusta	21,891	33,300	11,409	52
Columbus	10,123	17,303	7,180	71
Macon	12,749	22,746	9,997	78
Savannah	30,709	43,189	12,480	41
Kentucky				
Covington	29,720	37,371	7,651	26
Lexington	16,656	21,567	4,911	29
Louisville	123,758	161,129	37,371	30
Newport	20,433	24,918	4,485	22
Paducah	8,036	12,797	4,761	59
Louisiana				
Baton Rouge	7,197	10,478	3,281	46
New Orleans	216,090	242,039	25,949	12
Shreveport	8,009	11,979	3,970	50

not significantly alter the hierarchy of cities. Not a single one even approached metropolitan status—an expected but disappointing circumstance. Atlanta advanced to 65,500 people. Chattanooga and Little Rock moved forward as expected. Memphis underwent a quicker recovery than predicted, mainly because of a combination

Table 6 (*continued*)

City	Population		Increase	
	1880	1890	Number	Percent
Maryland				
Baltimore	332,313	434,439	102,126	31
Cumberland	10,693	12,729	2,036	19
Hagerstown	6,627	10,118	3,491	53
Mississippi				
Meridian	4,008	10,624	6,616	165
Natchez	7,058	10,101	3,032	43
Vicksburg	11,814	13,373	1,559	13
North Carolina				
Asheville	2,616	10,235	7,619	291
Charlotte	7,094	11,557	4,463	63
Raleigh	9,265	12,678	3,413	37
Wilmington	17,350	20,056	2,706	16
South Carolina				
Charleston	49,984	54,955	4,971	10
Columbia	10,036	15,353	5,317	53
Tennessee				
Chattanooga	12,892	29,100	16,208	126
Jackson	5,377	10,039	4,662	87
Knoxville	9,693	22,535	12,842	132
Memphis	38,592	64,495	30,903	92
Nashville	43,350	76,168	32,818	76
Virginia				
Alexandria	13,659	14,339	680	5
Danville	7,526	10,305	2,779	37
Lynchburg	15,959	19,709	3,750	24
Norfolk	21,966	34,871	12,905	58
Petersburg	21,656	22,680	1,024	5
Portsmouth	11,390	13,268	1,878	16
Richmond	63,600	81,388	17,788	28
Roanoke	669	16,159	15,490	2,315

of confidence in the sanitary reforms imposed after the 1870s epidemics and progress in the surrounding region. Macon and Montgomery experienced moderate growth, and both retained their importance as cotton markets while adding some manufacturing. Columbus supporters had expected their city to have more than its recorded 17,300 people in 1890. Vicksburg, the largest city in Mississippi, still functioned as a connecting link in the downstream cotton trade. The interior cities continued to reflect decisions made many decades earlier.

Population trends in the eighteen southern cities that first passed the 10,000 mark in the 1880s were fairly predictable. No new seaport cities of importance arose from Maryland through South Carolina. In Florida, Jacksonville increased by 9,500, reaching 17,200 inhabitants, Key West attained a population of 18,100, and Pensacola a population of 11,800. Only a few Louisiana and Mississippi River cities crossed the 10,000 mark—Baton Rouge, Shreveport, Meridian, and Natchez. Four commercial cities that moved past the 10,000 figure had modest urban pretensions—Jackson, Tennessee; Fort Smith, Arkansas; Paducah, Kentucky; and Hagerstown, Maryland. None of these places was crucial to southern urban progress. Of more potential consequence was the rise of a few Piedmont mill towns. Big Lick, Virginia, had 669 residents at the start of the 1880s, when textile factories financed by Yankee capitalists ushered in a boom. Under the new name of Roanoke, the place had 16,200 inhabitants in 1890. Danville, Virginia, showing a 37 percent rate of increase, went from 7,500 to 10,300 persons. In North Carolina, textile and cigarette manufacturing led to three moderately successful new mill towns; Charlotte, Raleigh, and Asheville. Two other localities, one old and one new, exhibited attributes associated with the New South. Knoxville finally started to display the success predicted by its early promoters. During the 1880s, Knoxville, helped by an infusion of industry, more than doubled in population, with an increase from 9,700 to 22,500. Birmingham was another case. The number of inhabitants grew from 3,100 to 26,200—a spectacular rise of 748 percent. As Knoxville, Birmingham, and the Piedmont towns demonstrated, manufacturing had more potential than cotton shipping for building towns in a hurry. Even so, once manufacturers had built the first mills, it took a new wave of factories to sustain growth.

Birmingham hoped to become a regional metropolis. The Louisville and Nashville Railroad connected Birmingham with a number of neighboring iron- and coal-producing towns, including Bessemer, Talladega, and Anniston. According to promotional literature, thirty-two iron furnaces operated in and around Birmingham. The editor of the *Birmingham Iron Age* claimed that more outside capitalists arrived every week. By 1890 Alabama was producing more iron and steel than any other southern state, and Andrew Carnegie remarked that the South was the "most formidable industrial enemy" that Pennsylvania encountered in the struggle for control of the American iron industry.[1] Northern money, some of it supplied by Carnegie, had provided the necessary resources to start a boom. Unfortunately for Birmingham's future aspirations, the building of a great city required more than outside money and a few small towns with furnaces and mines. Hinterland agricultural connections were of crucial importance, and as long as the farmlands around Birmingham stayed depressed, the city was bound to have problems in sustaining the rapid growth needed to make it a significant national center. Birmingham did not fit neatly into the South. Dixie's fragile agricultural economy simply did not require a proliferation of competing cities. After the construction and staffing of the mills, Birmingham, like the new industrial towns in the Piedmont, faced the rather unpromising prospect of competing with older towns for depressed agricultural markets; even with some outside help and a boldly stated program for industrial progress, city builders continued to encounter serious challenges.

In 1900 the South contained only nine more cities with populations of more than 10,000 than it had ten years earlier. The largest of the new places, none of which posed any immediate threat to the older communities, was Newport News, Virginia, which advanced from 4,400 to 19,600 inhabitants. Part of the complex of ports in the Norfolk area, it hardly had an independent status. An old seaport, Tampa, Florida, had 15,800 people and could count on future growth in relationship to progress along Florida's west coast. Two internal towns enjoyed some success: Owensboro, Kentucky, on the Ohio River between Paducah and Louisville, reached 13,200. Pine Bluff, Arkansas, on the Arkansas River, grew apace with the development of the rice industry on the Grand Prairie in east-central Arkansas. Pine Bluff had 11,500 residents but little immediate hope of being more than a farm marketing town. The chances of the agricultural and educational community of Athens, Georgia, which attained a population of 10,200 in 1900, were scarcely better. The four other places that crossed the 10,000 line were mill towns; the addition of so few new industrial centers reflected the general slowdown in the national economy that followed the Panic of 1893. Whether more limited growth than anticipated was good or bad depended on the viewpoint taken about the New South concept, because the more industry the South acquired, the more the section's economy depended on outside forces.

The 1900 census demonstrated that at best the South had only slightly improved its urban position in the United States during the Gilded Age. Whether southerners liked it or not, they had no choice except to judge their own progress by standards set in the North. If northerners decreed population totals important, people in the South had to follow suit. In 1900 there were 400 cities with more than 10,000 people in the United States. Only 57 of these were in the South. Twenty years earlier, 30 of 227 such cities had been in the South. Other indexes nullified the small gain. Of 82 American cities in 1900 in the 25,000-to-50,000 population class, only 10 were in the South. Of 40 cities with between 50,000 and 100,000, the South had but 5. Of 38 cities in excess of 100,000, there were 5 in the South. Dixie had added only one city in that category in twenty years; the rest of the country counted 17 more. The figures failed to convey a fundamental point about the southern urban network, however; as throughout much of its history, the South entered the new century with its regional metropolises, with the exception of Washington and to a lesser extent Baltimore, designed to serve sectional commercial needs. The South could do no better, given its inability to raise up a city capable of combating New York. The South never had the means of controlling its own credit. For that reason and because of the nature of the agricultural system, most southerners approached city building reasonably and realistically. Dixie's urban areas need separate consideration on their own merits; a statistical lag was inevitable, given the circumstances.

Failure to match the performance of the North did not mean stagnation or decline. The five largest southern cities all advanced in the 1890s. Memphis was the section's newest metropolis. It moved ahead, in part because of annexations, to 102,300 residents in 1900; 37,800 people had been added in ten years. Baltimore, continuing to feed on its carefully constructed midwestern connections, increased by 78,600. With 509,000 persons, it moved up a notch from 1890, ranking as the sixth largest city in the nation. The increased functions of the federal government helped to generate a 89,800 rise in the number of Washingtonians. At the dawn of the new century, the nation's capital ranked eleventh in the country, with 278,700 inhabitants. New Orleans grew by 25,900 to 242,000; Louisville by 43,600 to 204,700. The expansion rates were not out of line with those for numerous metropolises outside the South. For example, Detroit (285,700) added 79,800, Newark (246,000) added 65,200, and Providence (175,600) added 45,500. New York and its boroughs grew by 929,800, to 3.4 million, making it one of the largest world centers.

None of the other cities in the South of more than 50,000 people in 1900 had added as many as 25,000 inhabitants over the previous ten years. Atlanta had come the closest, pushing ahead by 24,400 to 89,900. The 12,200 augmentation for Birmingham (38,400) demolished the extravagant predictions by New South spokesmen that it would soon rival Pittsburgh, a city of 451,500 at the turn of the century. An increasingly settled state of urban relations in the South made it difficult for new and smaller cities to get ahead. By the dawn of the twentieth century, the 10,000 mark had lost relevance as a measurement of urbanism. Once metropolises had hewed out and established hinterlands, rapid advances by lesser places became difficult outside newly opened areas. The New South advocates did the South a disservice by claiming that the very adoption of a program designed to attract northern monies would soon allow Dixie to build a series of monster great cities. Such a statement made substantial achievements appear almost as failures.

Southern urbanization in the Gilded Age underscored the continuity of the section's experience. Economic, social, racial, religious, and political attitudes all had antebellum roots. Neither the Civil War nor Reconstruction had much more than a temporarily disruptive impact on southern cities. Indeed, there was little need to transform these cities so that they reflected northern images because they had mirrored national urban values since colonial times. The manner of their construction and their attempt to garner markets through transportation systems were all in line with the prevailing trends in American city making. Even so, the realization that the South lacked the resources to achieve urban and hence economic parity with the rest of the country dulled the spirit of many white southerners. An inferior agricultural system militated against a quick recovery. In the wake of the failed agrarian crusade, southern leaders concentrated on maintaining segregation and remembering the Lost Cause. A general acceptance of second-class status in the Union in exchange for a measure of social control over internal affairs gave the South the appearance of a failed and conservative bastion. The failure to realize the plans of the New South leaders obscured the continuity and the progress made in southern city building. At the same time the New South concept provided, as had J.D.B. DeBow in antebellum days, a rationale for building the very kind of urban society about which Thomas Jefferson had expressed ambivalence. Throughout the process the cities remained the best hope for a progressive South. Indeed, they continued to grow along logical lines. The next stratum developed in Florida.

Events that transpired in Florida, where northern capitalist Henry Morrison Flagler sought to become the Sunshine State's counterpart of empire builder James J. Hill in the Northwest, provided hope for the future. Henry Grady claimed that by 1889 Flagler had already invested $7 million in Florida hotel properties and superb winter homes. "The tide of travel," Grady wrote, "is turning again, and Florida is not only confirmed as the winter garden of the Republic, but its sanitarium."[2] According to the 1890 census, Florida was the last frontier in the continental United States. In 1888 Flagler, after a short Florida retirement, bought a short-line railroad that ran between Jacksonville and St. Augustine. Other acquisitions followed, leading to the creation of the Flagler System, which dominated Florida railroading. In 1896 Flagler's Florida East Coast Railroad reached Miami, 366 miles south of Jacksonville. In 1912, a year before his death, Flagler finished a spectacular extension of his railroad south from Miami through the Florida Keys over a series of bridges to Key West. In conjunction with his railroad properties, he started land companies, newspapers, cattle ranches, and utilities. Of special significance was his promotion of tourism, a relatively new and untried concept. Large Victorian-style resort hotels that he erected, including the elegantly named Ponce de Leon in St. Augustine, the Royal Poinciana in Palm Beach, and the Royal Palm in Miami, became national landmarks and symbols of vacation paradises. Flagler's promotional literature called St. Augustine the "Oldest City in America" and Key West "America's Gibraltar."[3]

As was to be expected, a few unreconstructed southern nationalists denounced Flagler as another in a long line of northern rascals bent on keeping the South in colonial bondage. This evaluation of course overlooked a fundamental postulate of the New South philosophy, namely the notion that the section could best advance by attracting such men as Flagler. According to this assumption, outside capital was actually beneficial because it would create jobs and provide the means by which the South would eventually break away from northern control.

Florida boomed in the first thirty years of the twentieth century. Promoters touted the eastern seaboard as the Gold Coast and the building of railroads down the West Coast helped to stimulate settlement further. Both the citrus and the cattle industries gained national markets, more and more retirees found Florida suitable to their needs, and tourism increased at a steady rate, especially during the general prosperity of the 1920s. Destructive hurricanes, overbuilding, environmental concerns, and recurrent land scandals failed to stop progress. The sudden surge was reminiscent of that in Ohio early in the nineteenth century.

The population of the Sunshine State rose from 528,500 in 1900 to 1.5 million in 1930, and the number of cities with more than 10,000 inhabitants increased from 4 to 14, as shown by Table 7. The 1930 census, using a 2,500 mark as the breaking point between rural and urban territory, showed Florida as 52 percent urban. In the South

Table 7. Thirty-Year Growth Percentages for Florida Cities over 10,000 in 1930

City	Population		Increase	
	1900	1930	Number	Percent
Daytona Beach	1,690	16,598	14,908	882
Gainesville	3,633	10,465	6,832	188
Jacksonville	28,429	129,549	101,120	556
Key West	17,114	12,831	−4,283	−25
Lakeland	1,180	18,554	17,374	1,472
Miami	1,681	110,637	108,956	6,482
Orlando	2,481	27,330	24,849	1,002
Pensacola	17,747	31,579	13,852	78
St. Augustine	4,272	12,111	7,839	184
St. Petersburg	1,575	40,425	38,850	2,467
Sanford	1,450	10,100	8,650	5,767
Tallahassee	2,981	10,700	7,719	259
Tampa	15,839	101,161	85,322	539
West Palm Beach	564	26,610	26,046	4,618

only Maryland, at 60 percent, had a larger percentage of urbanites. Miami, a village of 1,700 people in 1900, had 110,600 thirty years later. In the 1920s alone it added 81,100 inhabitants, for an increase of 274.1 percent. Two additional Florida cities had crossed the 100,000 mark by 1930—Jacksonville and Tampa. Many other places rose in spectacular fashion. Between 1900 and 1930 eight of the fourteen cities added over 10,000 people, and six increased by more than 1,000 percent. Key West was the single significant Florida city that decreased in size; its population dropped from 17,100 to 12,800 as a result of a decline in fishing and naval activities. The new urban centers led the way in furthering the fortunes of the Sunrise State. Many southerners felt uncomfortable with the rapid urbanization of Florida. They either ignored it, hoping that it would go away, or believed that the state reflected the further imposition of Yankee values upon Dixie.

Some southerners preferred to regard Texas and Oklahoma as part of the South. Somehow these states were considered more southern in a philosophical way than Florida, which tended to be associated with northern philistines, especially those from New York. It made little difference that considerable northeastern money went into southwestern petroleum and transportation projects. This influx of northern capital was not as obvious as northeastern tourists and migrants in Florida. Nor did it matter that most people in Texas and Oklahoma considered themselves westerners, with economic and social ties outside the South. They could not deny, however, that Texas had fought on the side of the Confederacy and that Oklahoma had Confederate connections.

The demographic result, whether intentional or not, was an arbitrary but considerable increase in the size and prowess of the urban South. In 1930 Texas had seventeen cities with populations of more than 25,000, and Oklahoma had four. Seven of the cities in the two states had in excess of 100,000 people.

Houston	292,400	Fort Worth	163,500
Dallas	260,500	Tulsa	141,300
San Antonio	231,500	El Paso	102,400
Oklahoma City	185,400		

The two biggest places in the Sooner State, Oklahoma City and Tulsa, grew by more than 100 percent in the 1920s. In the Lone Star State, which had very liberal annexation laws, so that it was fairly easy for larger communities to gobble up suburbs. Though the inclusion of El Paso and Tulsa in the South may have puzzled some observers, the first stirrings were occurring that would lead in the direction of a larger cultural, economic, and political superregion called the Sunbelt. Urban rather than agricultural values would shape new dispensations.

As 1930 statistics indicated, the biggest cities of the Progressive Age in the Old South continued to grow along rather predictable lines.

Baltimore	804,900	Memphis	253,100
Washington	486,900	Richmond	182,900
New Orleans	458,800	Nashville	129,700
Louisville	307,700	Chattanooga	119,800
Atlanta	270,400	Knoxville	105,800
Birmingham	259,700		

In all, these places accounted for eleven of the ninety-three cities in the United States with populations of more than 100,000. Another fifteen of the southern localities had more than 50,000 inhabitants.

Metropolitan area figures for the big cities made them seem even more impressive, with a few places adding more than 100,000 residents in the 1920s. Observers of the urban scene many decades later in the South often failed to notice, however, that so-called white flight from central cities started very early in the century. Suburbanization in and outside the South was part of a general fragmentation of metropolitan America. In 1930 Atlanta's metropolitan population was 440,900 and Birmingham's 431,500. In the first thirty years of the twentieth century, cities in the South represented bright spots in a perpetually depressed and racially divided society that felt oppressed and exploited by colonialism.

Northern capital lured into Dixie by various inducements, ranging from tax breaks to excellent railroad freight deferentials, helped create a number of medium-sized industrial towns. By 1930 industry had brought considerable progress in such places as Selma (18,000) in Alabama, Brunswick (14,000) in Georgia, and Kingsport (11,900) in Tennessee. Still, the largest number were in the Carolinas, where the "Cotton Mill Campaign" of the New South era eventually bore fruit. In addition, the tobacco industry expanded after the federal courts in 1911 ordered the breakup of the American Tobacco Company trust. Electrification and trunk railroads were additional factors. In 1929 the South had almost 64 percent of all the nation's textile spindles and produced 84 percent of all cigarettes.[4] At the start of the Great Depression, the South produced about 12 percent of the nation's manufacturing products, but most of the profits left the region. Outsiders quickly learned that for small initial investments they could pay low wages, engage in exploitative labor practices, buy politicians, charge high interest rates, and realize lucrative profits while reinvesting little in return. For unenlightened and ruthless capitalists willing to tolerate lethargic laborers, corrupt politicians, racial segregation, and hostility toward outsiders, the South was a land of opportunity.

Prophets of industry, in the belief that a continued expansion of manufacturing would solve any short-term difficulties, continued to claim that factories would allow the section to regain the greatness of its past. Edmonds of the *Baltimore Manufacturers' Record* remained convinced of what he considered the region's "boundless potentialities." In 1929, a year before his death, he claimed the South was "writing an Epic of Progress and Prosperity in Letters of Gold." He and his fellow promoters contended that the South of the Roaring Twenties was on the verge on an economic renaissance. "An electric spark has fired the South to build a new civilization," an enthusiastic promoter asserted in 1928. Two years later a North Carolina economist claimed, "The new industry of the South is part and parcel of a larger economy . . . a pecuniary society, whose economic ramifications extend over an ever widening area."[5] It followed that northern capital was a blessing rather than an evil. A job was a job, the reasoning went, and it made no difference where the investment capital came from. Wages were of course another matter. A 1922 survey indicated that average hourly earnings in Massachusetts textile mills were 40.9 cents compared with 32.5 cents an hour in Virginia and 21 cents in Alabama.[6] Industrial progress, despite the enthusiastic claims, carried a heavy price tag.

Northern interests had not moved South to help Dixie develop rival industrial components. Developments in the steel industry made this point abundantly clear. In the Birmingham area and elsewhere in Alabama the giant Tennessee Coal and Iron Company, a subsidiary of U.S. Steel of Pittsburgh, after a controversial 1907 merger, expanded its operations at a much slower rate than seemed warranted in the eyes of southerners. They argued that the slow rate of expansion was intended to protect already operating northern mills, a charge denied by Pittsburgh steel producers, who asserted that the South lacked markets. No one mentioned the fact that, since about the turn of the century, price fixing had prevailed under the patently unfair "Pittsburgh Plus" plan. Through this arrangement, Birmingham and other mills had to charge listed Pittsburgh prices, plus the freight rates from Pittsburgh. To make matters worse, agreements restricted Birmingham forges to the production of less profitable kinds of iron and steel. Fabricators in the South had to pay much more for their steel than competitors in the Pittsburgh area. Even after the Federal Trade Commission had outlawed Pittsburgh Plus in 1924, the southern mills remained at a disadvantage. A "multiple basing point" formula that lasted for the next fourteen years arbitrarily held Birmingham prices $3.00 to $5.00 a ton above those in Pittsburgh.[7] It was one thing for southerners to develop regional food processing, lumber, and paper industries but quite another to challenge the very heart of the northern manufacturing machine.

Southern white mill workers received lower wages and in general had poorer working conditions than their counterparts in the North. During the 1920s, southern promoters of industrial progress contended that the region's conservative "Anglo-Saxon" laborers hated unions, abhorred government interference, obeyed employers, and worked cheap. The Macon Chamber of Commerce claimed that local operatives were "thrifty, industrious, and one hundred per cent American." Kwanians in Marion, North Carolina, trying to lure northern money to their fair city, noted that "every factory or branch of industry is certain to be able to secure adequate, satisfactory and contented labor."[8] Rhetoric throughout the South emphasized the docility of workers and their willingness to work long hours under the harshest of conditions. In 1925 a writer in an Atlanta business publication wrote, "The New England mills are forced to operate largely with unruly, indifferent, ignorant foreign labor. Southern mill hands are now in their second generation, skilled, reliable and intelligent. The supply of native white labor is ample for present and future cotton manufacturing needs. It has been demonstrated, too, that the negro can be quickly trained for certain of the less important jobs."[9] No southern state had minimum-wage legislation, and many states resisted attempts to curtail the use of child labor. What passed for a reform in North Carolina limited women employees to twelve-hour days.

The prevailing situation helped make labor agitation inevitable. Prior to World War I most union activity in the South involved skilled workers. During hostilities union organizing resulted in bitter strikes in the steel and textile industries; in 1918 authorities used troops to break unpopular walkouts in Anderson and Columbus cotton mills. Most gains made by national unions were lost after the war. Nine thousand textile workers suffered defeat in 1921 North Carolina labor disturbances that followed massive layoffs during an economic downturn. In the round of prosperity that followed, unions lost influence. In 1927 and 1928, when textile owners, faced with growing competition and falling prices, introduced increased workloads, new organizing efforts followed. A great deal of violence occurred, especially in Elizabethton, Tennessee, and Marion, North Carolina. A 1929 communist-led strike in Gaston failed completely and convinced many southerners that there was a connection between unions and radicalism.[10] As a result of the harsh disputes, organized labor made little progress. Many textile mills, never very pleasant places to work, remained unorganized, the unhappy consequence of the New South philosophy. The conduct on the Piedmont of the erstwhile "Lords of the Loom," coupled with that of the hard-driving Pittsburgh steel makers, had a backlash in Dixie that would lead people to question the whole concept of an urban South.

Control of blacks persisted as an important white preoccupation in the urban South. The suppression of black rights took many forms. A severe race riot in Atlanta in 1906, in which whites invaded black neighborhoods to attack innocent victims, provided a brutal example of direct tactics. Blacks' boycott of Jim Crow streetcars failed. Residential segregation became more rigid and codified by law. Lynchings served as another means of keeping blacks aware that they were in a subservient position. Gains made by blacks in the World War I period, when manpower shortages opened up jobs previously held solely by whites, only intensified efforts to segregate and intimidate them further. The revival of the Ku Klux Klan shocked many people; in the urban South the nationwide organization—it had powerful Klaverns in Indiana and northern Wisconsin—while opposing Roman Catholicism and supporting its own version of moral purity, was known as a self-proclaimed bulwark of white supremacy. The Robert E. Lee Klan No. 1 in Birmingham claimed 10,000 members; Klansmen arrogantly and incorrectly called Atlanta the "Imperial City."[11] A Memphis newspaper called Booker T. Washington an "Alabama coon."[12]

Blacks had little recourse, apart from moving north, except to adjust as best they could. Their ghettos, usually hewed out of old shanty towns established on the edge of cities during Reconstruction, became "Hidden Communities," with commercial and political institutions divorced from the white world. Blacks lived a world apart, denied the vote and segregated by a growing body of ordinances that humiliated them by requiring them to use separate water fountains and seats in the back of public conveyances. Even though blacks performed the most menial and hardest jobs in the urban South, they had little to say about how cities were run. In 1920 Baltimore was 15 percent black and New Orleans 26 percent, but white officials determined the course of urban life.

At least two cities had classic urban political machines, which handled most public welfare for both whites and blacks. In Memphis, Edward "Boss" Crump, who originally gained power as a reformer, dominated the city for several decades, using ruthless political methods. Popular with the voters for his low tax policies, segregationist views, and improvement of the park and boulevard system, Crump was strongly probusiness. "Memphis," he said, "should be conducted as a great business corporation."[13] Crump's counterpart in New Orleans, Martin Behrman, was a former Jew from New York who converted to Roman Catholicism. His political organization, the Choctaw Club, dominated the Crescent City's political scene for most of the first quarter of the twentieth century. Large public works projects that Behrman championed, even ones that generated huge debts, gained massive voter support. Behrman and Crump both understood that the delivery of popular services more than compensated for the cost at election time.

Southern urban governments, despite a conservative image, quickly adopted much heralded improvements in governmental forms, designed to promote efficiency and professionalism. Staunton, Virginia, appointed the nation's first city manager in 1908. Chattanooga, Birmingham, Mobile, and Memphis all adopted the commission plan. Some observers believed the changes cosmetic. In 1927 William J. Robertson, a critic of southern urban governments, called the average mayor in the South "a weak vessel, subject to the beck and call of the unscrupulous politicians" and claimed that every city with a population of more than 75,000 had "a political organization as formidable as Tammany Hall in its machine rule, and in its ability to take care of its political friends." While this may have been the situation in a few places, rather benevolent business government was the rule throughout the urban South of the Progressive era. An exception was Washington, which was governed by Congress and three commissioners appointed by the president. Urban reformer Frederic C. Howe praised this undemocratic arrangement, claiming, "True, Washington is governed in an autocratic way, for in the Capital City the city is disfranchised. . . . Washington is probably as honestly governed as is any European municipality, and it has been for years. Its streets are clean, well lighted, and well protected by the police. Its school system is among the best, and its health, fire, and many other departments are beyond serious criticism."[14]

Southern city governments made the transition to larger and generally more efficient administrations far more readily than many of those in the North, where rapid economic, technological, and ethnic changes proved more than some leadership groups could handle. In the 1890s both Kansas City and Denver came close to social disintegration, when their business communities lost touch with the flow of events. In these places and others, including New York, Chicago, and Boston, only powerful machine rule stabilized affairs. James and Thomas Pendergast in Kansas City and several Tammany Hall leaders in New York were able through their ties to a wide range of groups in society to achieve a community consensus. In the South such a process was unnecessary—both Crump and Behrman relied primarily on native white support. White supremacy provided a common ground for most whites; the legacy of controlling blacks contributed to a general concern for stability. The slackening off of immigration and migration made for an increasingly homogeneous white population. Slower growth rates in the South were other contributing factors. The continuity that characterized southern urban development necessitated a different kind of response from that in the teeming northern immigrant cities.

Many urban changes took place in America in the first thirty years of the twentieth century. The "great cities" that had emerged by 1890 continued to grow. The need for urban services fueled a mounting professionalism in city government. The "Horse City" ended and the age of the automobile started. Not only did the motor vehicle substitute one form of pollution for another, but it affected everything from police responsibilities to the spatial characteristics of urban areas. Of special significance was the furthering of suburban development. Downtown areas made what amounted to a last stand.

The building of great skyscrapers provided a false sense of permanence, drawing attention away from the first suburban shopping centers. Zoning ordinances, an innovation, could potentially change the traditional appearance of cities. The ready availability of electricity and gas had important implications for energy use. Home ownership became a major goal of urban Americans. The agricultural nation receded into the past; in 1920 the census reported that more than half the people in the country lived in urban territory. The new urban identity did not bypass the South. Atlanta, Baltimore, and Washington gained networks of automobile suburbs.[15] Automobile dealerships became some of Dixie's fastest growing businesses. Tall buildings thrust toward the skies from Baltimore to New Orleans. To the extent that resources permitted, southern cities and urban dwellers embraced "modern urban America."

An important aspect of the Progressive era was the changing scope of urban planning, as the City Beautiful movement of the Gilded Age moved beyond parks and boulevards. Two important projects in Chicago helped to set the stage. George Pullman built an entire planned industrial town; Daniel H. Burnham directed the construction of the "White City" at the 1893 Columbia Exposition. Violent strikes ruined Pullman's paternalistic experiment. Critics called Burnham's emphasis on Classical or Renaissance styles outdated and undemocratic. Pullman received praise from many European experts, and 27 million people visited the White City. No matter what flaws were involved, both schemes tended to advance urban planning. An application of technology led to a new trend, the "City Efficient" movement, which applied the latest engineering principals to urban problems ranging from the construction of traffic intersections to the placement of water hydrants. So much structural reform occurred that municipal expert William Bennett Munro wrote in 1918, "American cities have made more progress in the direction of clean and efficient government within the last ten years than they were able to make during the preceding fifty."[16] Once people knew how to run modern cities, a consensus quickly developed that dictated the course of municipal administration for much of the twentieth century. Urban administration moved from the realm of experimentation to that of application, management, and funding levels.

The South, with its long tradition of urban planning stretching back to colonial Jamestown, was receptive to the new trends. A government report misleadingly claimed that only 71 of 786 official planning commissions in the country were in the South. Civic organizations, women's clubs, chambers of commerce, and professional groups provided the sinews of a fairly comprehensive planning network that augmented the efforts of official bodies. City-sanctioned planning commissions in Atlanta, Memphis, Knoxville, New Orleans, and Nashville all evolved from unofficial planning committees. Pie-in-the-sky proposals involving the moving of railroad stations and the building of great civic art galleries usually went for nought, although there were some solid achievements in the form of zoning and transportation ordinances. Plans for center cores and environs served cities well, especially the major ones, in ensuing years and sometimes decades down the line. An increasingly commonly view held that planning was the way to cope with the problems of the modern city.

Trying to keep pace with the need for increasingly complex levels of urban services taxed the resources of southern city governments. More than half of all municipal expenditures in the 1920s in cities were usually dedicated to police and fire protection plus education. Because the black voters remained disenfranchised, white electorates determined their needs, much to their disadvantage. The maintenance of separate school systems for blacks and whites taxed available resources. Even though a disproportionate amount of the funds went to the white schools, both white and black institutions failed to meet national standards. Still, given the depressing nature of "separate but equal" education, schools enjoyed widespread support. People at the bottom saw education as a way for their children to get ahead; conservatives approved the teaching of patriotism and societal values. Appropriations for the police continued to reflect a traditional strong sense of law and order among white southerners. Between 1920 and 1930 police appropriations in Atlanta increased from $468,900 to $903,500. The same trend prevailed in Birmingham and New Orleans. In 1928 law enforcement costs accounted for 14.5 percent of the city budget in Charleston, 10.5 percent in Birmingham, and 9.5 percent in Memphis. Fire departments gained larger and larger outlays in direct proportion to increased urban congestion and size. In the twenties the departments in New Orleans, Birmingham, Memphis, Nashville, and Knoxville sometimes received more money annually than the police.[17]

Other areas of concern required attention. The extension of sewer lines and street improvements continued to occupy city officials. Almost always, black districts got short shrift; most had inadequate sewerages and unpaved roadways. Charitable and health spending remained at low levels; the largest cost was usually a city medical facility, such as Henry Grady Hospital in Atlanta. By the 1920s systematic collections had resolved the "garbage question" in the South and elsewhere. The automobile reduced the amount of filth in the streets, and horses virtually disappeared. The Progressive era saw few refinements in municipal affairs beyond better-built machines and better-trained bureaucrats. Given the twin burdens of fiscal restraints and the issue of race, southern cities did quite well in dealing with their daily urban services—at least in regard to the needs of their white citizens.

By the 1920s it seemed to some observers that southerners had achieved a better understanding of an urban civilization and that the section was experiencing an urban rebirth. The process started during World War I. While hostilities did not last long enough to have an obvious impact on southern urbanization, war orders and military activities had caused an unexpected round of prosperity that extended into peacetime. A new spirit of progress and hope seemed abroad in Dixie.[18]

Numerous forms of boosterism swept through the urban South. The enthusiasm of the New South movement lived on. "Atlanta," a supporter gushingly proclaimed in 1924, "stands for the New South, the New South with all the romance of music, beauty, poetry, idealism of a fading past." The same year a resident of the Crescent City declared, "With 206 years to its credit, New Orleans is one of the oldest cities in the land. But its ways are young." A fiftieth anniversary tract for Birmingham proclaimed, "The dream of the founders of Birmingham has been more than fulfilled. . . . there are those of vision who see this city four-fold in numbers, in size, in worth. . . . And, viewed in the light of what has gone before, who shall say their vision is idle?"[19] In 1925 a reporter, trying to catch the spirit of the times, wrote, "The average Southern is a born booster, and the mood is contagious." Three thousand salesmen, including William Jennings Bryan for a handsome promotional fee, praised the virtues of Coral Gables, Florida. On the eve of the Great Depression the governor of Virginia said, "The South is being pointed to today as the West was in a former period—as the land of promise." A Journalist for the *New York Herald-Tribune* noted in 1930, "The clamor of Chambers of Commerce, the seductive propaganda of city and state industrial development boards, the rattling knives and forks and pepful jollities of Rotarians, Kiwanians, Lions, and Exchange Clubs are filling the erstwhile languorous wistaria-scented air with such a din these days that every visitor must recognize immediately a land of business progress."[20] *Babbitt*, Sinclair Lewis's penetrating novel about city life, could just as well have been set in the Buckhead section of Atlanta as in a composite midwestern city.

Some of the more ardent boosters were aspiring real estate operators and owners of small local businesses. These people expressed their concerns through service clubs, such as the Elks, Kiwanis, and Lions, plus promotional publications. Whether they believed their own propaganda (a tasteless piece in the *City Builder* of Atlanta in 1925 read: "Henry Woodfin Grady became the embodiment of the *Atlanta Spirit*. Indeed, Grady became the *Spirit of Atlanta*")[21] was beside the point. The boosters all had economic stakes, be it a haberdashery or vacant lot, in their communities, and it therefore behooved them to put their best foot forward. Frequently their plans were small and their sell too hard.

Just as often, boosters in the urban South actually had little to say about the broader contours of community direction and development. In the big cities, including Birmingham and Atlanta, formal or informal groups of leading businessmen, many of whom had political leaders at their beck and call, set policies. Each business leader, in addition to larger concerns, frequently had his own constituency to look after. The situation in medium-sized towns was somewhat different. In some older communities, one or maybe two mill or cotton press owners ran the town. They were usually unenthusiastic about change, fearing that it might upset a settled state and threaten their control. In many of the newer mill towns, local managers wielded considerable power, but they were merely the on-the-scene representatives of northern owners. To them, the price of Japanese textiles might be of greater importance than what transpired in some obscure southern mill town.[22]

Southern intellectuals criticized the booster spirit and what they saw as a trend toward urbanism calculated to undermine or destroy traditional values. "Everywhere people were pushing one another into the slums or the country," novelist Ellen Glasgow of Richmond observed in 1922. "Everywhere the past was going out with the times and the future was coming on in a torrent. . . . To add more and more numbers; to build higher and higher; to push harder and harder; and particularly to improve what had already been added or built or pushed—these impulses had united at last into a frenzied activity."[23] In 1923 Thomas Wolfe, from the vantage point of his New York apartment, scathingly criticized the "cheap Board of Trade Boosters, and blatant pamphleteers" who had, in his view, hurt rather than helped his hometown of Asheville, North Carolina. "I will say," Wolfe complained, "that 'Greater Asheville' does not necessarily mean '100,000 by 1930,' that we are not necessarily four times as civilized as our grandfathers because we go four times as fast in automobiles, because our buildings are four times as tall." Wolfe believed that southerners had emerged "into the kind of sunlight of another century."[24] The materialism of urban progress disturbed people of letters. "*Can we afford to be rich?*" Mary and Stanley Chapman asked in the *South Atlantic Quarterly.* "We must look well into our consciences before we answer this question, for the loss of our spiritual grace is too high a price to pay for any material gain."[25] Such attacks on city growth, very Jeffersonian in conception, placed leading southern intellectuals squarely in a national antiurban tradition of long standing. Certainly urban life had its deplorable features and a corresponding loss of rural values. Levels of antiurbanism increased in direct proportion to the movement of people from farms to cities.

The southern retrenchment of the 1890s did not mean a curtailment of progress. Rather, it served as recognition that no way existed for the South to regain parity with the North quickly within the federal Union. The sorry state of southern agriculture precluded the building of the kind of regional hinterlands that were needed to sustain rapid urban growth. The segregation system further complicated and aggravated an already unfortunate situation. City building proceeded within the limits imposed on a defeated society restricted by a lack of capital, inadequate transportation arrangements, poor proximity to major markets, and outside control. Under the adverse circumstances, urbanization proceeded quite well and usually at a steady pace in all except a few of the old Gilded Age cities. Atlanta and Birmingham flourished; Mobile and Charleston faded. In Florida another stratum of southern cities appeared. Even though promotional claims overreached, the Sunshine State achieved solid urban growth. On the western fringes of the South, Texas and Oklahoma gained major urban components. Throughout the South, manufacturing, even though hurt by outside marketing influences, advanced faster than ever before in the section's history. The poor working conditions and low wages in southern mills caused people to question the desirability of the trend. Heavily embellished promotionalism repelled southern intellectuals, and as a result some southerners began to question the desirability of more urbanization in Dixie. By the start of the Great Depression, this proposition, fundamental to the nature of the South, had yet to be resolved.

6

DEPRESSION, WAR, AND CIVIL RIGHTS

In 1930 a group of Vanderbilt University intellectuals collectively contributed to a book of essays, *I'll Take My Stand: The South and the Agrarian Tradition.* They attacked industrialism and applied science, deplored the trend toward urbanization in the South, and called for a return to agrarian values. They denigrated capitalism and communism as twin menaces that, given the "blind drift" of industrialism, would produce identical economic systems in both the United States and the Soviet Union.[1]

For the Vanderbilt group the choice for the future was not between communism and capitalism but between industrialism and agrarianism. The group's members envisioned a utopian South "in which agriculture is the leading vocation, whether for wealth, for pleasure, or for prestige." One of their number denounced mass education; another believed "the money economy" hurt farmers. A general suspicion of machines and a need to establish mastery over them permeated the book. "We can accept the machine," an essayist wrote, "but create our own attitude toward it." All the Nashville Agrarians deplored boosterism, calling upon their fellow southerners "to look very critically at the advantages of becoming a 'new South' which will be only an undistinguished replica of the usual industrial community."[2]

The deliberately provocative essays called attention to the continual drift away from Jeffersonian principles in Dixie. While many southerners, white and black, may have agreed in general with the thoughts expressed in *I'll Take My Stand,* a return to an idealized past was out of the question by 1930. Even the Nashville Agrarians lived in a metropolitan area. The South proceeded, as it and the rest

of the nation had for decades, down the road to an increasingly urbanized society.

The Nashville Agrarians came in for considerable ridicule and
disapproval. Critics called them "typewriter agrarians" and "tower-
of-ivory agrarians." H.L. Mencken, who denounced them as
"Agrarian Habakkuks," wrote, "Left to the farmers of Tennessee,
they would be clad in linsey-woolsey and fed on side-meat, and the
only books they could read would be excessively orthodox."
Thoughtful observers believed that the South should face reality,
accept industrialism, and work toward controlling its excesses. William Best Hesseltine, a young Virginia-born U.S. historian, declared
in a 1931 article in the *Sewanee Review*, "The South has the opportunity to regulate industry before industry gets a strangle hold
on the section. It . . . can profit from the experience of the rest of
the nation in such matters as the relations of capital and labor. . . . None of these results can be obtained by a policy of ob-
scurantism, or by fostering a spirit of reaction."[3]

The Nashville Agrarians welcomed such commentary even
though they did not agree with the sentiments. They envisioned a
great popular movement to promote an agrarian America. Although
nothing came of that sophistry—few people in a time of depression
cared about the philosophical positions of a few Vanderbilt scholars—a bitter irony was that, before the 1930s had ended, the South
in the popular mind had come to be regarded as more agrarian than
urban. The popular image, however, did not show the rural South
that the agrarians had in mind.

During the Great Depression many Americans outside the South
received the impression through a variety of sources that the South
was a land of dirt-poor croppers suffering from pellagra and hook-
worms. These unfortunates, blacks as well as whites, were depicted
as classic victims of economic unrest—rural folk in bib overalls and
worn dresses torn between old traditions and the brutality of modern
life. Secretary of Labor Frances Perkins helped set the tone in an
unfortunately worded 1933 statement in which she remarked, "A
social revolution will take place if you put shoes on the people of
the South."[4]

Social programs inaugurated by Tennessee Valley Authority officials aimed at helping southern agrarians adjust to modern life.
Sectional studies, especially Rupert Vance's *Human Geography of
the South* (1932) and Howard W. Odum's *Southern Regions in the
United States* (1936), which depicted croppers as victims of a lack
of regional planning, furthered perceptions of a crisis in the rural
South. Government writers, depression victims themselves, pro-

duced *These Are Our Lives,* a powerful collection of case histories that emphasized the grim lot of tenant farmers. Erskine Caldwell's *Tobacco Road* (1932), Herbert Harrison Kroll's *I Was a Sharecropper* (1937), and John Steinbeck's *Grapes of Wrath* (1935) helped illustrate the plight of croppers. Studies that combined the written word and photographic documentation, including Archibald MacLeish, *Land of the Free* (1938), and James Agee and Walker Evans, *Let Us Now Praise Famous Men* (1941), movingly showed rural life unadorned.

Photographers of the Farm Security Administration crisscrossed Dixie taking pictures of poor farmers. The photographs were often of great artistic quality. "Here," Alfred Kazin wrote, "was America. . . . Here was the greatest creative irony the reportorial mind could establish—a picture of Negro farmers wandering on the road, eating their bread under a billboard poster furnished by the National Association of Manufacturers—'America Enjoys the Highest Standard of Living in the World.' "[5] Here, seemingly, were useless, unwanted members of a society on its last legs, one that at a minimum still needed reconstruction.

Assessments of the state of southern agriculture culminated with the issuance by the National Emergency Council of a 1938 federal document, *Report on the Economic Condition of the South,* which reiterated that the rural South was in a sorry state. The report's chief architect, Clark Howell Foreman, a southerner with a Ph.D. who had done graduate work at Harvard University, Columbia University, and the London School of Economics, had served Secretary of Interior Harold Ickes as an adviser on black affairs. The sixty-four-page report, the draft of which took only a couple of weeks to write, reflected Foreman's acceptance of the assertions of Odum, Vance, and others that a ruthless brand of industrial paternalism held Dixie down. "The paradox of the South is that while it is blessed by Nature with immense wealth, its people as a whole are the poorest in the country," the *Report on Economic Conditions* claimed. "Lacking industries of its own, the South has been forced to trade the richness of its soil, its minerals and forests, and the labor of its people for goods manufactured elsewhere." The report, which focused on the states of the old Confederacy, plus Kentucky and Oklahoma, contained the usual recitation of bleak statistics about the South. The section had half the nation's farmers and only one-fifth the agricultural implements. Illiteracy was high in underfunded school districts. Industrial income remained the lowest in the country. The region ranked first in child labor. More than 4 million families lived in substandard housing. Excessive credit costs, absentee owners, high tariffs, and unfair freight rates prevented southerners from solving their own problems. "Penalized for being rural, and handicapped in its efforts to industrialize," the official paper stated, "the South, in fact, has been caught in a vise that has kept it from moving along with the main stream of American economic life."[6]

The conclusions prompted President Franklin D. Roosevelt to call the South the "Nation's No. 1 economic problem," but he failed in his attempts to use the document as part of a strategy to defeat senators and congressmen he did not like and to promote liberal social legislation. In the North, a writer for the *New York Times* resented the suggestion that outside capital was responsible for the plight of southern agriculture; the *Nation* attacked the impact of "the financial imperialism of Northern big business" on the southern way of life. On a different plane, many urban southerners, while offended by what they saw as a blatant attempt by Roosevelt to shape their politics, objected to the charges of backwardness in Dixie. Two viewpoints emerged. According to a journalist for the *Miami Herald,* the report showed that northerners were jealous of progress in the South. Reflecting the other viewpoint, an *Atlanta Journal* official said, "Just take off the differential freight rates and other discriminatory legislation; send some of your technological and scientific skill down here; lend us some money at lower interest rates and we'll do the rest."[7] Obviously, the kinds of abuses cited in the NEC report and enumerated by other observers did occur in the South. What went unsaid, even though it remained central to all discussions, was the issue of black equality. So too did the extent of urban growth in the South. The Nashville Agrarians, the publicists of farmer degeneracy, and the authors of the NEC report all ignored the long course of city building in the South. It was almost as if Dixie had no urban components.

When New Deal theorists did think of cities, they considered them in a national context rather than a regional one. A 1937 federal report by the Urbanism Committee to the National Resources Committee contended that cities had received more "widespread national neglect" than any other part of the "national existence." The report, *Our Cities: Their Role in the National Economy,* stated: "Whether this is to be attributed to the absorption of our best efforts by the demands of our commercial and industrial system, or by other pressing claims of national policy, it is evident that America must now set out to overcome the continual and cumulative disregard of urban policies and administration and to take into account the place of the urban community in the national economy."[8] The speed of urbanization accentuated the problem. Between 1900 and 1920 the urban population of the United States grew from 30 million to 69 million, representing an increase of about 130 percent. The rate slowed to 26 percent in the 1920s and to an estimated 3 percent from 1930 to 1935. The report enumerated a number of urban problems: dangers to public health, pollution, inadequate recreational facilities, congestion, unattractive districts, lags in public improvements, and the like.

The committee recommended that Congress continue to assist urban welfare programs, establish permanent public works projects, rehouse low income groups, and promote planning at various levels of government. In calling for a national urban policy, the committee members made the uninsightful observations that urban dwellers were "by no means of uniform type" and that cities "must be distinguished according to the principal function they serve." A proposed need to establish norms to delineate the nature of urban life left out the South. "The most significant industrial cities of the United States are concentrated in a belt extending from New England as far south as New Jersey and as far west as Illinois," their report stated. "It is in this area, therefore, that in general we may expect to find the most characteristic manifestations of urban life in the United States."[9] Even New Deal planners encouraged southerners to regard their cities as having a different legacy. Such thinking by policy makers about the development of cities in Dixie was enough to make Henry Grady roll over in his grave. Fortunately, in a time of national trial, such thinking did not stop federal money from flowing into urban Dixie.

Between 1933 and 1939 the national government spent more than $2 billion in the South. Much of the money helped cities either directly or indirectly. The Agricultural Adjustment Act, plus special legislation to help the marketing of cotton and tobacco, provided the basis for rejuvenating agriculture. These and other measures automatically helped cities by enhancing the quality of their hinterlands. The creation of the Tennessee Valley Authority did the same and more.

Despite its controversial aspects—critics charged it represented an attempt to socialize America—the TVA had the potential to improve the economic and social status of a whole region. In an immediate sense the huge new agency's dam building and electrification endeavors resulted in thousands of construction jobs. Some of the main southern industries, textiles, tobacco, food, pulp, and paper, did not decline percentage-wise between 1929 and 1933 to the extent that manufacturing did in the North. Unfortunately, industry in Dixie was not on as firm a ground as the statistical compilations could be interpreted to indicate, because southern firms had been on weak ground all through the 1920s. Moreover, the Birmingham steel industry went into a tailspin early in the depression. Consequently, the downturn, in spite of a few bright spots, in particular the cigarette industry in Richmond, was as serious in the urban South as elsewhere. Indeed, given the sorry state of agriculture and corresponding slumps in retail sales and commercial transactions, overall conditions may actually have been worse in Dixie's towns.

Early in the crisis much of the aid came from the stopgap Federal Emergency Relief Administration and the Civil Works Administration, but by the middle 1930s, as the New Deal became more institutionalized, a number of agencies engaged in relief endeavors. Certain small ones, the National Youth Administration and the Resettlement Administration, had only local significance. The first housing projects had little impact beyond setting precedents for future large developments. The biggest expenditures came from two gigantic agencies, the Works Progress Administration and the Public Works Administration. The New Deal worked mightily to help and, at the same time, to keep the Solid South in the Democratic column at election time.

The New Deal agencies underwrote a wide variety of projects in the urban South. Sometimes federal officials gave out the aid. At other intervals, it passed through state and local units of governments. In those instances, the risk of corrupt practices multiplied. Edward Crump of Tennessee, Huey Long of Louisiana, and Herman Talmadge of Georgia came under close scrutiny because of fear that they might divert relief funds for their own purposes. No major federal prosecutions resulted, but some excesses occurred. In Nashville the state WPA administrator in Tennessee erected a $2,497 monument in his honor and engaged in other questionable practices, including building a steeplechase course for a private riding club.[10]

Large sums of money were involved; expenditures in Birmingham, among the hardest hit of southern cities, amounted to $361 million alone between 1933 and 1937. Big projects funded throughout the urban South included sewerages, streets, buildings, and bridges. The WPA built airports in Tampa and Nashville. Richmond gained from a number of depression-inspired enterprises: a bridge over the James River, a state library, and a high school. New Deal funds made possible the construction in Knoxville of several University of Tennessee buildings. Even small communities gained street and curb improvements. These and other schemes involved the services of tens of thousands of workers. Other funding helped recovery following disastrous floods in the middle 1930s along the Ohio and Mississippi rivers.

Compared with conditions in the depths of the Great Depression, circumstances improved considerably as the decade progressed. Florida cities, helped by a national revival of tourism, actually experienced something close to a boom; in 1936 Miami Beach reported the construction of 47 hotels and 74 apartment houses.[11] Although some groups benefited more than others—black southerners profited the least—federal largess helped tremendously and established important precedents for the future.

Memphis was in the enviable position of having the necessary political connections to receive considerable federal funds with little price to pay in return. Boss Edward Crump was one of Franklin Roosevelt's floor managers at the 1932 Democratic National Convention, and members of the Tennessee congressional delegation had strong New Deal ties. Crump, long an advocate of public power projects, enthusiastically endorsed the creation of the Tennessee Valley Authority. The Memphis business community, after some initial fears about the cotton market, supported the policies of the first Agricultural Adjustment Administration. Businessmen in Memphis, as throughout the nation, first favored the National Recovery Administration and then turned against it.

Within Memphis, the Public Works Administration spent $8.5 million and the city $14 million, mostly raised through loans, to erect a number of buildings, notably a hospital and several public schools, and to finance street and other improvement projects. The United States Housing Authority, a spin-off from PWA, raised up several segregated housing projects. By 1938, the Works Progress Administration had spent $5.2 million to construct Crump Stadium, to build a municipal zoo, and to expand the airport. The various New Deal public works undertakings suited the needs of the machine. Tangible examples of progress, they provided jobs and thereby buttressed rather than undermined the authority of Crump's organization. As in other parts of the urban South, New Deal money did not alter the existing power structure.

The city showed considerable reluctance to spend local tax money on relief, in 1937 allocating one-tenth of 1 percent of its annual budget on welfare expenditures, less than that authorized for golf course maintenance. A WPA regional administrator observed, "Memphis gave the distinct feeling that a warm welcome was extended to government concerning itself with the plight of the unemployed and paying the bills—as long as it is the *Federal* government."[12] Memphis officials, claiming that 56 percent of all residents made it through the depression without going on welfare, gave only cursory attention to helping destitute blacks, rural migrants, and hard core poor. Almost all blacks fared badly and were forced to live in ramshackle houses in undesirable parts of town. Any aid they received from the New Deal came through the innately hostile machine. Crump, while continuing strongly to support Roosevelt's spending measures, including a 1937 flood control bill that aided Memphis, became increasingly disenchanted with social programs intended to help blacks. Because federal authorities continued to work through the Crump machine, he remained in charge of Memphis throughout the Great Depression.

On the surface the southern cities of the 1930s seemed much like those around the rest of the nation. When the average city in the United States contained 21,800 inhabitants, the only difference in the South was that it did not have as many cities in that class as other sections. In 1930 Alabama had four cities of between 15,000 and 25,000 people and North Carolina two; Massachusetts had eighteen and Iowa five. The same was true of the big metropolises; no matter that they were in Georgia or Florida rather than Wisconsin or California, they shared similar attributes with those throughout urban America. From the air, cities appeared as a sprawling mass of structures and characterized by irregular checkerboard street patterns. City centers remained crowded, filled with buildings built before the depression. The areas around downtown were usually in decay, with transportation facilities, light industries, and warehouses interspersed with dilapidated residences and roominghouses. Here recent migrants, blacks, and the homeless found refuge. Beyond that, middle-class apartment houses, usually close to local business districts, dotted the landscape.

These classic conditions did not mean that all cities had the same features. Rather they simply reflected the somewhat monotonous course of city development; one that in no small way related to land uses and values. "Gambling in land values had contributed to alternate booms and depressions, raising false hopes, encouraging over-ambitious structures, wiping out private investors, and, all in all, has been one of the major tragedies of American urban life," *Our Cities* claimed. "Inflated valuations have contributed to vertical expansion and over-intensive land utilization, with the result that the private use of land has far outgrown public facilities and services, including water, sewerage, health, police and fire protection, street and transit facilities, and has created all sorts of congestion."[13]

The very diversity that had characterized Dixie since colonial days, seen in architectural images, continued to give its cities a distinctive flavor. The red Georgian row houses of Baltimore contrasted with the one-story rambling bungalows, with ample front porches and spacious lawns, found in cities of all sizes in the lower South. The trend from north to south, in keeping with the needs of the climate, called for fewer basements, more windows, higher ceilings, thinner walls, and thicker screens. Public and commercial structures differed just as much. The eclectic styles of Washington set the tone. The older edifices combined the Georgian, Greek Revival, and Moorish vogues of the antebellum period with the later Victorian and Gothic designs of the Gilded Age. The newer buildings of the Federal Triangle were of Moderne designs.

The White House and Capitol both had some of the more attractive attributes of traditional antebellum southern architecture. In Nashville and Richmond, the state capitols also reflected the glories of the Old South; the Confederacy did not last long enough to produce a separate style. At New Orleans, the Roman Catholic cathedral, built along Moorish lines long before the Civil War, remained a landmark. The French Quarter, constructed in Spanish forms because of destructive fires in the late eighteenth century, featured two- and three-story buildings with ironwork balconies and courtyards. Mansions in Savannah, Charleston, and Mobile displayed varied Georgian and Greek Revival influences. Sharply different were the white Moderne hotels and apartments of the Florida Gold Coast. The downtown districts of Atlanta, Birmingham, Louisville, and Nashville, with streets walled by steel frame skyscrapers, looked like the commercial cores of numerous other large cities all over the country.

Many visitors were surprised to find that the urban South was not all magnolias, blossoms, camellias, and moss. Tremendous differences prevailed between the stately homes of the Garden District of New Orleans and the shacks of the Washington black quarter only a few blocks from the Capitol. Yet such differentiations could be found throughout America. Winnetka, a suburb on Chicago's North Side, was one of the land's swankest residential developments. Less than fifteen miles away was the South Side of Chicago, with its large black district, the poverty-stricken and unloved product of a black migration from the rural South in World War I. Sociologists had long commented on the extremes of wealth and poverty in Boston, New York, and Philadelphia. All had their black slums, as did many cities in the Midwest with very small black populations, including Grand Rapids, Racine, and Ottumwa.

What bothered an increasing number of observers of the South was the formal segregation system. It, plus the perceived poverty of the section, set southern communities off in northern eyes as much or more so than any other attribute. An influential southern intellectual blamed the situation on the section's agrarian roots. W.J. Cash in *The Mind of the South* (1941) said that city people in Dixie had accepted rural concepts of "violence, intolerance, aversion and suspicion toward new ideas . . . , an exaggerated individualism and a too narrow concept of social responsibility, attachment to fictions and false values, above all too great attachment to racial values and a tendency to justify cruelty and injustice in the name of these values."[14] Correct or not, philosophical rationales by southerners about the reasons for racial segregation fell on deaf ears above the Mason and Dixon Line. Many northerners' conception of attitudes in the South was conveyed by a cruel and inflammatory racist banner carried in a 1930 Ku Klux Klan parade in Atlanta: "Niggers, back to the cotton fields—city jobs are for White Folks."[15]

World War II wrought massive changes in Dixie. Unlike World War I, which had only limited impact because it lasted less than two years, mobilization and hostilities encompassed half a decade. The gigantic scope of the war effort directed against Germany, Japan, and their allies brought huge amounts of federal money into the South, far more than during the Great Depression, which came to an abrupt end. All of Dixie's ports boomed throughout the crisis. The movement of servicemen and materials of war taxed transportation facilities. The section by virtue of its warm climate, geographical features, and seniority of congressional members gained a great number of training facilities.

In the summer of 1941 more than 500,000 servicemen engaged in maneuvers in central Louisiana, helping the economies of Shreveport and Alexandria. During the war millions of soldiers, sailors, and marines trained in the South. During hostilities the federal government constructed more than $4 billion in training facilities, many located near cities, throughout the South. Of greater permanency was defense industry. Southern governors and other leaders worked hard to acquire a fair share of contracts—in the early stages of mobilization, eleven southern states received nearly $17 billion in contracts, a disproportionate number, in view of their much smaller share of industrial capacity. In a very competitive environment, Chester C. Davis, an FDR confidant who had a considerable say over the location of large war plants, said, "Nothing short of the most rigorous and most positive efforts to achieve recognition. . . . will suffice."[16]

In the course of hostilities, southern war plants received about

20 percent of the hundreds of billions of dollars spent by the federal government. Expenditures for the construction of war workshops amounted to roughly $4 billion. The shipbuilding industry expanded at a tremendous rate; seventeen yards, including ones in Mobile, Jacksonville, Tampa, and Norfolk, constructed $6 billion in ships. In New Orleans, A.J. Higgins Industries, a prewar maker of small plywood boats, converted to the production of landing craft and PT boats, expanding its workforce from 400 in 1941 to 20,000 in 1944. Ordnance works grew rapidly. The Volunteer Works in Chattanooga and the Redstone Arsenal in Huntsville, Alabama, reflected the huge requirements of the munitions industry.

Expansion in the chemical industry resulted in the construction of large facilities in Virginia and Louisiana. Petroleum production added luster to the economy of a number of Louisiana cities, including Shreveport and Baton Rouge. War contracts spurred great increases in steel production in Birmingham. A gigantic aircraft assembly plant in Marietta, an Atlanta suburb, made thousands of heavy bombers. The Oak Ridge, Tennessee, and Huntsville, Alabama, works of the Manhattan District were part of one of the most costly activities in the history of the federal government, the construction of the atomic bomb. The TVA eleric power network made Oak Ridge a desirable site; construction work occupied a staggering 82,000 people. The textile industry recovered completely from the depression. Tobacco production boomed as never before. Less noticed but equally important was the proliferation of small war plants, in many cases the suppliers of larger firms. Even though the bulk of war orders went to concerns outside the South, the influx of money into the region held the promise of radically changing its temperament and personality.[17]

Donald M. Nelson, the chairman of the War Production Board, believed the war would bring "the South into the vanguard of world industrial progress." He said, "A bird's-eye view of large-scale Southern industry makes you feel that the South has rubbed Aladdin's lamp."[18] Such hyperbole not withstanding, the South was changing. In agriculture, mechanization accelerated; the number of croppers decreased in the very period that government experts discovered them. The trend was already under way by the start of the war. Many southern cities experienced population increases during the Great Depression as former black and white cotton farmers moved into urban areas. Between 1930 and 1940 Birmingham grew by 3 percent to 267,600 people, Atlanta by 11.8 percent to 302,300, and Nashville by 8.8 percent to 107,400. In the same span numerous northern cities hardly grew at all; Milwaukee, for instance, enlarged by 1.6 percent and Chicago by 0.6 percent. Throughout the urban South, the impact of the war, while creating some of the kind of opportunities for industrial advancement that Nelson talked about, brought dislocations. Experts argued that southerners remained so rural in temperament that it was harder for them than for other Americans to adjust to an urban environment.

Social commentators sought to explain the significance of wartime change in the urban South. Washington, which in the 1930s increased in size by 36 percent to 663,000 inhabitants, continued to expand rapidly. Shortly before Pearl Harbor, Donald Wilhelm, writing in the *American Mercury*, described the hectic pace of events: "There are 240,000 men and women on one or another public payroll ... increasing at the rate of 5,000 a month. ... The horde of government employees go to work in all kinds of places. The government has taken over 200-odd mansions, hotels and apartment houses to use as offices. It is a bit startling to find the official with whom you have business sitting amid the shiny tiles of what last week, or yesterday, was obviously a bathroom. Sometimes the fixtures have been decently boxed in to serve as chairs or tables; sometimes not."[19]

Mobile, one of the wartime South's fastest growing places, came under intense scrutiny. According to novelist John Dos Passos, Mobile was "trampled and battered like a city that's been taken by storm. Sidewalks are crowded. Gutters are stacked with litter. ... Garbage cans are overflowing. Frame houses on treeshaded streets bulge with men in shirtsleeves. ... Cues wait outside of movies and lunchrooms." Agnes Meyer of the *Washington Post* found in Mobile a host of "primitive, illiterate backwoods people ... hostile, defiant, suspicious, and terrified," huddled in shacks, tent colonies, and trailer camps. Other writers discovered sin in Norfolk, where one exposé reported "girlie" camps and free-and-easy "VD-girls."[20] The war caused a social crisis in Washington, Mobile, Norfolk, and other southern metropolises. What saved the southern cities was that almost all of their citizens backed the war effort. They put up with rationing, raised victory gardens, and accepted the need for "dimouts" plus other restrictions. Many young men and women served in the armed forces. Patriotism helped southern urbanites to weather the crisis.

Following the war a great round of prosperity swept across the nation, fueled by wartime savings, a demand for civilian goods, and the needs of the new Cold War. The South shared in the boom. Technically, its industrial base experienced what economists called a "takeoff." The factories built during hostilities served the region well; in 1947 more than 2 million people worked in southern factories, compared with 1.3 million in 1939.[21] The emphasis in Dixie was on adding industry; few people cared that doing so meant actively seeking outside capital. The War Assets Administration disposed of many of the war plants to private interests for very low prices, big chemical and ammunition plants became fixtures, state governments established agencies to promote industrial development, and local units of governments offered northern owners everything from tax incentives to factory buildings. Despite widespread unionization during the New Deal and the war, the passage in several southern states of right-to-work legislation and generally lower wage scales than elsewhere made the South attractive to manufacturers.

Several large cities had mayors with a strong business orientation, including William B. Hartsfield in Atlanta and King High in Miami. In New Orleans a dynamic "reformer," De Lesseps Story Morrison, swept to victory in 1946, defeating entrenched politicians with ties to the Long interests. Early in his administration Morrison persuaded Kaiser Aluminum to build a large factory in suburban New Orleans. *Time* magazine virtually eulogized the mayor, stating in November of 1947, "Chep Morrison, symbol of the bright new day which had come to the city of charming ruins, also symbolized as well as anyone the postwar energy of the nation's cities."[22] Yet Morrison, for all his charm and ability, was a segregationist. Here, along with other usual political liabilities, lay a problem for him, New Orleans, and the rest of the South. Until the end of segregation, no matter what the hypocrisy in the North on the race issue, the South would remain a land apart.

Southern blacks had not shared to a full extent in the economic progress of the World War II period. In 1941 Roosevelt, responding to pressure from black leaders, had issued an executive order forbidding discrimination in defense industries and establishing the Committee on Fair Employment Practice (FEPC). The FEPC, which died an unlamented death for lack of funds in 1946, had little influence. It had no power to enforce directives and refused even to recommend action against violators. From the first it came in for attack from segregationists. Congressman John Rankin of Mississippi called it "the beginning of a communistic dictatorship." Newspaper editorials in the South called the members of the committee, chaired by the segregationist publisher of the *Louisville Courier-Journal*, "Roosevelt racial experts" and "halo-wearing missionaries of New Deal Socialism." If anything, the FEPC strengthened the resolve of segregationists. Its final report lamely stated that black war workers performed " 'h jobs': hot, heavy, and hard."[23]

By then blacks had already identified what they wanted in return for backing the war effort—nothing less than their full rights as American citizens. Talk about ending educational inequalities and voting restrictions upset and alarmed white southerners. They cautioned blacks that a sudden end to segregation would be a disaster for both races and worried about outside agitators who preached false doctrines. In a sign of things to come, a white extremist with Klan connections noted, "If there is room for a National Association for the Advancement of Colored People, there is need of a League to Maintain White Supremacy."[24]

Little of what happened in the civil rights field in the years immediately after the war had a direct impact on the urban South. City administrations confronted the problem with great caution. Token improvements involved appointing a few black police officers and upgrading black schools. Mayors established biracial commissions to write reports and argued that promoting business would help all classes. The slow pace of racial progress provided little leverage on the national level. In 1948 President Harry S. Truman desegregated the armed forces and banned discrimination in federal agencies, but his call for comprehensive civil rights legislation, ranging from anti-poll-tax to antilynching measures, was unsuccessful. Truman's very proposals aroused great ire among southern segregationists, who were thwarted in their efforts to oppose him in the 1948 presidential election, although Strom Thurmond's States' Rights party carried South Carolina, Louisiana, Mississippi, and Alabama. During Truman's full term in office he continued to promote civil rights and made racial concerns an important part of his Fair Deal.

His activities set the stage for action by the United States Supreme Court. A series of somewhat technical decisions that extended back into the 1930s and struck down segregation in institutions of higher education augured a challenge to the whole system of segregation in the South. Some southern leaders, seeing the threat coming, tried to head it off through token efforts and pious statements. Governor James F. Byrnes of South Carolina, an important New Deal official in the Roosevelt years, said in 1951, "It is our duty to provide for the races substantial equality in school facilities."[25]

While some changes followed, substantial inequities remained; Mississippi spent 75 percent more on a white student than a black one. In May 1954 in *Brown* v. *Board of Education of Topeka*, the Supreme Court unanimously called for the desegregation of the schools, striking down the "separate but equal" doctrine. The justices, who had several school cases before them, including one from rural South Carolina, acted on the Topeka case for a practical reason; they knew that the decision could be enforced in Kansas. The following year the justices added that *Brown* v. *Board* should be carried out "with all deliberate speed," whatever that phrase meant. This refusal to set a date invited opposition in the South.

A resistance movement quickly formed among white southerners.[26] The usual assortment of bigots railed against the prospect of the mongrelization of the white race, and the moribund Ku Klux Klan revived fitfully. Just about all the schools in Dixie remained segregated in an immediate sense, which helped restrain white southerners and provided leeway for the formation of a widely based, respectable antidesegregation movement. White Citizens' Councils garnered considerate support. In Mississippi membership grew in a year from only 14 people to 60,000. Soon the movement had more than 300,000 members. So-called moderate politicians were swept aside; the order of the day was "massive resistance." Federal court decisions and orders to desegregate individual school districts followed a predictable pattern: mob violence, delayed action by public officials, reluctant local enforcement of court orders, and formation of private white schools.

A notable clash in 1956 in Clinton, Tennessee, widely covered by the media, saw the burning of school buses. President Dwight D. Eisenhower, committed to building the Republican party in the South, avoided taking a stand on *Brown* v. *Board,* claiming he should not comment on a Supreme Court decision. A combination of the ambivalence of the judicial authorities, the vacillation of the president, and the obstinacy of the white southern resisters guaranteed a confrontation of national proportions over the federal government's readiness to enforce school desegregation. Urban progress in the South depended, in no small measure, on what would happen next.

A great national crisis—called by some commentators the worst since the Civil War—occurred in the fall of 1957 after a U.S. district court order to desegregate Little Rock Central High School. Governor Orval Faubus of Arkansas, supported by other segregationist governors, called out his state's National Guard to stop black students escorted by federal marshals from integrating the school. Mayor Woodrow Wilson Mann of Little Rock accused Faubus of trying to "put down trouble where none existed."[27] The governor, of course, wanted a confrontation. When the school board tried to comply with the court order, mobs gathered. Violence followed. Eisenhower, faced with an obvious threat to federal authority, after learning that a mob leader was a close associate of Faubus, acted decisively. He deactivated the Arkansas National Guard and in a calculated show of force ordered a paratroop division that made up the most battle-ready elements of the nation's strategic reserve into Little Rock to enforce the court's mandate.

Television brought the powerful and successful assertion of the authority of the federal government into homes throughout the country. When Faubus wrote Eisenhower a letter of protest, the president, his troops in place, did not bother to reply. Even though delaying actions, both peaceful and violent, continued in the South (Faubus closed Little Rock's four high schools in 1958-59), the federal government had reestablished its authority. This action did not lead to integrated schools. Throughout Dixie, white private schools had the effect of leaving public schools almost entirely black—segregation in reverse. For one reason or another, white patrons of public schools continued to resist the efforts of federal authorities to place their children in integrated schools. Yet the Little Rock crisis had tremendous implications for the urban South because it ensured that federal authority would ultimately triumph, foreshadowed a renewal of federal order in the South, and made cities attractive for investment capital.

The quest for racial equality moved beyond the issue of black and white schools. A limited civil rights act involving voting rights, passed with the cooperation of both major parties and signed by Eisenhower during the Little Rock crisis, broke a "logjam" going back to Reconstruction. Another technical voting act followed in 1960. Such actions furthered the acquiescence by Washington to attempts in the South designed to challenge segregation. A landmark boycott in 1955-56 that protested segregated seating on Montgomery buses brought to prominence a young minister, Dr. Martin Luther King, Jr., an organizer of the Southern Christian Leadership Conference. King used an important black urban institution, the church, as a basis for his movement.

The nucleus of SCLC support came from black ministers across the South. King and his followers believed in "nonviolent resistance," and in 1960 a SCLC auxiliary, the Student Nonviolent Coordinating Committee, started "sit-ins" at segregated facilities throughout the South. Many significant demonstrations occurred in cities, where regional and national television carried what happened far beyond local lunchrooms, swimming pools, hotels, and bus stations. Counter activities, such as the pouring of ketchup on well-dressed demonstrators by KKK members, hurt the white cause, as did the beating and jailing in Alabama of "Freedom Riders" from the Congress of Racial Equality.

In the spring of 1963 violence erupted when Dr. King and his followers carried their equality crusade to Birmingham. They expected trouble that would be televised, and the city's hard-line public safety commissioner, T. Eugene "Bull" Connor, accommodated them. He ultimately arrested thousands of blacks and turned dogs and hoses on countless others. In the process he made a spectacle of himself nationwide and created national sympathy for the black movement. Violent acts against blacks and the calling out of the National Guard by George Wallace, Alabama's segregationist Democratic governor, failed to restore complete peace. The brutal murder by bombing of four young black girls attending Sunday school in a Birmingham church appalled Americans, including many white segregationists.

August 1963 saw the March on Washington by 200,000 Americans that helped transform a regional movement into a national one. Speaking at the foot of the Washington Monument, Dr. King, who had become the leader of the Civil Rights movement, told a national television audience, "I have a dream that one day this nation will rise up and live out the true meaning of its creed."[28] This conviction, shared by countless millions of American citizens in all parts of the country, was to have a profound impact on the South. While the fact was not understood at the time, the Civil Rights crusade broke an economic logjam and set the stage for dramatic growth in the South.

In 1964 and 1965 Congress passed sweeping civil rights legislation dealing with public accommodations and voting rights. President Lyndon B. Johnson, a southerner or westerner, depending on his political predilections and the expediencies of the moment, said that he hoped civil rights legislation would dry up "the springs of racial poison."[29] More violence lay ahead. During the summer of 1964, in a squalid southern rural Mississippi backwater, white extremists brutally murdered three civil rights workers in cold blood. The following year, a freedom march in Alabama led by Dr. King, a recent recipient of a Nobel peace prize, resulted in still more violence. Other incidents occurred; in Atlanta, Lester Maddox dramatized his resistance to the federal legislation by issuing ax handles to white customers of his restaurant for use against blacks. Maddox parlayed his ensuing notoriety into election as governor of Georgia and became one of the last urban resisters to gain high office.

On the surface the majority of southern whites accepted black legal equality, but Dr. King did not do as well when he attempted to carry what had been a unique southern regional campaign into the North or when he turned to social issues. On April 4, 1968, while Dr. King was in Memphis to help striking garbage workers, an assassin gunned him down. Days of serious rioting followed in Baltimore, Washington, and other cities. King's death came at the end of a crucial period in the national experience. As for the urban South, the results of the civil rights revolution had the potential of providing the basis for bridging long-standing gaps between the sections and eradicating old boundaries.

The civil rights struggle obscured economic progress in the urban South. To be sure, some cities suffered for their role in supporting traditional southern urban policies. Montgomery, as a direct consequence of the bus boycott, supposedly lost bids for a DuPont plant and at least four other factories. Little Rock failed to attract any new factories of importance between 1958 and 1961. An official of the city's chamber of commerce was moved to tell southern businessmen, "Keep your public schools open. You will never regret it." Throughout the section, business leaders increasingly believed that violence, school closings, and uncompromising stands on integration questions retarded economic growth. Virginia commercial interests forced their state's governor to soften his massive resistance plans. In Atlanta, Mayor Hartsfield claimed that his city was "too busy to hate," which he tried to help prove in 1955 by successfully desegregating city-owned golf courses. In 1961, when Atlanta peacefully integrated its schools, the mayor treated the occasion as a gala promotional and media event and even hosted a cocktail party for the visiting press.[30]

Throughout the racial crisis the South continued to interest northern business. An obvious attraction was an antiunion attitude, furthered among whites by support for desegregation from national unions. Although much of the new and, for that matter, old southern industry was unionized, sectional attitudes translated into less militant members and a willingness to accept lower wages than those paid in the north. This was especially true in North and South Carolina, Georgia, and Florida, all of which attracted considerable industry throughout the 1950s. Old shibboleths about the wickedness of northern money and the adverse impact of colonialism no longer applied. Even in a period when northern interests with money and new managerial ideas sought to bring about fundamental changes in the South, the quest for outside funds seemed almost laudable.

The postwar years saw great gains in the South's industrial output. By 1960 the South had more than 200 steel fabricators and more than 100 large foundries. Seven hundred apparel plants and at least 100 shoe factories dotted the Dixie landscape. Industries were much more diversified than before the war, even though by 1952 some four-fifths of the cotton textile industry was in the South. The chemical industry expanded its wartime base; DuPont constructed ten new plants and General Electric built nineteen facilities. Food processing became the section's single biggest industry, followed by petroleum, coal, chemicals, and textiles. Very noteworthy was the movement into the South of large northern paper companies, attracted in part by abundant water and fast-growing pine. Over sixty pulp, paper, and consumer product mills were already in operation by the early 1950s. Soon more than 600,000 people, either directly or indirectly, worked in the paper industry.

New markets created all sorts of opportunities. Changes in farming, particularly the phasing out of the cropper system and the trend toward corporate agriculture, brought more prosperous hinterlands. Both farmers and city people had the money to buy new consumer goods. The Johnson Lawn Mower Corporation moved from Ottumwa, Iowa, to Brookhaven, Mississippi, in 1952 to take advantage of inducements offered by the state and nonunionized cheap labor.[31] In 1956 alone the South added more than a thousand new industrial concerns. The establishment in the late 1950s of the Research Triangle Park in North Carolina contributed to a coming of age of southern industry, adding potentially important research and development components. Southern manufacturers gradually acquired the means and technology to produce their own new product lines.[32]

A continued flow of federal money further enhanced the southern urban economy. Dire predictions that funds from the national government would dry up did not happen, despite the termination of depression projects during the war and the cancellation with the fall of Japan of billions of dollars in war orders. The Cold War, the Korean War, and the acceptance of the need for a large peacetime military establishment kept defense orders coming. Atlanta's Dobbins Air Force Base had more than 15,000 employees in 1959. The bomber plant built in Marietta in World War II employed thousands of people to produce B-47 bombers. Many places, including Jacksonville, Pensacola, Charleston, and Norfolk benefited from peacetime naval activities. Military posts, such as Fort Benning near Columbus and Camp Gordon in the Augusta vicinity, added millions of dollars monthly to local payrolls. Oak Ridge flourished as an Atomic Energy Commission facility; Huntsville and Cape Canaveral became centers of missile and space development. Federal dollars came as well from a number of other sources.

President Eisenhower, who said he opposed "creeping Socialism," actually increased federal expenditures. He kept the Tennessee Valley Authority, he acquiesced to broader social security coverage, and he carried on urban renewal and housing programs started under Truman. Of great significance was the Interstate Highway Act of 1956, designed to provide for the construction of a national system of free urban and rural expressways. An important consideration that requires emphasis was that the federal government did not overtly punish the urban South for its resistance to integration. Far from it. Without much notice, southern cities had derived advantage, in a very real sense, as a result of the actions of the federal government.

Throughout the 1950s the urban South increased rapidly in population, building on a base created decades earlier. How much cities grew and why they rose depended on the use of statistics. Moreover, many newcomers were displaced black and white farmers who had been forced off the land by mechanization and who had little choice except to move to town. Central city totals no longer conveyed an accurate idea of size. Annexation programs, as in the case of Atlanta, made some places seem to be growing faster than they actually were. Even casual observers in Atlanta could see, however, that a spirit of progress was in the air; a feeling that the city had all the ingredients necessary to become a national metropolis. Still, between 1950 and 1960, official census figures showed Atlanta increasing in population from 331,300 to 487,500, a solid but not spectacular rise. Equally deceptive were the compilations for Baltimore and Washington. The census indicated that both were in a state of decline, Baltimore falling from 949,800 to 939,000 and Washington from 802,200 to 764,000. In fact inner-city whites and new residents were moving to the suburbs. Thus a new government census definition for Standard Metropolitan Statistical Areas presented a much different picture. The metropolitan area statistics showed Baltimore moving ahead in size during the 1950s from 1.5 million to 2.1 million and Atlanta from 727,000 to 1 million.

The SMSA aggregates indicated solid growth throughout the urban South: Memphis, for example, went from 529,600 to 674,600 and Miami nearly doubled, increasing from 495,100 to 935,000. Out in Texas, Dallas rose from 708,800 to 1.1 million and Houston from 806,700 to 1.4 million. Although the population rises were not as great as for some of the big metropolitan areas in the Far West—in the 1950s Los Angeles surged ahead from 4.2 million to 6 million and San Francisco from 2.1 million to 2.6 million—there was no question that unprecedented urban growth was under way in the South. Without much fanfare, even as the media focused its attention on racial discord, Dixie's cities began to display all the symptoms associated with sustained long-term progress.

The relationship between the urban South and the federal government underwent tremendous changes between 1930 and 1960. The Great Depression in the South, as in the rest of the country, set significant precedents. City fathers began to take influxes of federal funds for granted; in many ways urbanization and the larger domestic concerns of the United States became one and the same. The extent to which spending in Washington pulled the United States out of the depression is open to question, but certainly it did not hurt the urban South. World War II saw a continuation and intensification of the flow of federal monies. Southern cities benefited from their desirable climates, from low labor rates, and from local congressmen with a great deal of seniority. In a general way, the federal government had promised blacks that in exchange for supporting the war effort they would receive civil rights. Postwar efforts to promote racial equality in the South, furthered by President Truman, helped lead to the civil rights revolution.

The civil disobedience campaigns of Dr. Martin Luther King, Jr., played a great role in gaining attention and generating a consensus for national legislation. Violence directed against integrationists shocked Americans. The Civil Rights acts of 1964 and 1965 ended the segregation system. Through it all, federal money for defense and civilian purposes continued to be pumped into the South. Money from various "Great Society" projects, many financed through the huge and bureaucratic Office of Economic Opportunity, proved an unexpected bonus, sort of a throwback to the WPA and PWA, but in a time of relative prosperity rather than depression. Northern investors found the South fertile ground. A general introduction of air conditioning changed working conditions. Agricultural change transformed rural Dixie, with cotton picking becoming increasingly mechanized. By the 1960s the region was well on the way to regaining the modern equivalent of its antebellum position in the Union. For many reasons, the urban South played a major role in the section's resurgence.

7

AN URBAN RENAISSANCE

The trends that characterized southern urban progress continued following the changes wrought by the civil rights revolution. The long period of retrenchment came to an end. Industry steadily increased in importance and threatened to make the South more and more like the rest of the nation. A goal of state governments, in the wake of unsuccessful attempts to stop integration, was to fight delaying actions against unionization. Concern about air pollution, exhaustion of resources, and depletion of water supplies were, in the main, considerations that took second place to material progress. Nor did it seem to matter that certain expected growth industries, in particular chemicals and petroleums, involved serious environmental risks. In much the same way, the social consequences of the move toward corporate agriculture, although deplored by some observers, was submerged in a flood of statistics showing growing farming prosperity. The procurement of more and more federal and outside money became almost an end in itself. The Vietnamese War, which public opinion polls showed received considerable support in the South, saw huge military and arms expenditures. This condition continued under President Ronald Reagan's program to "rearm America."

Of even greater importance was the continued general improvement in the southern economy, which manifested itself in the massive advance of the country's gross national product. Consumer industries multiplied throughout the region. Increasingly, market prospects rather than other incentives loomed important in the decisions of northern corporations to move into Dixie. The building of a huge new General Motors plant in Tennessee served as a symbol of changed dispensations. Southern promoters claimed that the national financial recessions of the 1970s and early 1980s hardly hurt the section's cities. Even though this statement was open to question, little doubt remained that the South had gradually reemerged as a full partner in the life of the nation.

The formal end of segregation did not usher in an era of racial harmony. During the 1980s riots in the Liberty City and Overhill districts of Miami and disturbances in the streets of Tampa provided ample evidence that black urban southerners continued to hold grievances toward authorities. Racial hatred involving blacks, Hispanics, and the police appeared to be the immediate sources of the trouble, with poverty and a lack of opportunity as underlying causes. Still, Liberty City appeared a special case, given the racial mix in the Miami area that resulted from influxes of refugees from Cuba. The Tampa outbreaks seemed to be isolated events.

Throughout Dixie a general racial accommodation signaled the advent of cooperation between whites and blacks. In 1989 several large southern cities—including Atlanta, Baltimore, Birmingham, New Orleans, and Washington—had black mayors. Southerners tended to gloss over "white flight" to the suburbs and an exodus to predominantly white private schools; it was argued that much the same thing had happened in the North. The 1980 census indicated that some of the largest central cities in the South were more than 50 percent black. Although a great many of the millions of blacks who left the land in the post-World War II period went North to the mean streets of such places as Chicago and Philadelphia, enough moved to southern cities to affect their racial profiles in dramatic fashion. In 1980 blacks outnumbered whites 283,200 to 138,200 in Atlanta, 158,200 to 124,700 in Birmingham, and 308,000 to 238,200 in New Orleans.

As cities' racial characteristics changed, their tax bases deteriorated. The loss of whites, especially those from the middle class, hurt. Another negative factor involved cutbacks in federal spending for social programs. The New Deal era ended. While both major parties agreed that the poor needed help, arguments centered on the quality of programs and levels of funding. Some authorities believed that southern cities would soon experience fiscal emergencies of the same kind as those which in the 1970s and 1980s had afflicted Cleveland, New York, and other northern cities. During much of southern urban history money problems had of course been a thorn, but few leaders seemed outwardly distressed. By 1988 a significant issue facing administrators revolved around neither race nor money. Rather, the urban sites of the South had to contend with the stresses and strains associated with progress.

Census returns indicated that the South had achieved metropolitan dimensions in line with the rest of the country. American cities grew so rapidly in the 1960s that by the end of the decade more than 70 percent of the nation's inhabitants lived in Standard Metropolitan Statistical Areas. Some demographers predicted that the percentage would rise significantly in the twenty-first century, but in the 1970s metropolitan growth slowed. Several of the country's largest SMSAs either lost population or grew very slowly. Most of the losses came in the northeastern and the north-central census divisions. Thirty of thirty-two SMSAs that lost population were in those parts of the United States.

Much of the 9.1 percent growth in the metropolitan populations occurred in newer parts of the country, but the South registered impressive increases. All of the twenty-five fastest growing SMSAs were in either southern or western census regions. Equally noteworthy was the growth of central cities. In sharp contrast to the severe losses in older parts of the nation, forty-six of sixty southern cities with more than 50,000 inhabitants gained in population. While black and Hispanic minorities made up the largest number of the new inner city residents—not to the liking of some whites—growth attested to striking economic differentials that favored the South as opposed to the "old industrial heartland."[1]

A new census designation, Consolidated Metropolitan Statistical Areas, applied to urbanized areas of more than a million people. Estimates made by the census in 1984 indicated that the United States had thirty-seven CMSAs. The three largest were New York (17.8 million), Los Angeles (12.4 million), and Chicago (8 million). Of the rest, ten were in the South, as the following tabulation indicates.

Houston	3.6 million
Dallas-Forth Worth	3.5 million
Washington	3.4 million
Miami-Fort Lauderdale	2.8 million
Atlanta	2.4 million
Baltimore	2.2 million
Tampa-St. Petersburg	1.8 million
New Orleans	1.3 million
Norfolk	1.3 million
Charlotte	1.0 million

Other big southern metropolises, which the census now called Metropolitan Statistical Areas, included Louisville (962,600), Memphis (934,600), and Birmingham (895,200). Some of the CMSAs grew very rapidly between 1980 and 1984—Houston by 15 percent, Dallas-Fort Worth by 14.2 percent, and Atlanta by 11.3 percent. These increases came despite a recession in the early 1980s. By the last half of the decade, downturns in the petrochemical and petroleum industries had put the brakes, at least temporarily, on rapid progress in Louisiana, Texas, and Oklahoma. The situation's effect on the South as a whole would be an important measure of the economic condition and continued potential of the section's rising urban components.

State and local southern development boards continued to work hard to encourage manufacturing. Some states, all the time in competition with each other and development agencies in other parts of the country, did better than their counterparts. North Carolina, which had much to offer in way of resources, became the leading industrial state in the South. Mississippi, which started its regional pioneering "Balance Agriculture with Industry" program of industrial subsidization back in 1936, continued to rank at the bottom of all national indexes fifty years later. In a sense, development boards were a throwback to colonial times when government authorities tried to designate town sites. Development boards gave hope and sometimes actually obtained factories for out-of-the-way communities with small prospects under the best of circumstances.

The pursuit of progress continued, as it had for more than a hundred years, to take precedence over antebellum intellectual agrarian traditions. By the late 1980s it was unclear whether or not the South had completed the basic stages of industrialism, passing from the takeoff stage to a settled manufacturing economy. In short, was it time to calculate the human cost of industrialization and close the books? Many of the workers in the expanding industries of the modern South were men and women forced off the land by the transformation of southern agriculture. They were, although many were older, the twentieth-century equivalent of the immigrant and native American peasants and farm workers who staffed the northern foundries and machine shops of the Gilded Age.

A young southern historian, James C. Cobb, wrote movingly about what the transition from an unprofitable farm to a factory job had meant to his father in the early 1960s:

His move into industry produced the largest and steadiest income my family had ever enjoyed. My father's new job was not by any means an unmixed blessing, however. As a farmer he had often worked a dawn-to-sunset day during the planting and harvesting periods. Yet eight hours at an indoor, sit-down job left him drained and listless, and he so obviously dreaded his daily toil that his morning "goodbyes" to us were protracted and almost pathetic. . . . On his tractor he had been the master of his domain. . . . In the factory, however, he fought a losing battle with machines that mystified and humiliated him, often to the delight of some of his younger and crueler co-workers. . . . Certainly as a family we felt we were experiencing progress. Yet for my father there was an important sacrifice of both status and, unfortunately, self-respect.

Such a response was a little hard for many northerners to understand because their families had made the transition much earlier. It was, though, a very real and human consideration in the modern South. "The sacrifices that accompanied industrial development," Cobb concluded, "became all too apparent in the Sunbelt era as southerners and northerners alike acknowledged that there had been more to the southern way of life than racism and demagoguery, and asked whether the South, which they had once hoped would be saved by industrialism, could now be saved from it."[2]

Governmental services were increasingly significant in the building of the metropolitan South. New Orleans had a number of federal facilities, including the Eighth Naval District and the U.S. Department of Agriculture Marketing Service; Atlanta had more than 30,000 federal employees. No place was as directly tied to "Big Government" as Washington; by the late 1970s more than 411,000 persons, both civilian and military personnel, in the District of Columbia area worked for the national government. Another million individuals engaged in a wide variety of related efforts—lobbying, legal services, trade associations, and so on. The gigantic role played by the government required a massive concentration of people and resources. From a strictly financial standpoint, the cutting of the political deal in the early days of the Republic that placed the nation's capital at a southern site worked ultimately to the advantage of Dixie. Here was the kind of urban advance that could not be accessed in the short run. The building of Washington back in the Early National period had initially hurt Baltimore and had resulted in a real estate debacle. It reflected the sometimes unpredictable factors associated with city building.

Tourism had become big business in many parts of the metropolitan South. Long important, furthered by the warm climate and geographical features, the southern vacation industry expanded beyond the expectations of all except the most ardent boosters in the 1970s and 1980s. The growing affluence of many Americans, coupled with better security and increased vacation benefits, contributed to the trend. Vacations became accepted annual endeavors, not something planned and saved for years in advance. Indeed, in an age of deregulation and relatively low airline fares, people thought little of flying halfway across the country and back over a couple days. The availability of decent motels and hotels, standardized restaurants and fast-food establishments, and toll-free reservation services eliminated some of the uncertainty associated with travel.

Interstate limited-access highways made it fairly easy for automobile travelers to cover several hundred miles a day. When people arrived by air, all the major southern cities could be reached in only a few hours from any place in the continental United States. A higher quality of attractions helped in luring tourists; while some snake farms and seashell shops remained, many had given way to lavish amusement parks and gardens, some run by religious organizations. As in the nineteenth century, promotional activities were important in luring tourists. Advertisements, as expected, accentuated the positive, emphasizing good times and playing down high prices, crowded facilities, poor service, insects in season, and unreasonable weather. As a governor of Louisiana proclaimed, "Let the good times roll." And so they did, for millions of visitors to the South.

Some large southern cities reaped great rewards from tourism. Washington became, as the Republic grew in power and importance, almost a mandatory tourist stop—the Capitol Building, the White House, the Washington Monument, the Jefferson and Lincoln memorials, the Supreme Court, and the Arlington National Cemetery were the great shrines and working symbols of the nation. The District of Columbia's many museums, especially those for air and space, art, history and technology, and natural history, were open to the public free of charge and drew more than 20 million visitors a year from the United States and around the world. The National Air and Space Museum, located a short distance from the Capitol, averaged more than 6 million visitors a year.

The large number of visitors to Washington artificially forced up prices for entertainment and hotel rooms, especially for accommodations. Much the same was true in New Orleans. Always a great attraction, more people than ever before had the means to visit the French Quarter to sample its supposedly excellent food and other allures. The Mardi Gras celebration was one of the greatest events of its kind in America. The building of the Super Dome and the renovation of New Orleans's center core—an old brewery adjacent to the French Quarter became a trendy arcade—helped the Crescent City, according to the Greater New Orleans Tourist and Convention Commission, to attain the position of the country's second greatest tourist mecca.

Other places gained from special entertainment features. Graceland, the home of the late entertainer Elvis Presley, brought thousands of people to Memphis. In Nashville, the Grand Ole Opry, Opryland U.S.A., and Andrew Jackson's home, the Hermitage, annually drew hundreds of thousands of visitors. Through aggressive marketing, Atlanta became a convention center. In 1988 the Democrats held their national convention in Atlanta, and the Republicans met in New Orleans. The Kentucky Derby in Louisville and the Preakness in Baltimore, two of the nation's premier horse racing events, attracted vast numbers of spectators. According to promoters, major league professional sports, especially baseball, football, and basketball, brought considerable numbers of visitors to Baltimore, Washington, Atlanta, Miami, New Orleans, and Tampa.

In 1984 a Super Bowl football game in Tampa attracted tremendous crowds and gave the city excellent free national publicity. The contest was said to have brought $70 million into the city; the amount was open to question. Even more difficult to ascertain was the tourist value of late-season major league baseball games between noncontenders. In a larger sense, the quest for tourist and convention dollars placed the urban South in direct competition with itself and with centers throughout the country and, indeed, in other countries. Changes in Ontario nonresidence fishing licenses, discount air fares between New York and London, unsettled political conditions in Fiji, and convention rates in Reno all had an impact on the South. Competition in the tourist, sport, and convention businesses rekindled the spirit of urban rivalry in America. For the urban South this presented an excellent opportunity to see how well the section could do competing against outside interests for business, unfettered by colonial restraints. It could be argued that, for the first time since antebellum days, the South had started with an advantage over New York.

Tourism helped build twentieth-century urban Florida. Naturally, in the 1980s almost all the promotional literature emphasized the increasing significance of other activities: aircraft parts factories in West Palm Beach, 5,000 light manufacturing plants in Miami, and breweries in Tampa. Still, few people claimed that Florida had achieved the status of a manufacturing giant; even aerospace money had failed to launch Titusville, which had an 1980 population of 31,900, into the upper levels among cities of the Sunshine State. Miami had been among the first areas in the state to boom as a tourist center. By 1940 more than 2 million vacationers were arriving every year. The number grew after the war to more than 5.5 million in 1960 and to a claimed 12.6 million in 1980.[3]

Undeniably, the drying up of mass tourism in Fidel Castro's Cuba and the failure of the Bahamas to attract as much vacation business as expected helped the Florida tourist business. Fort Lauderdale-Hollywood gained attention as the gathering place during the spring of hundreds of thousands of college students; Palm Beach, a suburb of West Palm Beach, was one of the country's richest resorts. High-rise hotels and condominiums stretched for miles along the shore from West Palm Beach through Miami Beach. On the west coast, Tampa-St. Petersburg was at the northern end of a vacation district that extended South for 150 miles through Sarasota, Fort Myers, and Naples. In central Florida, Walt Disney World, near Orlando, every year drew crowds of more than 13 million. The massive facility was a logical extension of earlier pleasure grounds, such as Busch Gardens in Tampa and Marineland of Florida near St. Augustine. Despite much social comment about the tackiness and superficiality of Florida's "Vacation Land," millions of visitors continued to pour money into the state's coffers.

Florida continued to improve its position as a prime retirement center and winter home. The idea of retiring to the Sunshine State had begun to take hold in the nineteenth century but had initially been a dream that few Americans could ever hope to realize. Florida had many qualities, including flora and vegetation unlike that in the rest of the country, that continued to attract people in the twentieth century. Particularly appealing was the warm climate despite its humidity except during the winter months. From the very first, Florida publicists conjured up pleasing visions of sand, sun, and surf. The construction of railroad lines connected towns throughout the state with the big metropolises in the North. By the 1930s St. Petersburg had a large retirement community, and Daytona Beach had many winter residents.

Following World War II, the southeast coast attracted millions of retirees and seasonable residents, touching off a huge boom in condominium construction. The move of large numbers of older permanent residents into the state changed the state's congressional politics and forced leaders to place a greater emphasis on social security and issues related to old age. Miami Beach and St. Petersburg had much older populations than almost all places of similar size in the United States. Although winter residents did not vote in Florida, they added to the state's cosmopolitan image.

One community lured at least 10,000 Canadian "Snow Birds" every season. Canadian social commentator Richard Gwyn noted in his 1985 book *The Forty-Ninth Paradox,* "On any day in January or February, there are about one million Canadians, or 4 percent of the total population in Florida." Canadian political leader Jean Chretien, commenting on the pull of Florida on his countrymen, observed, "Canadians love Canada, but not for fifty-two weeks of the year."[4] Like tourism, the attracting of retirement and seasonable residents was a business. It placed Florida in direct competition with Arizona, California, and Hawaii for affluent elderly citizens.

Pundits and media experts alike observed that a new spirit of progress seemed abroad in the urban South. Even the term South was passé, replaced by one that had broader connotations, Sunbelt or Sun Belt. The expression, attributed to political consultant Kevin Philips in his 1969 book *The Emerging Republican Majority,* was worthy of Madison Avenue. It implied that the sun did not shine in the North or Frostbelt, although South Dakota claimed to have more sunny days on average than any other state. At the same time the term "Sunbelt," denoting by implication a region that cut across traditional sectional lines, blurred racial questions by linking the fortunes of southern cities with those in the Southwest and the Far West. The concept of a Sunbelt represented a public relations triumph, generally bought uncritically by the national weekly news magazines and by the television networks. The phraseology sounded good, and maybe it was true. Much of the message, however, had been heard before. It was nothing new to equate the South with the golden West or to gloss over racial disharmony. Another problem was very fundamental: no one seemed to agree on how to define the Sunbelt.

The Sunbelt idea had—depending on the observer—certain economic, political, geographic, demographic, and lifestyle characteristics. Some analysts associated the Sunbelt with a probusiness climate. The title of an article in *Fortune* gushed, "Business Loves the Sunbelt (and vice versa)." According to a Georgia trade official, "The Sunbelt is not sunshine. Its an attitude . . . conducive to business. The North has lost that attitude." Oklahomans, quick to see the possibilities, placed a rising sun logo on their automobile license plates. Some political definitions were mean spirited. One New York writer saw the Sunbelt in terms of military spending, or in terms of areas that received more defense dollars than the Northeast. In 1976 journalist Kirkpatrick Sale equated the "Southern Rim" with right-wing politics, which he regarded as a threat to the nation's progressive traditions. Sale wrote, "It hardly seems an accident that there is indeed a cartographic line that sets off this area almost precisely: the boundary line which runs along the northern edges of North Carolina, Tennessee, Arkansas, Oklahoma, New Mexico, Arizona, or generally the 37th parallel." Demographers appeared as confused as anyone else. One included St. Louis and Kansas City. Another, in separate essays in the same book, placed Memphis in both the Sunbelt and Frostbelt. Quality-of-life studies provided still another measurement. An article entitled, "The Sunning of America," claimed, "The Sunbelt offers both more 'sun' and more 'fun.' Outdoor living, informal entertaining, and golf the year round—all afford the new lifestyles which Americans have adopted."[5]

Virtually the only statement with which everyone agreed was that a Sunbelt existed. The extent of the boundaries—if there were any; some people considered it a state of mind—were entirely another matter. Richard M. Bernard and Bradley R. Rice summed matters up, noting, "The very concept of a Sunbelt is a novel and somewhat controversial notion in American geography . . . .General usage, however, has not led to a common definition of the American Sunbelt."[6] Further complicating affairs was that some experts discounted the region's very existence. Census bureaucrats ignored the Sunbelt. Under their definitions, the South consisted of the Old Confederacy, plus Oklahoma, Kentucky, West Virginia, Maryland, Delaware, and the District of Columbia. The West included all the intermountain states and those on the Pacific slope. At the same time Department of Commerce officials delineated a "Sunbelt-South" as the census South minus Maryland, Delaware, and the District of Columbia. Joel Garreau, the author of a 1981 book entitled *The Nine Nations of North America*, argued that the very idea of the Sunbelt was "spurious" and "misleading."[7] No matter how proper Garreau's sentiments, the term had gained common coinage by the 1980s and was used by the media in reference to cities with warmer climes or conservative politics.

Carl Abbott, a professor of urban studies at Portland State University, produced a grandiose and controversial definition of Sunbelt that was based on census and other data. Abbott's Sunbelt was a phenomenon of the decades after 1940. Applying historical analysis to his statistical evidence, he concluded that "real shifts" of population, wealth, and industrial capacity created a new regional pattern.[8] In his view, the South had overcome racism and poverty; the West faced new problems of maturity and continuing growth. "The overall result of economic growth in the last generation has thus been the convergence of South and West," he stressed. "They are no longer exceptions to the American standard—a charmed golden West, a South of massive resistance and rural starvation."[9]

Per capita income figures, business location indicators, comparative social and socioeconomic characteristics, and population ratios allowed Abbott to define the limits of his version of the Sunbelt in terms of fast-growing metropolitan areas. Under his definition the new region included a great rim of states running from Delaware through Florida, omitted Alabama, Mississippi, and Louisiana, and swept through Texas, New Mexico, and Arizona and on to California, Oregon, and Washington. Excluded as well from his arbitrary definition were Arkansas, Tennessee, and Kentucky; Nevada, Utah, and Colorado were included. "Overall, it has been the warm coasts of the Pacific, the Gulf of Mexico, and the Atlantic Ocean southward from Chesapeake Bay that have exerted the strongest pull on the American population," Abbott explained. "The Sunbelt-Southeast can be considered as the South Atlantic slope, for all its fast-growing metropolitan areas lie southeastward of a line drawn parallel to the Appalachian front from the Mason-Dixon Line to the Gulf of Mexico. Indeed, this line recognizes growth differences within Alabama by splitting Mobile from the less prosperous cities upstate."[10]

However flawed Abbott's statistically based conclusions, his vision of the Sunbelt's potential magnificence was new in discussions of the urban South's future. He showed that several decades of urbanization had helped to change the nature and shape of the region. Then too, his attempt to exclude integral parts of the Old Confederacy from a definition of the Sunbelt indicated in dramatic fashion the need to think about the South in new terms. He demonstrated that modern urban metropolitan trends had started prior to World War II and long before the end of the segregation system. If nothing else, his statistics indicated the consistency of southern urban growth. Furthermore, they provided the basis for the bold conclusions that linked the fortunes of Los Angeles, San Francisco, and Denver with those of Norfolk, Miami, and Atlanta. DeBow or Grady, even in their most visionary moments, never went so far. In one fell swoop, Abbott gave the South great commercial centers and then some. His urban Sunbelt united forces that reduced New York and its northeastern and midwestern hinterlands to subordinate positions.

Abbott's use of statistical data and his sweeping interpretations harked back to the mid-nineteenth-century studies of William Gilpin and Jesup W. Scott. Gilpin had combined theories of geographical and gravitational determinism to "prove" in 1855 that by 1955 the West would contain a monster "Centropolis" of 50 million people and various preeminent cities. Scott was able to demonstrate to his satisfaction using demography that railroads would lead to dramatic population and commercial shifts from the Northeast to Midwest, especially to Toledo, where he owned considerable property. Abbott went even further; he envisioned a whole new super region. Such visionary conceptual thinking was needed as a starting point in discussions about the probable course of twenty-first-century southern urbanization. It showed in vivid terms that the identity of American's regions would continue to change.

The leaders in southern cities continued to think along traditional developmental lines. Politicians had to worry about reelection; businessmen needed to consider their annual bottom lines. All dire predictions by white supremacists to the contrary, it made little difference who was in charge of city hall—whites, blacks, or Hispanics. Nor did the form of government—be it commission, city manager, mayor and council, or metro—seem to have an appreciable impact. The emphasis fell on immediate progress and urban boosterism. Politicians had to consider the consequences of alienating major local concerns because they usually had the option of leaving town. William B. Hartsfield of Atlanta had admitted as much on one occasion when he told a friend that in every act as mayor he kept in mind that Atlanta was the headquarters of Coca-Cola.[11] He set forth another basic function of office, declaring, "We roll out the red carpet for every damn Yankee who comes in here with two strong hands and some money. We break our necks to sell him."[12]

A later Atlanta mayor, Andrew Young, a national black leader who had served as U.S. ambassador to the United Nations, reacted with appropriate civic rage when he decided that a television miniseries had unfairly represented the police and judicial procedures in his city which had preceded the conviction of a young and talented black man for murder. Young won elections fought along racial lines, but his victories did not translate into a purely black administration. In the modern South, black mayors, beset by the forces afflicting urban leaders throughout the nation's history, had little choice except to support traditional progrowth policies.

Even though the old white dominant groups, by virtue of their economic holdings, continued to have a say in shaping the direction of urban policy throughout the South, blacks received better urban services than they had in segregation days. On the surface their public schools, despite enforced busing and virtual resegregation, seemed better. Both white and black political organizations courted black voters, and increasing numbers of blacks served in elected and nonelected positions. For the first time since Reconstruction, blacks held positions of authority in police and fire departments. As always in the South, money for services remained a serious problem. What happened in New Orleans in the 1960s was typical. According to the mayor, the city "lost 125,000 people—most white and affluent—moving out to the suburbs, and in their place, 90,000, mostly poor and black, moved in."[13] Miami faced a more complicated situation. In 1980 its total population of 346,900 included 87,100 blacks plus another 194,100 citizens of Spanish origin; many were Cuban immigrants and their children.

The ethnic mix taxed the capabilities of the Miami metro government, as did the growing role of the area as an organized crime and drug center. National magazines called it "Mob City" and compared the situation with that in Chicago during Prohibition. Concern about law and order continued to mount in the urban South, with the major change that crime fighting in most parts no longer served as an excuse to keep black populations in line. As cities struggled to increase the efficiency of police departments and generally to improve services in the face of diminishing revenues, annexation seemed a logical panacea. With some justification, central city residents argued that they paid for parks, cultural centers, sport facilities, and airports used by everyone in their metropolitan areas.[14] If, as many experts predicted, Sunbelt central cities started to experience more and more of the development problems associated with those in the Frostbelt, annexation promised to become a burning issue of the 1990s.

In the meantime, a cautious optimism prevailed, generating a belief that the southern metropolis of the 1980s would prevail, overcoming the challenge of economic, social, and political fragmentation. Promotional prognostications smacked of a throwback to the nineteenth century. The *Miami Herald* claimed: "Nowhere in America is the cutting edge of 20th century change more evident than in Miami."[15] The historian Gary R. Mormino, who lived in Tampa, felt that growth was the "manifest challenge" facing the city, even though he admitted blacks had not fared very well inasmuch as they had elected their first member of the city council only in 1983. "Tampa Bay is a collection of dynamic and recklessly growing communities, held together by vigorous and administrative climate—business and natural—and brought together by the fortunes—cathartic and athletic—of its football team," Mormino enthusiastically declared. "For a city that was once known as the

'Hell Hole of the Gulf Coast,' the journey to metropolitan status has been dizzying. Demographers predict that Tampa should reach a population of 400,000 by the year 2000, and the metropolitan region should spiral to three and a half million persons."[16]

Arnold R. Hirsch, a historian and regional planner at the University of New Orleans, while noting that economic growth in the Gulf region brought "a growing number of increasingly dangerous industrial accidents and more pollution to the already carcinogen-laden Mississippi River," saw hope for the future. "Regional, national, and international currents," he said, "regularly lap at the Crescent City and there is tangible evidence of a new worldliness."[17] Even intellectuals accepted the premise that the urban South continued to be on the move.

Perhaps as never before, a spirit of optimism pervaded thinking throughout much of urban Dixie. The cities of the South seemed alive to change, ready to seize upon the latest technological innovations to advance their interests, while places in the Northeast and the Midwest appeared old and tired by comparison. In the nineteenth century, a great technological innovation, the railroad, had welded the two sections together and had created the basis for a hundred years of northern domination. During the 1980s, at the end of the railroad era, and at the advent of what many popular writers proclaimed the "new technological age," the South gave signs of enjoying certain advantages in air transportation.

At Kitty Hawk in North Carolina in 1903, the Wright brothers flew a plane heavier than air, and the United States first launched manned space flights in the 1960s from the beaches of eastern Florida. During World War II, hundreds of thousands of airmen trained at southern bases. Many of these facilities came under local control following hostilities. During much of the year southern skies provided superior flying conditions. Most important was the early establishment of air freight and passenger airlines in the South. By the time jet travel began, the more important southern carriers were in a position to play major national and international roles. They extended their services into other parts of the country and competed on equal terms or better with airlines outside the South.

By the 1980s the urban South had excellent commercial aviation components. Delta Air Lines, Inc., one of the nation's most successful major carriers, was an Atlanta corporation. Eastern Airlines, among the largest passenger lines in the country, was a Miami company until its ownership changed in 1987. Pan American, the first large American carrier to fly overseas routes, started in Miami. Southern congressmen had helped Pan American acquire Latin

American connections. Another pioneer overseas airline, Mackey, until its demise in the 1970s, flew out of Fort Lauderdale to the Bahamas. A larger Atlanta-based regional line, Southern, merged with several others across the United States and eventually became part of Republic, a Minneapolis-St. Paul concern, which in turn merged with Northwest in 1986. On the one hand, some southern airlines failed, ranging from the small Flamingo, a commuter line that served Florida and the Bahamas, to the larger Air Florida, a Miami regional carrier that in the early 1980s expanded its routes too fast. On the other hand, Federal Express, a rapidly expanding mail and freight line founded by northern interests, used Memphis as its main collection and distribution point.

Deregulation of routes and a general increase in the number of travelers between large cities helped the South. The adoption of the hub concept by large passenger airlines resulted in a tremendous increase in Atlanta's volume of traffic. By the mid-1980s Atlanta's Hartsfield International Airport and Dallas/Fort Worth International Airport rivaled O'Hare in Chicago and Los Angeles International as America's busiest airports. Miami International, with more than 13 million air travelers annually, handled great numbers of Latin American visitors and northern vacationers. Fort Lauderdale and West Palm Beach were two other important South Florida airports much favored by tourists. The Washington and Baltimore areas had three passenger jet airports, including the venerable and busy National Airport, near downtown Washington. Memphis served as a regional hub for major carriers and benefited from its central location.

The air industry, despite numerous problems—Eastern habitually hovered on the brink of financial disaster and had continual labor-management problems—was very big business. More than 160,000 employees in Miami and 30,000 in Atlanta directly or indirectly worked in the aviation industry as a whole. Both cities had large air maintenance and repair facilities; the annual payroll alone in Atlanta approached the billion dollar mark. The broader implications of the business remained imperfectly understood. Although no one had as yet formulated a generally accepted theory about aviation developments in geopolitical terms, there appeared a growing realization that more was involved than simply carrying people and moving goods. Air transportation had the power to alter the face of urban America radically and fundamentally.

Large southern centers of the late twentieth century had already assumed many of the attributes of their counterparts throughout the country. Suburbanization trends that started following World War

II continued over the next forty years. Architectural designs in southern suburbs were much the same as those elsewhere, with ranch-style dwellings predominating. Some larger homes featured fake white columns, plantation house imitations that could be found all the way from Maine to California. In short, the form was no longer distinctively associated with the South; no true regional architecture flourished in Dixie. If anything, air conditioning, which in the years after 1960 became a common feature, worked against sectional designs.[18] High ceilings, verandas, and porches were no longer necessary. Accompanying suburbanization was a trend toward shopping centers. Those in Atlanta, New Orleans, and Baltimore looked the same as ones in Denver, Milwaukee, and Hartford. The shopping centers—the largest in North America was purportedly one in Edmonton, Alberta—had a fundamental impact on downtowns, altering their traditional roles as merchandising centers. City people no longer felt a need to go downtown as often as they had in the past.

Downtowns increasingly became centers for business and entertainment and lost most of their traditional merchandising functions. Specialty shops and convenience stores rather than department stores appeared the wave of the future; from a retail standpoint, this development seemed to be a curious throwback to the era that preceded the ascendancy of department and chain stores. Some downtowns became places to leave at night; that of Washington was a classic example. All sorts of schemes emerged, designed to attract everything from convention delegates to suburban shoppers. The tangible results accomplished by what seemed a countless number of downtown development boards were usually confined to never enacted plans and rhetorical predictions of impending greatness. Walls came down, replaced by parking lots and terraced parks.

Some places did accomplish significant changes. Baltimore tore down and rebuilt portions of its central core, with the previously decrepit waterfront district becoming the site of a magnificent national aquarium. Atlanta business interests constructed a huge urban extravaganza called Peachtree Center, an area of more than twenty acres that attempted to blend rural and urban forms, with large hotels and office buildings thrusting toward the sky in the middle of parklike splendor that reminded enthusiastic residents of the Tivoli Gardens in Copenhagen.[19] Peachtree Center, which was located near Atlanta's convention and sports arenas, supposedly contained the tallest hotel in the United States. Even so, Peachtree Center failed to become an attraction on the same level as the historic French Quarter in New Orleans. The redevelopment and preservation of whole old central districts, including those in Savannah and Charleston, represented the better side of southern urban architecture. A key fact was that a combination of urban renewal, public housing, and expressways had destroyed much of the urban South's architectural heritage. Anonymous architecture, in which "form follows function" prevailed over aesthetic considerations, predominated almost everywhere.

The southern cities, which had a special attraction as the late twentieth century advanced, became the the kind of places in which many Americans wanted to live. The climate, always a winter inducement, became even more attractive as air conditioning became more widespread in offices, factories, stores, homes, and automobiles. Urban expressways greatly increased commuter ranges. String cities of a new sort emerged in some parts of the South. Conrad Treuber, a population expert, noted in 1974 after flying over North Carolina, "You fly over that section of the country at night and look down and it looks like one big long urban area," he said. "But it's really nothing like the sort of tight clustering that you see in the Northeast. I think we'll see a lot more of that sort of thing. People there can live in uncrowded conditions but still have a reasonable choice of jobs to choose from."[20]

By 1988 the emergence of what the media called "megacounties," for example Fairfax County in the Washington area and Gwinnett County just northeast of Atlanta, tended to confirm the trend. For those who could afford it, southern suburban living represented a relaxed and congenial way of life, complete with barbecue grills, two or more cars, above-average schools, carpools, volunteer activities, and all sorts of opportunities for outdoor recreation.

A wide range of cultural activities characterized late twentieth-century Dixie. In many places symphony orchestras and art galleries were gaining prominence. Although the most publicized institutions were in the rising national metropolises of Houston, Dallas, and Atlanta, a life of refinement and polish was increasingly available in medium-sized cities such as Corpus Christi and Alexandria, Louisiana. Television, videocassettes, movies, radio, and regional newspapers gave southerners much the same worldview as Americans elsewhere in the nation. The sexual revolution, feminism, AIDS, teenage rebellion, abortion and the drug culture all affected the South as well as other regions of the country. Isolation was no longer a feature of the southern condition. Even though prophets of doom feared that Dixie would lose its identity, the prospect seemed remote. Southern mores appeared too strong to fall before "Yankee Culture."

A black Chicagoan from Tuskegee said it best: "Chicago ain't where I live. It's where I stay. Chicago's *existin*.' Tuskegee is *livin*.' "[21]

Southern intellectuals and social commentators worried about the impact of urbanization on agrarian institutions that they regarded as traditional. In 1973 John Egerton expressed concern that "the South and the nation are not exchanging strengths as much as they are exchanging sins,. more often than not, they are sharing and spreading the worst in each other, while the best languishes and withers." Marshall Frady, a leading southern journalist and writer, feared that the "tinfoil-twinkly simulation" of southern California threatened to engulf the South. "Faulkner's Flem Snopes has evolved into a relentlessly bouncy and glitter-eyed neo-Babbitt with an almost touching lust for new chemical plants, glassy-maized office parks and instant subdivisions," he wrote. "The mischief is that, in its transfiguration into What-a-Burger drive-ins and apartment wastelands, the South is being etherized, subtly rendered pastless, memoryless and vague of identity."[22] While this trend was not exactly new, it represented a variation on the familiar theme that undesirable outside forces would eventually overwhelm Dixie and, although they might fail to destroy it, would corrupt and compromise its identity.

Implicit in the analysis of Egerton, Frady, and others was a call for a review of agrarian values, a restudy of the fundamental principles of Jeffersonianism or of the sentiments expressed in *I'll Take My Stand*. Yet these observers did not want a return to segregation— far from it. They feared a loss of something nebulous but at the same time associated with traditional values; they sought to reaffirm the South's religious heritage, the uniqueness of the landscape, and the heroism of Confederate leaders. It was as if the South had remained a rural bastion until cities suddenly overwhelmed it. Living in a period of tremendous sectional change, the thoughtful southerners sought to preserve old values even as they acquiesced to the new. Surely, as long as such sentiments as those expressed by Jefferson and the authors of *I'll Take My Stand* were abroad, the South would endure, both in fact and in mind.

Although the southern boundaries might change or be open to dispute, the concept of regionalism refused to die in America. In the aftermath of the civil rights revolution, northerners, as at the end of Reconstruction, showed little inclination to tell southerners how to conduct their affairs. Moreover, as a new era dawned in the South of the 1980s, they no longer had the power to do so. Colonialism in Dixie was not even an issue. Once it became clear that northern money, mills, and media would not destroy the best of southern culture, the section's nationalists turned to other questions. Through the use of outside capital the South, at considerable cost and just as the men of the New South creed had predicted, achieved equality in the Union. At long last the region put behind it the defeat of 1865. Southern per capita income levels, to be sure, remained lower than in the North. In the 1880s the difference was significant; in the 1980s it was increasingly irrelevant, given variations in prices, changing land values, and cost-of-living adjustments.

Racial relations in the modern South, as widely noted, remained strained. Busing to achieve school desegregation was generally unpopular, blacks and whites attended their own churches, and residential districts remained almost totally segregated. Much the same situation existed outside the South. With regard to race relations, sentiments in urban America, North and South, increasingly dovetailed. That was to beg the question. Throughout southern history, cities in the South had been more like those in the North than had the section's agrarian components. Perhaps it would have been more accurate to put things the other way around, to say that northern cities gradually became more similar to their southern neighbors. Urbanization in the United States, from the earliest days to the present, always crossed sectional lines.

Southern urban development had traditionally moved ahead at a pace that seemed appropriate in view of sectional needs. Of great import was that cities in the South had never grown in isolation from the rest of America. It has been argued that southern urbanites retained rural values. "But the southern city is different because the South is different," regional southern historian David R. Goldfield, a transplanted New Yorker teaching in North Carolina, has written. "In that region, the city is much closer to the plantation than it is to Chicago and New York."[23] This viewpoint may have had some validity, but it did not take southern cities outside the mainstream. Exactly the same thing could be said about cities in the North. After all, Central Park in New York helped spawn the City Beautiful movement, and Chicago authorities had deliberately set aside huge tracts of land on the city's outskirts as forest preserves. A dedication to rural values united city people, as did what an older generation called urbanity: a commonality of values associated with the urban condition.

The history of the urban South progressed within a sectional framework, all the while making a significant contribution to the southern way of life. After more than 350 years of city building, two decades stood out as more important than all the others. Of special significance were the 1880s and the 1950s, give or take a few years on either side. The two periods encompassed the great leaps forward in southern urbanization. In colonial days leaders built the first foundations (which probably seem more important in retrospect than they did at the time), established basic levels of urban services, pioneered a planning tradition, and built necessary economic institutions. The antebellum years featured the careful construction of regional strata of cities concurrent with a reckless and relentless expansion in the North.

The South could not compete in building boom towns, as members of the ill-fated commercial convention movement concluded. The twin agonies of Civil War and Reconstruction impeded progress in the defeated communities and in those outside the Confederate States of America that escaped the direct ravages of war. The goal of all concerned was hardly to advance but rather to get back to the situation before the start of hostilities. In the early metropolitan period, southern urban leaders held the line, presided over steady but generally unspectacular growth, promoted growing professionalism in city administration, and entertained a high degree of unwarranted optimism. During the Great Depression the South's cities hung on, helped immeasurably by federal relief funds. In World War II, with the depression past, the urban centers overcame the threat of a grave social crisis and advanced rapidly as war-related ventures brought a large measure of prosperity. The decades after the postwar era led to so much economic progress that in the 1980s the cities of the South had achieved a common ground or better with their counterparts around the nation.

Both the 1880s and 1950s were activist decades that set courses for the future. I mean to imply not that all developments were positive but rather that both key decades were watersheds in the southern experience in America. The 1880s saw basic decisions in regard to levels of services, relationships between towns, and the establishment of segregation systems. The South was tentatively moving in the direction of urban maturity and was seeing the beginnings of industrialization. In effect, the "modernization" of southern cities started during the 1880s. In the 1950s *Brown* v. *Board* brought tremendous changes in race relations in the South as a whole. The postwar period saw an upswing in the economy and especially the start of a major new industrial thrust. Everything from real estate divisions to suburban shopping centers helped to make southern cities more and more like those in other regions. Many things—air conditioning, interstate highways, urban renewal, public housing, tax breaks for home owners, and air transportation—changed the face of Dixie. As in the 1880s, a "modernization" process was under way.

Trends that began in the 1880s gave every indication of continuing into the twenty-first century. In the years ahead southern cities would confront a future at once regional and national in its implications. I do not mean that Jefferson or the writers of *I'll Take My Stand* were wrong and that the men of the New South creed were right. The South's response to future challenges, however, would reflect the influence of the city in determining the course of modern civilization.

NOTES

1. THE CONSTRUCTION OF COLONIAL CITIES

1. Quoted in Charles N. Glaab and A. Theodore Brown, *A History of Urban America,* 3d ed. (New York, 1983), 53. See Martin White and Lucia White, *The Intellectual versus the City: From Thomas Jefferson to Frank Lloyd Wright* (Cambridge, Mass., 1962); Lewis Mumford, *The City in History: Its Origins, Its Transformations, and Its Prospects* (New York, 1961).

2. Quoted in John W. Reps, *Town Planning in Frontier America* (Princeton, 1969), 107. See also John W. Reps, *Tidewater Towns: City Planning in Colonial Virginia and Maryland* (Charlottesville, 1972); William B. Hesseltine and David L. Smiley, *The South in American History* (Englewood Cliffs, N.J., 1960).

3. Edward M. Riley, "The Town Acts of Colonial Virginia," *Journal of Southern History* 16 (Aug. 1950):307-23.

4. Quoted in ibid., 307. See also John C. Rainbolt, "The Absence of Towns in Seventeenth-Century Virginia," *Journal of Southern History* 35 (Aug. 1969):343-60; John W. Reps, *The Making of Urban America: A History of City Planning in the United States* (Princeton, 1965).

5. Quoted in Riley, "Town Acts," 321. See Paul Clemens, *The Atlantic Economy and Colonial Maryland's Eastern Shore: From Tobacco to Grain* (Ithaca, 1980).

6. Quoted in Reps, *Town Planning,* 115. The "safe harbor" passage appears in Carville Earle and Ronald Hoffman, "The Urban South: The First Two Centuries," in Blaine Brownell and David R. Goldfield, eds., *The City in Southern History and the Growth of Urban Civilization in the South,* National University Publications Interdisciplinary Urban Series (Port Washington, N.Y., 1977), 31.

7. Reps, *Town Planning,* 124; Reps, *Making of Urban America;* Everett B. Wilson, *Early Southern Towns* (South Brunswick, N.J., 1967).

8. John A. Ernst and H. Roy Merrens, " 'Camden's turrets pierce the Skies!': The Urban Process in the Southern Colonies during the Eighteenth Century," *William and Mary Quarterly* 30 (Oct. 1973):549-74. See Henry Bacon McKoy, *Wilmington, N.C.—Do You Remember When?* (Greenville, S.C., 1957).

9. Quoted in Earle and Hoffman, "Urban South," in Brownell and Goldfield, *City in Southern History,* 37; Robert Rhett, *Charleston: An Epic of Carolina* (Richmond, 1940).

10. Quoted in George E. Waring, Jr., comp., "The Southern and the Western States," in *Report on the Social Statistics of Cities, Tenth Census of the United States, 1880,* vol. 10, pt. 2 (Washington, D.C., 1886-87), 2:97. Volume 9, part 1, is entitled "The New England and the Middle States." Hereinafter cited as *Social Statistics of Cities,* (1 or 2). See Rhett, *Charleston.*

11. Quoted in *Social Statistics of Cities*, 2:6. See Hamilton Owens, *Baltimore and Chesapeake* (New York, 1941); J. Thomas Scharf, *History of Baltimore and County*... (Philadelphia, 1881); Paul G.E. Clemens, *The Atlantic Economy and Colonial Maryland's Eastern Shore: From Tobacco to Grain* (Ithaca, 1980); David R. Goldfield, *Cotton Fields and Skyscrapers: Southern City and Region, 1607-1980* (Baton Rouge, 1982), 14-16.

12. Quoted in *Social Statistics of Cities*, 2:9.

13. For a good general summary of northern urban development and its relationship to the South, see Bayrd Still, *Urban America: A History with Documents* (New York, 1974), 13-57. See also Glaab and Brown, *A History of Urban America*, 1-51; Blaine Brownell and David R. Goldfield, *Urban America: From Downtown to No Town* (Boston, 1979).

14. The quoted passages appear in Carl Bridenbaugh, *Cities in Revolt: Urban Life in America, 1743-1776* (1955; repr. New York, 1970), 99-106; *Social Statistics of Cities*, 2:16.

15. The quoted passages appear in Bridenbaugh, *Cities in Revolt*, 377-78. See also Carl Bridenbaugh, *Cities in the Wilderness: The First Century of Urban Life in America, 1625-1742* (1938; repr. New York, 1970). The two volumes represent the standard accounts of urban conditions in the colonial South.

16. Quoted in Bridenbaugh, *Cities in Revolt*, 377-78.

17. Quoted in ibid., 242; Lawrence H. Larsen, "Nineteenth Century Street Sanitation: A Study of Filth and Frustration," *Wisconsin Magazine of History* 52 (Spring 1969):239-47. See Rhett, *Charleston*, also see *Social Statistics of Cities*, 2:95-98.

18. Quoted in Bridenbaugh, *Cities in the Wilderness*, 406; idem, *Cities in Revolt*, 130.

19. Quoted in Reps, *Town Planning*, 107-8. See Reps, *Tidewater Towns*; Reps, *Making of Urban America*.

20. Reps, *Town Planning*, 235-38.

21. Ibid. See also Goldfield, *Cotton Fields and Skyscrapers*, 16-7.

22. Quoted in Reps, *Town Planning*, 239-40. For a modern example of the southern urban planning tradition, see Margaret Ripley Wolfe, *Kingsport, Tennessee: A Planned American City* (Lexington, Ky., 1987).

23. Quoted in *Social Statistics of Cities*, 2:9. See Bridenbaugh, *Cities in Revolt*.

2. The Building of an Antebellum System

1. Quoted in *Social Statistics of Cities*, 2:10. See Sherry Olson, *Baltimore: The Building of an American City* (Baltimore, 1980); Scharf, *History of Baltimore*.

2. Quoted in *Social Statistics of Cities*, 2:29. See Reps, *The Making of Urban America*; William Howard Taft and James Bryce, *Washington: The Nation's Capital* (Washington, D.C., 1915); Constance McLaughlin Green, *Washington*, vol. 1, *Village and Capital, 1800-1878* (Princeton, 1962).

3. *Social Statistics of Cities*, 2:79-80. See William Christian, *Richmond: Its People and Its Story* (Philadelphia, 1923); John P. Little, *History of Richmond* (Richmond, 1933).

4. Quoted in *Social Statistics of Cities*, 2:228. See also John P. Moore, *Revolt in Louisiana: The Spanish Occupation, 1776-1780* (Baton Rouge, 1976); John G. Clark, *New Orleans, 1718-1812: An Economic History* (Baton Rouge, 1966).

5. See a standard account: Julius Rubin, *Canal or Railroad? Imitation and Innovation in the Response to the Erie Canal in Philadelphia, Baltimore, and Boston,*

Transactions of the American Philosophical Society, n.s., vol. 51, pt. 3 (Philadelphia, 1961). See also the appropriate sections of any standard urban history text, especially Still, *Urban America;* Glaab and Brown, *A History of Urban America.* A contemporary view is "Commercial Delusions-Speculations," *American Review* 71 (Oct. 1845):341-57.

6. Edward Ingle, *Southern Sidelights: A Picture of Social and Economic Life in the South a Generation before the War* (New York, 1896), 98; Thomas J. Wertenbaker, *Norfolk: Historic Southern Port,* edited by Marvin Schlegal (1931; repr. Durham, 1962); De Saussure and J.L. Dawson, *Census of the City of Charleston, for the Year 1848: Exhibiting the Condition and Prospects of the City. Illustrated by Many Statistical Details, Prepared Under the Authority of the City Council* (Charleston, 1849); William Harden, *A History of Savannah and South Georgia,* 2 vols. (Chicago, 1913).

7. See Lawrence H. Larsen, "Chicago's Midwest Rivals: Cincinnati, St. Louis, and Milwaukee," *Chicago History: The Magazine of the Chicago Historical Society* 5 (Fall 1976):151-61; Richard C. Wade, *The Urban Frontier: Pioneer Life in Early Pittsburgh, Cincinnati, Lexington, Louisville, and St. Louis* (Chicago, 1959); Wyatt Belcher, *The Economic Rivalry between St. Louis and Chicago, 1850-1880* (New York, 1947); Allan Pred, *Urban Growth and City-Systems in the United States, 1840-1860* (Cambridge, Mass., 1980).

8. *Social Statistics of Cities,* 2:157 (Atlanta), 135-36 (Chattanooga), 169 (Macon), 209-10 (Vicksburg), 211-12 (Little Rock), 199-200 (Montgomery), 140-43 (Memphis). For Columbus, see *Georgia: A Guide to Its Town and Countryside,* American Guide Series (Athens, Ga., 1940), 217-18. See also Belcher, *Economic Rivalry;* James Neal Primm, *Lion of the Valley: A History of St. Louis* (Boulder, 1981).

9. David R. Goldfield, "Cities in the Old South," in Brownell and Goldfield, *City in Southern History,* 77-78. See also John W. Reps, *Town Planning;* idem, *Making of Urban America; Social Statistics of Cities,* 2:81 (Richmond), 107 (Columbia), 163 (Augusta), 118-19 (Lexington), 268 (New Orleans), 194 (Mobile), 200 (Montgomery), 211-12 (Little Rock), 143 (Memphis), 209 (Vicksburg), 136 (Chattanooga).

10. Basil Hall, *Travels in North America, in the Years 1827 and 1828,* 3 vols. (Edinburgh, 1829), 3:139-40. See William Casey, *An Architectural Monograph: Charleston Doorways, Entrance Motives from a South Carolina City,* White Pine Series, vol. 14, monograph 81 (New York, 1928).

11. Anne Royall, *Sketches of History, Life and Manners in the United States* (New Haven, 1826), 131. See *An Omnibus of the Capitol,* House of Representatives, Doc. 412, 2d ed., 8th Cong., 2d sess. (Washington, D.C., 1959).

12. Joseph H. Ingraham, *The South-West. By a Yankee,* 2 vols. (1825; repr. New York, 1966), 1:99.

13. Quoted in Still, *Urban America,* 113.

14. Both quoted passages appear in Lyle W. Dorsett and Arthur H. Shaffer, "Was the Antebellum South Antiurban? A Suggestion," *Journal of Southern History* 38 (Feb. 1972):97-98.

15. Quoted in Harriet E. Amos, *Cotton City: Urban Development in Antebellum Mobile* (University, Ala., 1985), 59. See Peter Hamilton, *Mobile of the Five Flags: The Story of the River Basin and Coast about Mobile from the Earliest Times to the Present* (Mobile, 1913); Caldwell Delancy, *The Story of Mobile* (Mobile, 1953).

16. Quoted in Amos, *Cotton City,* 193.

17. Quoted in Dorsett and Shaffer, "Was the Antebellum South Antiurban?," 96.

18. Quoted in Amos, *Cotton City,* 136-37.

19. Quoted in Goldfield, "Old South," in Brownell and Goldfield, *City in Southern History,* 76. See also Leonard P. Curry, *Urban Life in the Old South* (St. Louis, 1976), 8-9; David R. Goldfield, "Planning for Urban Growth in the Old South," *South Atlantic Urban Studies* 4 (Charleston, 1980): 243-45.

20. Quoted in Amos, *Cotton City,* 172-73, 188-92.

21. Goldfield, "Old South," in Brownell and Goldfield, *Cities in Southern History,* 74-75, 79; Curry, *Urban Life,* 7-10; Goldfield, "Planning for Urban Growth in the Old South," 243-44; Leonard P. Curry, "Urbanization and Urbanism in the Old South: A Comparative View," *Journal of Southern History* 40 (Feb. 1974):53-56; David R. Goldfield, *Cotton Fields and Skyscrapers: Southern City and Region, 1607-1980* (Baton Rouge, 1982).

22. *Social Statistics of Cities,* 2:13-14 (Baltimore), 253 (New Orleans); Thomas D. Clark, *Kentucky: Land of Contrast* (New York, 1968), 122; Amos, *Cotton City,* 143. On violence in New Orleans, see Fredrick Marcel Spletstoser, "Back Door to the Land of Plenty: New Orleans as an Immigrant Port, 1820-1860," 2 vols. (Ph.D. diss., Louisiana State University, 1978).

23. *Social Statistics of Cities,* 2:72 (Petersburg), 164 (Augusta), 123 (Louisville); John B. Clark, Jr., "The Fire Problem in Kentucky, 1778-1865: A Case History of the Ante-bellum South," *Register of the Kentucky Historical Society* 51 (April 1953):97-122.

24. *Social Statistics of Cities,* 2:122-23 (Louisville), 253 (New Orleans), 13 (Baltimore), 142 (Memphis).

25. Quoted in E. Merton Coulter, "The Great Savannah Fire of 1820," *Georgia Historical Quarterly* 23 (March 1939):1-27.

26. Quoted in Joseph Ioor Waring, "The Yellow Fever Epidemic of Savannah in 1820, with a Sketch of William Coffee Daniell," *Georgia Historical Quarterly* 52 (Dec. 1968): 398-404; M. Foster Farley, "The Mighty Monarch of the South: Yellow Fever in Charleston and Savannah," *Georgia Review* 27 (Spring 1973):56-70; David R. Goldfield, "The Business of Health Planning: Disease Prevention in the Old South," *Journal of Southern History* 42 (Nov. 1976):557-70.

27. Quoted in David R. Goldfield, *Cotton Fields and Skyscrapers,* 61.

28. The quoted passages are in Herbert Collins, "Southern Industrial Gospel before 1860," *Journal of Southern History* 12 (Aug. 1946):383-402. See also Ernest M. Lander, Jr., "The Iron Industry in Ante-Bellum South Carolina," *Journal of Southern History* 20 (Aug. 1954):337-55; Fletcher M. Green, "Duff Green: Industrial Promoter," *Journal of Southern History* 2 (Feb. 1936):365-88; Broadus Mitchell, *William Gregg: Factory Master of the Old South* (Chapel Hill, 1928); Herbert Collins, "The Idea of a Cotton Textile Industry in Ante-Bellum North Carolina, 1870-1900," *North Carolina Historical Quarterly* 34 (May 1927):358-92; Diffee W. Standard and Richard Griffin, "The Cotton Textile Industry in Ante-Bellum North Carolina," *North Carolina Historical Review* 34 (Jan. 1951):15-37; 34 (April 1957):131-66; Norris W. Preyer, "Why Did Industrialism Lag in the Old South," *Georgia Historical Quarterly* 55 (Fall 1971):378-96.

29. Raymond L. Cohn, "Local Manufacturing in the Antebellum South and Midwest," *Business History Review* 54 (Spring 1980):80-91.

30. See Richard C. Wade, *Slavery in the Cities: The South, 1826-1860* (New York, 1964); Claudia Dale Golden, *Urban Slavery in the American South, 1820-1860: A Quantitative History* (Chicago, 1976); Robert S. Starobin, *Industrial Slavery in the Old South* (New York, 1970); Clement Eaton, *Slave-Hiring in the Upper South* (New York, 1974); Mariane Buroff Sheldon, "Black-White Relations in Richmond, Virginia, 1782-1820," *Journal of Southern History* 45 (Feb. 1979):27-44; John T.

O'Brien, "Factory, Church, and Community: Blacks in Antebellum Richmond," *Journal of Southern History* 44 (Nov. 1978):509-36; Goldfield, *Cotton Fields and Skyscrapers*, 44-53.

31. Quoted in Wade, *Slavery in the Cities*, 245. See also Leonard P. Curry, *The Free Black in Urban America, 1800-1880: The Shadow of the Dream* (Chicago, 1981).

32. Quoted in Amos, *Cotton City*, 97. See L.P. Jackson, "Free Negroes of Petersburg, Virginia," *Journal of Negro History* 12 (July 1927):365-88; E. Horace Fitchett, "The Origin and Growth of the Free Negro Population of Charleston, South Carolina," *Journal of Negro History* 26 (Oct. 1941):421-37; Ira Berlin, *Slaves without Masters: The Negro in the Antebellum South* (New York, 1974).

3. THE RAVAGES OF CIVIL WAR AND RECONSTRUCTION

1. The quoted passage appears in Herbert Wender, *Southern Commercial Conventions, 1837-1859*, Studies in Historical and Political Science, ser. 48, no. 4 (Baltimore, 1930), 11; Amos, *Cotton City*, 222-39. See Jered W. Roberson, "The Memphis Commercial Convention of 1853: Southern Dreams and 'Young America,' " *Tennessee Historical Quarterly* 33 (Fall 1974):279-96; William M. Burwell, "Virginia Commercial Conventions," *DeBow's Review* 12 (Jan. 1853):30; "Competition of the Gulf and Atlantic Ports," *DeBow's Review* 24 (Jan. 1858):47-48.

2. Quoted in Wender, *Commercial Conventions*, 72-73.

3. Quoted in ibid., 207.

4. Hinton Rowan Helper, *The Impending Crisis of the South: How to Meet It* (New York, 1857), 331-34. See J.D.B. DeBow, "Contests for the Trade of the Mississippi Valley," *DeBow's Review* 3 (Feb. 1847):98.

5. Lawrence H. Larsen, "New Orleans and the River Trade: Reinterpreting the Role of the Business Community," *Wisconsin Magazine of History* 61 (Winter 1977-78):112-24; Merl E. Reed, *New Orleans and the Railroads: The Struggle for Commercial Empire, 1830-1860* (Baton Rouge, 1966); Harold Sinclair, *The Port of New Orleans* (New York, 1942); "The Banks and Insurance Companies of New Orleans," *DeBow's Review* 25 (Nov. 1858):561. John G. Clark, "New Orleans and the River: A Story in Attitudes and Responses," *Louisiana History* 8 (Spring 1967):117-36; R.B. Way, "The Commerce of the Lower Mississippi in the Period 1830-1866," *Mississippi Valley Historical Review* Extra Number (July 1920):57-68; Frank H. Dixon, *A Traffic History of the Mississippi River System*, National Waterways Commission, Doc. 11 (Washington, D.C., 1909); *Report of Israel Andrews on the Trade and Commerce of the British North American Colonies, and Upon the Trade of the Great Lakes and Rivers*, Senate Executive Document 112, 32d Cong., 1st sess., Serial 622 (Washington, D.C., 1854); Robert T. Reinders, *End of an Era: New Orleans, 1850-1860* (New Orleans, 1964).

6. William Burwell, "The Commercial Future of the South," *DeBow's Review* 30 (Feb. 1961):147; Ulrich P. Phillips, *A History of Transportation in the Eastern Cotton Belt to 1860* (New York, 1913).

7. Quoted in Jo Ann Carrigan, "Yellow Fever in New Orleans, 1853: Abstractions and Realities," *Journal of Southern History* 25 (Aug. 1959):339-55.

8. Quoted in Thomas H. Wertenbaker, *Norfolk: Historic Southern Port*, ed. Marvin Schlegel (1931; repr. Durham, 1962), 247.

9. Quoted in Carrigan, "Yellow Fever in New Orleans," 342. See Jo Ann Carrigan, "Privilege, Prejudice, and Strangers Disease in Nineteenth-Century New Orleans," *Journal of Southern History* 36 (Nov. 1970):568-78.

10. See John Duffy, *Sword of Pestilence: The New Orleans Yellow Fever Epidemic of 1853* (Baton Rouge, 1966); Donald Everett, "The New Orleans Yellow Fever Epidemic of 1853," *Louisiana Historical Quarterly* 33 (Oct. 1950):380-405; John Duffy, "Nineteenth Century Public Health in New York and New Orleans: A Comparison," *Louisiana History* 15 (Fall 1974):325-37.

11. Quoted in Carrigan, "Yellow Fever in New Orleans," 343.

12. Quoted in *Social Statistics of Cities*, 2:265.

13. Quoted in ibid., 2:266.

14. Quoted in Phillip S. Foner, *Business and Slavery: The New York Merchants and the Irrepressible Conflict* (Chapel Hill, 1941), 10.

15. See Goldfield, *Cotton Fields and Skyscrapers*, 80-85; Noah Brooks, *Washington in Lincoln's Time* (New York, 1895); Catherine Copeland, *Bravest Surrender: A Petersburg Patchwork* (Richmond, 1961); Florence Corley, *Confederate City: Augusta, Georgia, 1860-1865* (Columbia, 1960); Barry Fleming, *Autobiography of a City in Arms: Augusta, Georgia, 1861-1865* (Augusta, 1938); John Coleman, *Lexington during the Civil War*, rev. ed. (Lexington, Ky., 1939); Peter Walker, *Vicksburg: A People at War, 1860-1865* (Chapel Hill, 1960); Emory M. Davis, *The Confederate State of Richmond: A Biography of the Capital* (Austin, 1971); Joseph Parks, "A Confederate Trade Center under Federal Occupation: Memphis, 1862-1865," *Journal of Southern History* 7 (Aug. 1941):289-314. See also Mary Loughborough, *My Cave Life in Vicksburg: With Letters of Trial and Travail* (Little Rock, 1882); Osborn Oldroyd, *A Soldier's Story of the Siege of Vicksburg* (Springfield, Ill., 1885); Adolph Hoehing and the editors of the Army Times Publishing Company, *Vicksburg: Forty-seven Days of Siege* (Englewood Cliffs, N.J., 1969); Samuel Carter III, *The Siege of Atlanta, 1864* (New York, 1973).

16. Quoted in Leonard P. Curry, *Rail Routes South: Louisville's Fight for the Southern Market, 1865-1872* (Lexington, Ky., 1969), 28. See John L. Kerr, *The Louisville and Nashville: An Outline History* (New York, 1933); Maury Klein, *History of the Louisville and Nashville Railroad* (New York, 1972); Kincaid Herr, *The Louisville and Nashville Railroad, 1850-1963* (Louisville, 1963).

17. Quoted in C. Vann Woodward, ed., *Mary Chesnut's Civil War* (New Haven, 1981), 343.

18. The quoted passages appear in J.G. Randall, *The Civil War and Reconstruction* (1937; repr. Boston, 1953), 666-67. See Gerald M. Capers, *Occupied City: New Orleans under the Federals, 1862-1865* (Lexington, Ky., 1965); Dale A. Somers, "New Orleans at War: A Merchant's View," *Louisiana History* 14 (Winter 1973):49-68; Dale A. Somers, "War and Play: The Civil War in New Orleans," *Mississippi Quarterly* 26 (Winter 1972-73):3-28. Samuel Derrick, *Centennial History of South Carolina Railroads* (Columbia, 1930); Richmond Price, *Georgia Railroads and the West Point Route* (Salt Lake City, 1962).

19. E. Merton Coulter, *The South during Reconstruction, 1865-1877*, A History of the South, vol. 8 (Baton Rouge, 1947), 263-64.

20. Ernst S. Griffith, *A History of American City Government: The Conspicuous Failure, 1870-1900* (New York, 1974), 31-43; Bobby L. Lovett, "Memphis Riots: White Reaction to Blacks in Memphis, May 1865-July 1866," *Tennessee Historical Quarterly* 38 (Spring 1979):9-33.

21. The passages quoted appear in Terry L. Seip, "Municipal Politics and the Negro: Baton Rouge, 1865-1880," in Mark T. Carleton, Perry H. Howard, and Joseph B. Parker, eds., *Readings in Louisiana Politics* (Baton Rouge, 1975), 248, 250.

22. The standard survey on southern railroading in the last half of the nineteenth century is John F. Stover, *The Railroads of the South, 1865-1900: A Study in Finance*

and Control (Chapel Hill, 1955). See Maury Klein, *The Great Richmond Terminal: A Study in Businessmen and Railroad Strategy* (Charlottesville, 1970); Jesse C. Burt, Jr., "Four Decades of the Nashville, Chattanooga and St. Louis Railway, 1873-1916," *Tennessee Historical Quarterly* 9 (June 1950):99-130; Samuel Derrick, *Centennial History of South Carolina Railroads* (Columbia, 1930).

23. The quoted passages appear in C. Vann Woodward, *Origins of the New South, 1877-1913,* A History of the South, vol. 9 (Baton Rouge, 1951), 107.

24. "The Grain Trade of the United States and Tables on the World's Wheat Supply and Trade," Bureau of Statistics, Department of the Treasury, *Monthly Summary of Commerce and Finances, January 1900,* n.s., no. 7 (Washington, D.C., 1900). See Larsen, "New Orleans and the River Trade," 123-24.

25. *Social Statistics of Cities,* 2:142 (Memphis), 266 (New Orleans); James H. Ellis, "Business and Public Health in the Urban South during the Nineteenth Century: New Orleans, Memphis, and Atlanta," *Bulletin of the History of Medicine* 44 (May-June 1970):197-212.

26. Quoted in *Social Statistics of Cities,* 2:146-47. See John H. Ellis, "Memphis' Sanitary Revolution, 1880-1890," *Tennessee Historical Quarterly* 23 (March 1964):59-72; Lawrence H. Larsen, *The Rise of the Urban South* (Lexington, Ky., 1985), 123-24.

27. Quoted in *Social Statistics of Cities,* 2:287.

28. Quoted in Paul M. Gaston, *The New South Creed: A Study in Southern Mythmaking* (New York, 1970), 25.

29. Quoted in Lawrence J. Friedman, *The White Savage: Racial Fantasies in the Postbellum South* (Englewood Cliffs, N.J., 1970), 43.

30. Henry W. Grady, *The New South* (New York, 1890), 91-92.

31. Quoted in Gaston, *New South Creed,* Prolouge.

32. Quoted in Hesseltine and Smiley, *The South in American History,* 393. See James M. Russell, *Atlanta, 1847-1890: City Building in the Old South and the New* (Baton Rouge, 1988).

33. Grady, *New South,* 104.

34. Quoted in Gaston, *New South Creed,* 117 (Edmonds), 126 (Watterson).

35. Quoted in Friedman, *White Savage,* 54.

4. The Advent of the New South

1. Both quoted passages appear in Gaston, *The New South Creed,* 43. See Larsen, *The Rise of the Urban South;* Roger L. Ransom and Richard Sutch, *One Kind of Freedom: The Economic Consequences of Emancipation* (Cambridge, England, 1977).

2. Quoted in Gaston, New South Creed, 87-90. See Jonathan M. Wiener, *Social Origins of the New South: Alabama, 1860-1885* (Baton Rouge, 1978). He believes that southern industrialism followed a "Prussian Road." Another Marxist view is expressed in Dwight B. Billings, Jr., *Planters and the Making of the New South: Class, Politics, and Development in North Carolina, 1865-1900* (Chapel Hill, 1979).

3. C. Vann Woodward, *The Strange Career of Jim Crow* (New York, 1955); John W. Blassingame, *Black New Orleans, 1860-1880* (Chicago, 1973); Constance Mc-Laughlin Green, *The Secret City: A History of Race Relations in the Nation's Capital* (Princeton, 1967); Robert E. Perdue, *The Negro in Savannah, 1865-1900* (New York, 1973); Dale A. Somers, "Black and White in New Orleans: A Survey of Race Relations, 1865-1900," *Journal of Southern History* 40 (Feb. 1974):19-42; Howard N. Rabinowitz,

Race Relations in the Urban South, 1805-1900, History of Urban America Series (New York, 1978); Pete Daniel, "The Metamorphosis of Slavery, 1865-1900," *Journal of American History* 66 (June 1979):88-99; Goldfield, *Cotton Fields and Skyscrapers,* 103-18.

4. Dieter Cunz, *The Maryland Germans: A History* (1948; repr. Port Washington, N.Y., 1972); Robert T. Clark, "Reconstruction and the New Orleans German Colony," *Louisiana Historical Quarterly* 23 (April 1940):501-24; Bob Cyrus Rauchie, "The Political Life of the Germans in Memphis, 1848-1900," *Louisiana Historical Quarterly* 51 (Summer 1968):165-75; Earl Niehaus, *The Irish in New Orleans, 1800-1860* (Baton Rouge, 1965). General studies that have materials on the South include Stephen Byrne, *Irish Emigration to the United States: What it has Been, and What it is* (New York, 1873); Albert Faust, *The German Element in the United States,* 2 vols. (New York, 1912); Carl Wittke, *We Who Built America: The Saga of the Immigrant* (Cleveland, 1939); Stanley C. Johnson, *History of Emigration from the United Kingdom to North America, 1763-1912* (London, 1913). Of Special value is Stephan Thernstrom, ed., *Harvard Encyclopedia of American Ethnic Groups* (Cambridge, Mass., 1980).

5. Grady, *New South,* 184-86. See Ray Allen Billington, *The Protestant Crusade, 1800-1860: A Study of the Origins of American Nativism* (New York, 1933); Charles Reagan Wilson, "The Religion of the Lost Cause: Ritual and Organization of the Southern Civil Religion, 1865-1920," *Journal of Southern History* 46 (May 1980):219-38; Kenneth K. Bailey, "Southern White Protestantism at the Turn of the Century," *American Historical Review* 68 (April 1963):618-35; Kenneth K. Bailey, *Southern White Protestantism in the Twentieth Century* (New York, 1964).

6. *Report on Statistics of Churches in the United States, Eleventh Census of the United States, 1890* (Washington, D.C., 1894), 9:91, 112-15. See Hunter D. Farish, *The Circuit Rider Dismounts: A Social History of Southern Methodism, 1865-1900* (Richmond, 1938); W.W. Bames, *The Southern Baptist Convention, 1845-1953* (Nashville, 1954); Paul N. Garber, *The Methodists Are One People* (Nashville, 1939); Carter Woodson, *The History of the Negro Church* (1921; repr. Washington, D.C., 1945); John M. Cromwell, "First Negro Churches in the District of Columbia," *Journal of Negro History* 7 (Jan. 1922):64-106; Leonard Dinnerstein and Mawy Dale Palsson, *Jews in the South* (Baton Rouge, 1973); Isaac Fein, *The Making of an American Jewish Community: The History of Baltimore Jewry from 1773 to 1920* (Philadelphia, 1971); Eli N. Evans, *The Provincials: A Personal History of Jews in the South* (New York, 1973); Myron Berman, *Richmond's Jewry: Shabbat to Shookoe, 1796-1976* (Charlottesville, 1979); Steven Hertzberg, *Strangers within the Gate City: The Jews of Atlanta, 1845-1915* (Philadelphia, 1978).

7. Monroe Lee Billington, *The American South* (New York, 1971), 278-79; C. Vann Woodward, *Origins of the New South, 1877-1913,* A History of the South, vol. 9 (Baton Rouge, 1951), 60-64; Howard N. Rabinowitz, "Half a Loaf: The Shift from White to Black Teachers in the Negro Schools of the Urban South, 1865-1890," *Journal of Southern History* 40 (Nov. 1974):565-94; Edgar Knight, *The Influence of Reconstruction on Education in the South* (1913; repr. New York, 1969); *Report of the Commissioner of Education, 1880: Report of the Secretary of Interior,* vol. 3 (Washington, D.C., 1882), 8, 420-62.

8. *Report of the Commissioner of Education,* 640-75.

9. Frederic C. Howe, *The City: The Hope of Democracy* (New York, 1912), 9. See Gunther Barth, *City People: The Rise of Modern City Culture in Nineteenth-Century America* (New York, 1980).

10. *Report of the Manufacturers of the United States, Tenth Census of the*

United States, 1880 (Washington, D.C., 1883), 2:379-80; 383-443; Herbert Collins, "The Idea of a Cotton Textile Industry in Ante-bellum North Carolina, 1870-1900," North Carolina Historical Quarterly 34 (July 1927):358-92; Jack Blicksilver, Cotton Manufacturing in the Southeast: An Historical Analysis (Atlanta, 1959); Broadus Mitchell, The Rise of Cotton Mills in the South, Studies in Historical and Political Science, ser. 39, no. 2 (Baltimore, 1921); Broadus Mitchell and George Mitchell, The Industrial Revolution in the South (Baltimore, 1930); James C. Cobb, Industrialization and Southern Society, 1877-1984 (Lexington, Ky., 1984); David L. Carlton, Mill and Town in South Carolina, 1880-1920 (Baton Rouge, 1982); N.M. Tilley, The Bright-Tobacco Industry, 1860-1929 (Chapel Hill, 1948); J.K. Winkler, Tobacco Tycoon: The Story of James Buchanan Duke (New York, 1942).

   11. J.R. Killick, "The Transformation of Cotton Marketing in the Late Nineteenth Century: Alexander Sprunt and Son of Wilmington, N.C., 1866-1956," Business History Review 55 (Summer 1981):143-69; Edward King, The Great South, ed. W. Magruder Drake and Robert R. Jones (1878; repr. Baton Rouge, 1972), 373 (Columbus), 582 (Petersburg); William Best Hesseltine, Confederate Leaders in the New South (1950; repr. Westport, Conn., 1970).

   12. Grady, New South, 213. See Ransom and Sutch, One Kind of Freedom; Gilbert C. Fite, Cotton Fields No More: Southern Agriculture, 1868-1980 (Lexington, Ky., 1984).

   13. Green, Washington, vol. 1 Village and Capital, 1800-1878, 339-62; Christopher Tunnard and Henry Hope Reed, American Skyline: The Growth and Form of Our Cities and Towns (New York, 1955); Frederick Gutheim, Worthy of the Nation: The History of Planning for the National Capital (Washington, D.C., 1977); John W. Reps, Monumental Washington: The Planning and Development of the Capital Center (Princeton, 1967).

   14. Social Statistics of Cities, 2:27 (Washington and Georgetown), 3 (Baltimore), 213 (New Orleans), 122 (Louisville); Report on Valuation, Taxation, and Public Indebtedness, Tenth Census of the United States, 1880 (Washington, D.C., 1884), 7:684-99; Eugene J. Watts, Social Bases of City Politics: Atlanta, 1865-1903 (Westport, Conn., 1978).

   15. Social Statistics of Cities, 2:177 (Savannah), 100 (Charleston), 160 (Atlanta), 170 (Macon), 274-75 (New Orleans).

   16. Ibid., 2:18-19 (Baltimore), 39-40 (Washington). See Albert Fein, Frederick Law Olmsted and the American Environmental Tradition (New York, 1972).

   17. Winston A. Walden, "Nineteenth Century Street Pavements" (M.A. thesis, University of Missouri—Kansas City, 1967); Blake McKelvey, The Urbanization of America, 1860-1915 (New Brunswick, 1963), 88-89; Clay McShane, "Transforming the Use of Urban Space: A Look at the Revolution in Street Pavements, 1880-1924," Journal of Urban History 5 (May 1979):279-307; George A. Soper, Modern Methods of Street Cleaning (New York, 1909).

   18. Social Statistics of Cities, 2:32-33 (Washington), 272 (New Orleans), 99 (Charleston), 159-60 (Atlanta).

   19. Ibid., 58 (Alexandria), 143 (Memphis), 170 (Macon); Larsen, Urban South, 117-18.

   20. Social Statistics of Cities, 2:124 (Louisville), 58 (Alexandria), 165 (Augusta).

   21. Lawrence H. Larsen, "Nineteenth-Century Street Sanitation: A Study of Filth and Frustration," Wisconsin Magazine of History 52 (Spring 1969):239-47; Soper, Street Cleaning, 7-22; Otto L. Bettmann, The Good Old Days—They Were Terrible (New York, 1974); Goldfield, Cotton Fields and Skyscrapers, 92.

   22. Social Statistics of Cities, 2:121 (Lexington), 149 (Memphis), 59 (Alexandria),

68 (Norfolk), 115 (Covington), 171 (Macon), 108 (Columbia), 161 (Atlanta), 179 (Savannah), 287-88 (New Orleans), 21-2 (Baltimore), 84 (Richmond), 102 (Charleston); see Larsen, *Urban South*, 118-20.

23. *Social Statistics of Cities*, 2:22 (Baltimore), 46 (Washington), 59 (Alexandria), 102 (Charleston), 197 (Mobile). The quoted passage is from this source. See Larsen, *Urban South*, 120.

24. *Social Statistics of Cities*, 2:46. See Martin W. Melosi, *Garbage in the Cities: Refuse, Reform, and the Environment* (College Station, 1980).

25. *Social Statistics of Cities*, 2:121 (Lexington), 167 (Augusta), 171 (Macon), 201 (Montgomery), 19 (Baltimore); Larsen, *Urban South*, 121-25.

26. *Social Statistics of Cities*, 2:273 (New Orleans), 144-47 (Memphis).

27. The primary study of waterworks is Nelson Blake, *Water for the Cities: A History of the Water Supply Problem in the United States* (Syracuse, 1956); Walter G. Elliott, "Report on the Water-Supply in Certain Cities in the United States," *Report on the Water-Power of the United States, The Tenth Census of the United States, 1880*, vol. 17, pt. 2 (Washington, D.C., 1887), 1-272. *Social Statistics of Cities*, 2:76 (Portsmouth), 119 (Lexington), 144 (Memphis), 201 (Montgomery), 99 (Charleston), 137 (Chattanooga), 67 (Norfolk), 273 (New Orleans); Larsen, *Urban South*, 125-26.

28. *Social Statistics of Cities*, 2:72 (Petersburg), 76 (Portsmouth), 107 (Columbia), 170 (Macon), 119 (Lexington), 201 (Montgomery), 99 (Charleston), 165 (Augusta), 32 (Washington), 124 (Louisville), 273 (New Orleans), 62 (Lynchburg); Larsen, *Urban South*, 128-29.

29. *Social Statistics of Cities*, 2:32 (Washington), 81 (Richmond), 176 (Savannah), 160 (Atlanta); Larsen, *Urban South*, 129.

30. *Social Statistics of Cities*, 2:120 (Lexington), 114-15 (Covington), 133 (Newport), 161 (Atlanta), 108 (Columbia), 202 (Montgomery), 138 (Chattanooga), 148 (Memphis). See John H. Ellis, "Business and Public Health in the Urban South during the Nineteenth Century: New Orleans, Memphis, and Atlanta," *Bulletin of the History of Medicine* 44 (May-June 1970):197-212; Larsen, *Urban South*, 130-32.

31. *Social Statistics of Cities*, 2:139 (Chattanooga), 74 (Petersburg), 103 (Charleston), 128-29 (Louisville), 23-24 (Baltimore). The quoted passage appears in this source. See Larsen, *Urban South*, 134-35.

32. Quoted in *Social Statistics of Cities*, 2:129.

33. Ibid., 2:47 (Washington), 292 (New Orleans), 23 (Baltimore), 203 (Montgomery), 167 (Augusta), 139 (Chattanooga), 172 (Macon), 508-9 (Chicago), 528 (Peoria), 649 (Fond du Lac), 681 (Oshkosh). See Raymond Fosdick, *American Police Systems* (New York, 1920); James F. Richardson, *Urban Police in the United States* (Port Washington, N.Y., 1974); Larsen, *Urban South*, 135-41. See Eugene Watts, "The Police in Atlanta, 1890-1905," *Journal of Southern History* 39 (May 1973):165-82.

34. *Social Statistics of Cities*, 2:139 (Chattanooga), 167 (Augusta), 172 (Macon), 69 (Norfolk).

35. Ibid., 2:23 (Baltimore), 49 (Washington), 103 (Charleston), 149 (Memphis), 167 (Augusta).

36. The quoted passages appear in Albert Bushell Hart, *The Southern South* (New York, 1910), 217; Howard N. Rabinowitz, *Race Relations in the Urban South, 1865-1890* (New York, 1978), 53-54; *Alexandria Weekly Town Talk*, June 18, 1892; Goldfield, *Cotton Fields and Skyscrapers*, 103-12.

37. Rabinowitz, *Race Relations*, 52-54; Howard N. Rabinowitz, "The Conflict between Blacks and the Police in the Urban South," *Historian* 39 (Nov. 1976):62-76.

38. The quoted passages appear in Woodward, *Origins of the New South*, 137-38. See Ethel M. Ames, *The Story of Coal and Iron in Alabama* (Birmingham, 1910).

39. Quoted passages appear in Woodward, *Origins of the New South*, 138.

40. Grady, *New South*, 162; Goldfield, *Cotton Fields and Skyscrapers*, 115-32.

41. Robert P. Porter et al., "Progress of the Nation," in *Total Population, Eleventh Census of the United States: 1890*, vol. 1, pt. 1 (Washington, D.C., 1895), lxvi. See Larsen, *Urban South*, 142-64.

42. *Report on Manufacturing Industries in the United States at the Eleventh Census: 1890, Eleventh Census of the United States, 1890*, vol. 6, pt. 1 (Washington, D.C., 1895), 3-8.

43. Ibid., pt. 2, xiv, 30-38, 62, 450, 486.

5. HOLDING THE LINE

1. Quoted in Woodward, *Origins of the New South*, 125-27. Mitchell and Mitchell, *The Industrial Revolution in the South*; Ames, *The Story of Coal and Iron in Alabama*.

2. Grady, *New South*, 265. See Gaston, *New South Creed*.

3. Quoted in Andrew M. Modelski, *Railroad Maps of North America: The First Hundred Years* (Washington, D.C., 1984), 72-73.

4. George Brown Tindall, *The Emergence of the New South, 1913-1945*, A History of the South, vol. 10 (Baton Rouge, 1967), 75-80. See Ronald D. Eller, *Miners, Millhands, and Mountaineers: Industrialization of the Appalachian South, 1880-1920* (Knoxville, 1982).

5. The quoted passages appear in Tindall, *Emergence of the New South*, 70-71.

6. Ibid., 771. See Pete Daniel, *Standing at the Crossroads: Southern Life since 1900*, American Century Series (New York, 1986), 42-49.

7. Tindall, *Emergence of the New South*, 81-82; Cobb, *Industrialization*, 20.

8. Quoted in Tindall, *Emergence of the New South*, 319.

9. Quoted in Charles Paul Garofalo, "The Sons of Henry Grady: Atlanta Boosters in the 1920s," *Journal of Southern History* 42 (May 1976): 188-89.

10. Tindall, *Emergence of the New South*, 343-48; Daniel, *Standing at the Crossroads*, 103-8.

11. Blaine Brownell, "The Urban South Comes of Age, 1900-1940," in Brownell and Goldfield, *City in Southern History*, 147; August Meier and Elliott Rudwick, "The Boycott Movement against Jim Crow Streetcars in the South, 1900-1906," *Journal of American History* 55 (March 1969):756-75; Roger L. Rice, "Residential Segregation by Law, 1910-1917," *Journal of Southern History* 34 (May 1968):179-99; Kenneth T. Jackson, *The Ku Klux Klan and the City, 1915-1930* (New York, 1967).

12. Quoted in Roger Biles, *Memphis in the Great Depression* (Knoxville, 1986), 14.

13. Quoted in David R. Goldfield, *Cotton Fields and Skyscrapers: Southern City and Region, 1607-1980* (Baton Rouge, 1982), 100. See Biles, *Memphis*, 29-47; William D. Miller, *Memphis during the Progressive Era, 1900-1917* (Memphis, 1957); Joy L. Jackson, *New Orleans in the Gilded Age: Politics and Urban Progress, 1880-1896* (Baton Rouge, 1969); William D. Miller, *Mr. Crump of Memphis* (Baton Rouge, 1964).

14. Frederic C. Howe, *The City: The Hope of Democracy* (New York, 1912), 48. Quoted in Brownell, "The Urban South Comes of Age," 152.

15. See Howard L. Preston, *Automobile Age Atlanta: The Making of a Southern Metropolis, 1900-1935* (Atlanta, 1979).

16. William Bennett Munro, *Principles and Methods of Municipal Administration* (New York, 1915), 1.

17. Ibid., 154-57; Blaine A. Brownell, *The Urban Ethos in the South, 1920-1930* (Baton Rouge, 1975), 158-63; Blaine A. Brownell, "The Commercial-Civic Elite and City Planning in Atlanta, Memphis, and New Orleans in the 1920s," *Journal of Southern History* 41 (Aug. 1975):339-68; Goldfield, *Cotton Fields and Skyscrapers,* 150.

18. Goldfield, *Cotton Fields and Skyscrapers,* 130.

19. The quoted passages appear in Brownell, *Urban Ethos,* 191, 214-15.

20. The quoted passages appear in Tindall, *Emergence of the New South,* 98-99, 106.

21. Quoted in Garofalo, "The Sons of Henry Grady," 188.

22. Carl V. Harris, *Political Power in Birmingham, 1871-1921* (Knoxville, 1977); Robert J. Hopkins, "Status, Mobility, and Dimensions of Change in a Southern City: Atlanta, 1870-1910," in Kenneth T. Jackson and Stanley K. Schultz, eds., *Cities in American History* (New York, 1972), 216-31; Eugene J. Watts, *Social Bases of City Politics: Atlanta, 1865-1903* (Westport, Conn., 1978); Samuel M. Kipp III, "Old Notables and Newcomers: The Economic and Political Elite of Greensboro, N.C., 1880-1920," *Journal of Southern History* 43 (Aug. 1977):373-94.

23. Quoted in Brownell, "The Urban South Comes of Age," 123.

24. Quoted in Goldfield, *Cotton Fields and Skyscrapers,* 160-62.

25. Quoted in Tindall, *Emergence of the New South,* 109.

6. Depression, War, and Civil Rights

1. Twelve Southerners, *I'll Take My Stand: The South and the Agrarian Tradition* (1930; repr. Baton Rouge, 1977), xli. Quoted in Tindall, *Emergence of the New South,* 577. See W.J. Cash, *The Mind of the South* (New York, 1941); Carl N. Degler, *Place over Time: The Continuity of Southern Distinctiveness* (Baton Rouge, 1977); C. Vann Woodward, *The Burden of Southern History* (1960; repr. Baton Rouge, 1968); Frank E. Vandiver, ed., *The Idea of the South: Pursuit of a Central Theme* (Chicago, 1964); Henry Savage, Jr., *Seeds of Time: The Background of Southern Thinking* (New York, 1959).

2. *I'll Take My Stand,* xlvii, 214, 355, xxxviii-xxxix. Quoted in Tindall, *Emergence of the New South,* 578-79; Goldfield, *Cotton Fields and Skyscrapers,* 162-63.

3. The quoted passages are in Tindall, *Emergence of the New South,* 578-79.

4. Quoted in ibid., 575.

5. Quoted in ibid., 590.

6. Quoted in ibid., 589-90; Steve Davis, "The South as 'The Nation's No. 1 Economic Problem': The NEC Report of 1938," *Georgia Historical Quarterly* 62 (Summer 1978):119-32; James Samuel Ezell, *The South since 1965* (New York, 1963), 428-52. See Fite, *Cotton Fields No More.*

7. Quoted in Davis, "The NEC Report of 1938," 128. See Howard W. Odum, *Southern Regions of the United States* (Chapel Hill, 1936).

8. Report of the Urbanism Committee to the National Resources Committee, *Our Cities: Their Role in the National Economy* (Washington, D.C., 1937), x.

9. Ibid., 8.

10. James A. Burran, "The WPA in Nashville, 1935-1943," *Tennessee Historical Quarterly* 34 (Fall 1975):293-306. See Douglas L. Smith, *The New Deal in the Urban South* (Baton Rouge, 1988); Jo Anne E. Argersinger, *Toward a New Deal in Baltimore:*

People and Government in the Great Depression (Chapel Hill, 1988); Don H. Doyle, *Nashville since the 1920s* (Knoxville, 1925); Daniel, *Standing at the Crossroads*, 117-34.

11. Goldfield, *Cotton Fields and Skyscrapers*, 181.

12. Quoted in Biles, *Memphis*, 79.

13. *Our Cities*, 59. See Marston Fitch, *American Building: The Forces That Shape It* (1948; repr. New York, 1977); Thomas Tallmadge, *The Story of Architecture in America* (New York, 1936); Christopher Tunnard and Henry Hope Reed, *American Skyline: The Growth and Form of Our Cities and Towns* (New York, 1955).

14. Quoted in Goldfield, *Cotton Fields and Skyscrapers*, 164. See Rupert B. Vance and Nicholas J. Demearth, eds., *The Urban South* (Chapel Hill, 1954).

15. Quoted in Goldfield, *Cotton Fields and Skyscrapers*, 165.

16. Quoted in Tindall, *Emergence of the New South*, 695.

17. Ibid., 696-700; Goldfield, *Cotton Fields and Skyscrapers*, 182-84; Edward F. Haas, "The Southern Metropolis, 1940-1976," in Brownell and Goldfield, *City in Southern History*, 160; Michael J. McDonald and William Bruce Wheeler, *Knoxville, Tennessee: Continuity and Change in an Appalachian City* (Knoxville, 1983); Daniel, *Standing at the Crossroads*, 136-38.

18. Quoted in Tindall, *Emergence of the New South*, 700.

19. Quoted in Bayrd Still, *Urban America*, 444. See Constance McLaughlin Green, *Washington*, vol. 2, *Capital City, 1879-1950* (Princeton, 1963).

20. Quoted in Tindall, *Emergence of the New South*, 701-3.

21. Ibid., 701.

22. "Old Girl's New Boy," *Time* 50 (Nov. 24, 1947):26-29; Haas, "The Southern Metropolis," 164; Edward F. Haas, *DeLesseps S. Morrison and the Image of Reform: New Orleans Politics, 1946-1961* (Baton Rouge, 1974); Harold H. Martin, *William Berry Hartsfield: Mayor of Atlanta* (Athens, 1978).

23. The quoted passages are in Tindall, *Emergence of the New South*, 714-16; Daniel, *Standing at the Crossroads*, 150-71.

24. Quoted in Tindall, *Emergence of the New South*, 717.

25. Quoted in Charles P. Roland, *The Improbable Era: The South since World War II* (Lexington, Ky., 1975), 34; Donald McCoy and Richard T. Ruetten, *Quest and Response: Minority Rights and the Truman Administration* (Lawrence, 1978); Daniel, *Standing at the Crossroads*, 150-71; David R. Goldfield, *Promised Land: The South since 1945*, The American History Series (Arlington Heights, Ill., 1987), 50-84.

26. Numan V. Bartley, *The Rise of Massive Resistance: Race and Politics in the South during the 1950s* (Baton Rouge, 1969). Neil R. McMillen, *The Citizens' Council: Organized Resistance to the Second Reconstruction, 1954-1964* (Urbana, 1971); Goldfield, *Promised Land*, 85-121.

27. Quoted in Roland, *Improbable Era*, 40. See Robert L. Branyan and Lawrence H. Larsen, *The Eisenhower Administration, 1953-1961: A Documentary History*, vol. 2 (New York, 1971), 1118-41.

28. Quoted in Roland, *Improbable Era*, 49-53. See Michael R. Belknap, *Federal Law and Southern Order: Racial Violence and Constitutional Conflict in the Post-Brown South* (Athens, Ga., 1987); J.W. Pettason, *Fifty-eight Lonely Men: Southern Federal Judges and School Desegregation* (New York, 1961); Daniel, *Standing at the Crossroads*, 204-17.

29. Quoted in Billington, *American South*, 414.

30. Both passages are from James C. Cobb, *The Selling of the South: The Southern Crusade for Industrial Development, 1936-1980* (Baton Rouge, 1982), 128-129;

Elizabeth Jacoway and David R. Colburn, eds., *Southern Businessmen and Segregation* (Baton Rouge, 1982).

31. John Samuel Ezell, *The South since 1865* (New York, 1966), 444-51.

32. See Ernest J. Hopkins, *Mississippi's BAWI Plan*, Federal Reserve Bank of Atlanta (Atlanta, 1944).

7. AN URBAN RENAISSANCE

1. Quoted in Glaab and Brown, *Urban America*, 345-50. See Richard M. Bernard and Bradley R. Rice, eds., *Sunbelt Cities: Politics and Growth since World War II* (Austin, 1983), 40; Roland, *Improbable Era*; David R. Goldfield, *Promised Land: The South since 1945* (New York, 1987); Daniel, *Standing at the Crossroads*.

2. James C. Cobb, *Industrialization and Southern Society, 1877-1984*, New Perspectives on the South (Lexington, 1984), 3-4. See Fite, *Cotton Fields No More*.

3. Raymond A. Mohl, "Miami: The Ethnic Caldron," in Bernard and Rice, *Sunbelt Cities*, 72-73.

4. Quoted in Richard Gwyn, *Forty-ninth Paradox* (Toronto, 1985), 177. See Charles P. Roland, "The South, America's Will-o-Wisp Eden," *Louisiana History* 11 (Spring 1970):101-19.

5. The passages quoted appear in Bernard and Rice, "Introduction," *Sunbelt Cities*, 4-16. See Bernard L. Weinstein and Robert E. Firestine, *Regional Growth and Decline in the United States: The Rise of the Sunbelt and the Decline of the Northeast* (New York, 1978).

6. Bernard and Rice, *Sunbelt Cities*, 2-3.

7. Joel Garreau, *The Nine Nations of North America* (Boston, 1981).

8. Carl Abbott, *The New Urban America: Growth and Politics in Sunbelt Cities* (Chapel Hill, 1981), 15.

9. Ibid., 22.

10. Ibid., 32.

11. Goldfield, *Cotton Fields and Skyscrapers*, 159.

12. Quoted in Rice, "Atlanta," in Bernard and Rice, *Sunbelt Cities*, 37. See Erla Zwingle, "Atlanta: Energy and Optimism in the New South," *National Geographic* 174 (July 1988):2-29.

13. Quoted in Edward F. Hass, "The Southern Metropolis, 1940-1976," in Brownell and Goldfield, *City in Southern History*, 185.

14. See McDonald and Wheeler, *Knoxville, Tennessee*; Christopher Silver, *Twentieth-Century Richmond: Planning, Politics, and Race* (Knoxville, 1982); Don H. Doyle, *Knoxville since the 1920s* (Knoxville, 1985); David M. Tucker, *Memphis since Crump: Bossism, Blacks, and Civic Reformers, 1948-1968* (Knoxville, 1980).

15. Quoted in Mohl, "Miami," in Bernard and Rice, *Sunbelt Cities*, 91.

16. Quoted in Gary R. Mormino, "Tampa: From Hell Hole to the Good Life," in Bernard and Rice, *Sunbelt Cities*, 156.

17. Hirsch, "New Orleans," in Bernard and Rice, *Sunbelt Cities*, 131.

18. See Raymond Arsenault, "The End of the Long Hot Summer: The Air Conditioner and Southern Culture," *Journal of Southern History* 50 (Nov. 1984):597-628.

19. Rice, "Atlanta," in Bernard and Rice, *Sunbelt Cities*, 39; Goldfield, *Cotton Fields and Skyscrapers*, 156-57; Roland, *Improbable Era*, 154-56.

20. Quoted in Glaab and Brown, *Urban America*, 292. For the legacy of the school desegregation case, see Philip B. Kurlari, " 'Brown vs. Board of Education* was

the Beginning': The School Desegregation Cases in the United States Supreme Court: 1954-1979," *Washington University Law Quarterly* 1979 (Spring 1979):309-405.

21. Quoted in Cobb, *Industrialism*, 142.

22. The quoted passages appear in ibid.

23. Goldfield, *Cotton Fields and Skyscrapers*, 3.

ESSAY ON SOURCES

This essay is designed to acquaint readers with sources that have proved useful in studying southern urban history. In it I also hope to provide ideas for further research projects and to help those readers who wish to extend their general knowledge of the history of the South. I have listed here only a representative portion of the materials that I consulted in preparing this book, primarily those upon which I drew extensively. The rich materials pertaining to the history of the urban South encompass a variety of primary and secondary sources.

Useful urban history surveys that contain information on southern city building are Bayrd Still, *Urban America: A History with Documents* (Boston, 1974); Charles N. Glaab and A. Theodore Brown, *A History of Urban America*, 3d ed. (New York, 1983); Blaine Brownell and David R. Goldfield, *Urban America: From Downtown to No Town* (Boston, 1979); Constance McLaughlin Green, *American Cities in the Growth of the Nation* (1957; repr. New York, 1965); Zane Miller and Patricia M. Melvin, *The Urbanization of Modern America: A Brief History* (1973; repr. New York, 1987); Howard P. Chudecoff, *The Evolution of American Urban Society* (Englewood Cliffs, N.J., 1975). Brownell and Goldfield, two pioneering southern urban historians, have provided excellent comparative data on the urbanization of the South. General histories of the American South contain scattered information on city building: William B. Hesseltine and David L. Smiley, *The South in American History* (Englewood Cliffs, N.J., 1960); Francis Butler Simkins and Charles Pierce Roland, *A History of the South* (New York, 1972); Monroe Lee Billington, *The American South: A Brief History* (New York, 1971). John Samuel Ezell, *The South since 1865* (New York, 1966), has helpful cultural material. None of the general histories contains special chapters on southern urbanization.

There are a few excellent theoretical essays and anthologies. David R. Goldfield, *Cotton Fields and Skyscrapers: Southern City and Region, 1607-1980* (Baton Rouge, 1982), the first attempt to develop a hypothesis relating to southern urbanization, advances the premise that cities in the section are unique. The hypothesis is tested in Roger Biles, "Cotton Fields or Skyscrapers? The Case of Memphis, Tennessee," *Historian: A Journal of History* 50 (Feb. 1988):210-33. A compilation, Blaine A. Brownell and David

R. Goldfield, eds., *The City in Southern History: The Growth of Urban Civilization in the South*, National University Publications Interdisciplinary Urban Series (Port Washington, N.Y., 1977), contains six original scholarly essays. Two selections by Leonard P. Curry, "Urbanization and Urbanism in the Old South: A Comparative View," *Journal of Southern History* 40 (Feb. 1974):43-60, and a monograph, *Urban Life in the Old South* (St. Louis, 1971), demonstrate that the Old South had a significant urban dimension. T. Lynn Smith, "The Emergence of Cities," in Rupert B. Vance and Nicholas J. Demearth, eds., *The Urban South* (Chapel Hill, 1954), shows how the South steadily lost ground relative to the rest of the nation. Urbanization in the South differed from that in the rest of the United States, according to Blaine A. Brownell in "Urbanization in the South: A Unique Experience," *Mississippi Quarterly* 26 (Spring 1973):105-20. David R. Goldfield, "The Urban South: A Regional Framework," *American Historical Review* 86 (Dec. 1981):109-34, claims that southern city building was "urbanization without cities." See also Vernon Burton and Robert C. McMath, Jr., eds., *Toward a New South? Studies in Post-Civil War Southern Communities* (Westport, Conn., 1982).

Conceptual materials that help to place the rise of the urban South in perspective include C. Vann Woodward, *The Burden of Southern History* (1960; repr. Baton Rouge, 1968); Twelve Southerners, *I'll Take My Stand: The South and the Agrarian Tradition* (1930: repr. Baton Rouge, 1977); Carl N. Degler, *Place over Time: The Continuity of Southern Distinctiveness* (Baton Rouge, 1977); W.J. Cash, *The Mind of the South* (New York, 1941); V.O. Key, Jr., *Southern Politics in State and Nation* (New York, 1949); J. Isaac Copeland, ed., *Democracy in the Old South and Other Essays by Fletcher Melvin Green* (Nashville, 1969); Grady McWhiney, *Southerners and Other Americans* (New York, 1973); Benjamin Burks Kendrick and Alex Mathews Arnett, *The South Looks at Its Past* (Chapel Hill, 1955); William H. Nichols, *Southern Tradition and Regional Progress* (Chapel Hill, 1960); Harriet Chappell Owsley, ed., *The South: Old and New Frontiers: Selected Essays of Frank Lawrence Owsley* (Athens, Ga., 1969); Henry Savage, Jr., *Seeds of Time: The Background of Southern Thinking* (New York, 1959); Donald Davidson, ed., *Selected Essays and Other Writings of John Donald Wade* (Athens, Ga., 1966); T. Harry Williams, *Romance and Realism in Southern Politics* (Athens, Ga., 1961); Frank E. Vandiver, ed., *The Idea of the South: Pursuit of a Central Theme* (Chicago, 1964); Dewey W. Grantham, Jr., ed., *The South and the Sectional Theme since Reconstruction* (New York, 1967); William Best Hesseltine, "Regions, Classes, and Sections in American History," *Journal of Land and Public Utilities Economics* 1 (Feb. 1944):35-44; W.T. Couch, ed., *Culture in the South* (Chapel Hill, 1934); Clement Eaton, *The Waning of the Old South Civilization, 1860-1880's*, Lamar Memorial Lectures, No. 10 (Athens, Ga., 1968); Albert Bushnell Hart, *The Southern South* (New York, 1910); Howard W. Odum, *Southern Regions of the United States* (Chapel Hill, 1936); Arthur S. Link and Rembert W. Patrick, eds., *Writing Southern History: Essays in Historiography in Honor of Fletcher M. Green* (1965; repr. Baton Rouge, 1967); Louis D. Rubin, Jr.,

South: Portrait of a Culture (Baton Rouge, 1980); Richard H. King, *A Southern Renaissance: The Cultural Awakening of the American South* (New York, 1980); John B. Boles and Evelyn Nolan, *Interpreting Southern History: Historiographical Essays in Honor of Sanford W. Higginbotham* (Baton Rouge, 1987).

Students of southern urbanization have not made sufficient use of contemporary printed federal documents. A primary source of special importance is a remarkable survey, George E. Waring, Jr., comp., "The Southern and the Western States" and "The New England and the Middle States," *Report on the Social Statistics of Cities, Tenth Census of the United States, 1880,* vols. 9 and 10, pts. 1 and 2 (Washington, D.C., 1886-87). Thousands of individuals from all across the country, mostly public officials, provided the primary information collected in the *Social Statistics of Cities.* Material is included on 222 of the 227 cities in the United States with populations of 10,000 or more in 1880. The *Tenth Census of the United States, 1880,* was the most comprehensive American census taken to date and represented a response to congressional desires for a survey of the progress of the nation at the end of its first hundred years. The *Report on Statistics of Churches in the United States, Eleventh Census of the United States,* vol. 9 (Washington, D.C., 1894), has the best available nineteenth-century religious tabulations. (Attempts to take a religious census in 1880 failed because of faulty methodology.) These tables, which were set in small type, with the statistics spread across two pages, are difficult to use. Much easier to read are manufacturing statistics, such as those contained in *Report on Manufacturing Industries in the United States at the Eleventh Census: 1890, Eleventh Census of the United States, 1890,* pts. 1 and 2 (Washington, D.C., 1895), which summarizes the progress of American manufacturing to that point in time. Later statistics on industrial development can be obtained from the census or from a wide variety of secondary sources. The general data largely suffer from differing definitions of the southern region.

A variety of other federal documents contain helpful information. A detailed source for educational statistics in the Gilded Age is the report of the secretary of the interior, *Report of the Commissioner of Education, 1880,* vol. 3 (Washington, D.C., 1882). Basic to understanding the grain trade is Bureau of Statistics, Department of the Treasury, "The Grain Trade of the United States and Tables on the World's Wheat Supply and Trade," *Monthly Summary of Commerce and Finances, January 1900,* n.s., no. 7 (Washington, D.C., 1900). Despite the limited scope of the title, this long report has historical tables and a lengthy economic analysis. Information on waterworks appears in *Report on the Water-Power of the United States, Tenth Census of the United States, 1880,* vol. 17, pt. 2 (Washington, D.C., 1887). For late nineteenth-century urban financial data, see *Report on Valuation, Taxation, and Public Indebtedness, Tenth Census of the United States, 1880,* vol. 7 (Washington, D.C., 1884). The problems of modern cities are discussed in a report of the Urbanism Committee to the National Resources Committee, *Our Cities: Their Role in the National Economy* (Washington, D.C., 1937). Florida is examined as a last continental frontier in Robert P.

Porter et al., "Progress of the Nation," in *Total Population, Eleventh Census of the United States: 1890*, vol. 1, pt. 1 (Washington, D.C., 1895). A magnificent survey of the American railroad net is Andrew M. Modelski, *Railroad Maps of North America: The First Hundred Years* (Washington, D.C., 1984).

Numerous local histories, many of which are not analytical in structure and are confusing in organization, provide valuable background information and contribute to a better understanding of larger themes. Representative older works, some of them primary sources in their own right, include De Saussure and J.L. Dawson, *Census of the City of Charleston, for the Year 1848: Exhibiting the Condition and Prospects of the City, Illustrated by Many Statistical Details, Prepared Under the Authority of the City Council* (Charleston, 1849); Charles Fraser, *Reminiscences of Charleston: Lately Published in the Charleston Courier and Now Revised and Enlarged by the Author* (Charleston, 1854); Jacob Cardozo, *Reminiscences of Charleston* (Charleston, 1866); *Baltimore: Past and Present, with Biographical Sketches of Its Representative Men* . . . (Philadelphia, 1881); J. Thomas Scharf, *History of Baltimore City and County* . . . (Philadelphia, 1881); John Porter, *The City of Washington: Its Origin and Administration* (Washington, D.C., 1885); Charles Todd, *The Story of Washington: The National Capital* (New York, 1889); Richard Jackson, *The Chronicles of Georgetown, from 1751 to 1878* (Washington, D.C., 1878); H.W. Burton, *History of Norfolk, Virginia: A Review of Important Events and Incidents Which Occurred from 1736 to 1877* . . . (Norfolk, 1874); Samuel Mordecai, *Virginia, Especially Richmond in By-gone Days, with a Glance at the Present, Being Reminiscences and Last Words of an Old Citizen*, 2d ed. (Richmond, 1860); Benjamin Casseday, *The History of Louisville from Its Earliest Settlement till the Year 1852* (Louisville, 1852); George Ranck, *History of Lexington, Kentucky: Its Early Annals and Recent Progress, Including Biographical Sketches and Personal Reminiscences of the Pioneer Settlers, Notices of Prominent Citizens, etc., etc.* (Cincinnati, 1872); John Martin, *Columbus, Geo. from its Selection as a "Trading Town" in 1827, to its Partial Destruction by Wilson's Raid in 1865: History-Incident-Personality* (Columbus, 1874); James Davis, *The History of Memphis* (Memphis, 1873); John Keating, *History of the City of Memphis and Shelby County, Tennessee, with Illustrations and Biographical Sketches of Some of Its Prominent Citizens* (Syracuse, 1888); Edward Clarke, *Illustrated History of Atlanta, Containing Glances at its Population, Business, Manufactures, Industries, Institutions . . . and Advantages Generally, with Nearly One Hundred Illustrations, and a Lithographic Map of the City* (Atlanta, 1878); *Past, Present, and Future of Chattanooga, Tennessee* . . . (Chattanooga, 1885); and H.G. McCall, *A Sketch, Historical and Statistical of the City of Montgomery, Outlining Its History, Location, Climate, Health* . . . (Montgomery, 1885).

Among local histories of more recent vintage are Robert Rhett, *Charleston: An Epic of Carolina* (Richmond, 1940); Hamilton Owens, *Baltimore and Chesapeake* (New York, 1941); Francis F. Beirne, *The Amiable Baltimoreans* (1951; repr. Hatboro, Pa., 1968); Charles Hirschfield, *Baltimore,*

1870-1900: Studies in Social History (Baltimore, 1941); Sherry Olson, *Baltimore: The Building of an American City* (Baltimore, 1980); William Howard Taft and James Bryce, *Washington: The Nation's Capital* (Washington, D.C., 1915); William Stevens, *Washington: The Cinderella City* . . . (New York, 1943); Marshall Butt, *Portsmouth under Four Flags, 1752-1961* (Portsmouth, 1961); Henry Bacon McKoy, *Wilmington, N.C.—Do You Remember When?* (Greenville, S.C., 1957); Nettie Voges, *Old Alexandria: Where America's Past Is Present* (McLean, Va., 1975); George Holbert Tucker, *Norfolk Highlights, 1854-1881* (Norfolk, 1940); William Harden, *A History of Savannah and South Georgia,* 2 vols. (Chicago, 1913); Mills Lane, *Savannah Revisited: A Pictorial History* (Savannah, 1973); Besty Fancher, *Savannah: A Renaissance of the Heart* (Garden City, 1976); William Christian, *Richmond: Its People and Its Story* (Philadelphia, 1923); John P. Little, *History of Richmond* (Richmond, 1933); James G. Scott and Edward A. Wyatt IV, *Petersburg's Story: A History* (Petersburg, 1960); Rosa Faulkner Yancey, *Lynchburg and Its Neighbors* (Richmond, 1935); Dorothy T. Potter and Clifton W. Potter, Jr., *Lynchburg: "The Most Interesting Spot"* (Lynchburg, 1976); Helen Kohn Hennig, ed., *Columbia: Capital City of South Carolina, 1786-1936* (Columbia, 1936); Charles Nash, *The History of Augusta, First Settlements and Early Days as a Town, Including the Diary of Mrs. Martha Moore Ballard (1785-1812)* (Augusta, 1904); Isabella McMeekin, *Louisville: The Gateway City* (New York, 1946); John D. Wright, *Lexington: Heart of the Bluegrass* (Lexington, Ky., 1982); William McRaven, *Nashville: "Athens of the South"* (Chapel Hill, 1949); Alfred Crabbe, *Nashville: Personality of a City* (Indianapolis, 1960); Wilbur Creighton, *Building of Nashville* (Nashville, 1969); Henry Rightor, *Standard History of New Orleans,* 3 vols. (New York, 1952); Lyle Saxon, *Fabulous New Orleans* (Chicago, 1928); Harriet Kane, *Queen New Orleans: City by the River* (New York, 1949); Peter Hamilton, *Mobile of the Five Flags: The Story of the River Basin and Coast about Mobile from the Earliest Times to the Present* (Mobile, 1913); Caldwell Delaney, *The Story of Mobile* (Mobile, 1953); Nancy Telfair, *A History of Columbus, Georgia, 1828-1928* (Columbus, 1929); Etta Blanchard Worsley, *Columbus on the Chattahoochee* (Columbus, 1951); Ida Young, *History of Macon, Georgia* (Macon, 1950); Dallas Herndon, *Why Little Rock Was Born* (Little Rock, 1933); Ira Richards, *Story of a Rivertown: Little Rock in the Nineteenth Century* (Benton, Ark., 1969); Thomas Martin, *Atlanta and Its Builders: A Comprehensive History of the Gate City of the South* (New York, 1902); Walter Cooper, *Official History of Fulton County* (Atlanta, 1934); and Zella Armstrong, *The History of Chattanooga County and Chattanooga, Tennessee,* 2 vols. (Chattannoga, 1931-40).

Also see Thomas J. Wertenbaker, *Norfolk: Historical Southern Port,* edited by Marvin Schlegel (1931; repr. Durham, 1962); Gerald Capers, *The Biography of a Rivertown: Memphis: Its Heroic Age* (Chapel Hill, 1939); David M. Tucker, *Memphis since Crump: Bossism, Blacks, and Civic Reformers, 1948-1968* (Knoxville, 1980); Constance McLaughlin Green, *Washington,* vol. 1, *Village and Capital, 1800-1878* (Princeton, 1962), and *Washington,* vol. 2, *Capital City, 1879-1950* (Princeton, 1963); James M.

Russell, *Atlanta, 1847-1890: City Building in the Old South and the New* (Baton Rouge, 1988); James Neal Primm, *Lion of the Valley: A History of St. Louis* (Boulder, 1981); Don H. Doyle, *Nashville in the New South, 1880-1930* (Knoxville, 1988); Don H. Doyle, *Nashville since the 1920s* (Knoxville, 1985); D. Clayton James, *Antebellum Natchez* (Baton Rouge, 1968); William D. Miller, *Memphis during the Progressive Era, 1900-1917* (Memphis, 1957); Joy L. Jackson, *New Orleans in the Gilded Age: Politics and Urban Progress, 1880-1896* (Baton Rouge, 1969); Robert C. Reinders, *End of an Era: New Orleans, 1850-1860* (New Orleans, 1964); Christopher Silver, *Twentieth-Century Richmond: Planning, Politics, and Race* (Knoxville, 1982); Michael J. McDonald and William Bruce Wheeler, *Knoxville, Tennessee: Continuity and Change in an Appalachian City* (Knoxville, 1983).

Books and articles concerning the Civil War and Reconstruction experiences of southern cities include Noah Brooks, *Washington in Lincoln's Time* (New York, 1895); James Whyte, *The Uncivil War: Washington during the Reconstruction, 1865-1878* (New York, 1958); Catherine Copeland, *Bravest Surrender: A Petersburg Patchwork* (Richmond, 1961); Marvin Lucas, *Sherman and the Burning of Columbia* (College Station, 1976); Earl Schenck Miers, ed., *When the World Ended: The Diary of Emma LeConte* (New York, 1957); Florence Corley, *Confederate City: Augusta, Georgia, 1860-1865* (Columbia, 1960); Barry Fleming, *Autobiography of a City in Arms: Augusta, Georgia, 1861-1865* (Augusta, 1938); John Coleman, *Lexington during the Civil War*, rev. ed. (Lexington, Ky., 1939); Gerald M. Capers, *Occupied City: New Orleans under the Federals, 1862-1865* (Lexington, Ky., 1965); Mary Loughborough, *My Cave Life in Vicksburg: With Letters of Trial and Travail* (Little Rock, 1882); Osborn Oldroyd, *A Soldier's Story of the Siege of Vicksburg* (Springfield, Ill., 1885); Peter Walker, *Vicksburg: A People at War, 1860-1865* (Chapel Hill, 1960); Adolph Hoehing and the editors of the Army Times Publishing Company, *Vicksburg: Forty-seven Days of Siege* (Englewood Cliffs, N.J., 1969); Samuel Carter III, *The Siege of Atlanta, 1864* (New York, 1973); Emory M. Davis, *The Confederate State of Richmond: A Biography of the Capital* (Austin, 1971); Dale A. Somers, "New Orleans at War: A Merchants's View," *Louisiana History* 14 (Winter 1973):49-68; Dale A. Somers, "War and Play: The Civil War in New Orleans," *Mississippi Quarterly* 26 (Winter 1972-73):3-28; Perry A. Snyder, "Shreveport, Louisiana, 1861-1865: From Secession to Surrender," *Louisiana Studies* 11 (Spring 1972):50-70; Joseph H. Parks, "A Confederate Trade Center under Federal Occupation: Memphis, 1862-1865," *Journal of Southern History* 7 (Aug. 1941):289-314; C. Van Woodward, *Mary Chesnut's Civil War* (New Haven, 1981).

The role of blacks in southern cities has naturally attracted a great deal of attention. Of special importance for antebellum times are Richard Wade, *Slavery in the Cities: The South, 1820-1860* (New York, 1964); Claudia Dale Golden, *Urban Slavery in the American South, 1820-1860: A Quantitative History* (Chicago, 1976); Leonard P. Curry, *The Free Black in Urban America, 1800-1850: The Shadow of the Dream* (Chicago, 1981); Robert S. Starobin, *Industrial Slavery in the Old South* (New York, 1970); L.P. Jackson, "Free Negroes of Petersburg, Virginia," *Journal of Negro History* 12 (July 1927):365-88; E. Horace Fitchett, "The Origin and Growth of the Free Negro Population of Charleston, South Carolina," *Journal of Negro History* 26 (Oct. 1941):421-37; Dorothy Provine, "The Economic Position of Free Blacks in the District of Columbia," *Journal of Negro History* 58 (Jan. 1973):61-72; Ira Berlin, *Slaves without Masters: The Negro in the Antebellum South* (New York, 1974); Clement Eaton, "Slave-Hiring in the Upper South: A Step toward Freedom," *Mississippi Valley Historical Review* 55 (March 1960):663-73; John T. O'Brien, "Factory, Church, and Community: Blacks in Antebellum Richmond," *Journal of Southern History* 44 (Nov. 1978):509-36; Marianne Buroff Sheldon, "Black-White Relations in Richmond, Virginia, 1782-1820," *Journal of Southern History* 45 (Feb. 1979):27-44; Clement Eaton, *Slave-Hiring in the Upper South* (New York, 1974).

Items for the Gilded Age include John W. Blassingame, *Black New Orleans, 1860-1880* (Chicago, 1973); Constance McLaughlin Green, *The Secret City: A History of Race Relations in the Nation's Capital* (Princeton, 1967); Robert E. Perdue, *The Negro in Savannah, 1865-1900* (New York, 1973); Dale A. Somers, "Black and White in New Orleans: A Survey of Urban Race Relations, 1865-1900," *Journal of Southern History* 40 (Feb. 1974):19-42; Howard N. Rabinowitz, *Race Relations in the Urban South, 1865-1890*, History of Urban America Series (New York, 1978); Lawrence J. Friedman, *The White Savage: Racial Fantasies in the Postbellum South* (Englewood Cliffs, N.J., 1970); Howard N. Rabinowitz, "The Conflict between Blacks and the Police in the Urban South," *Historian* 39 (Nov. 1976):62-76; C. Vann Woodward, *The Strange Career of Jim Crow* (New York, 1955); Terry L. Seip, "Municipal Politics and the Negro: Baton Rouge, 1865-1900," in Mark T. Carleton, Peter H. Howard, and Joseph B. Parker, eds., *Readings in Louisiana Politics* (Baton Rouge, 1975):242-66; David C. Rankin, "The Origins of Black Leadership in New Orleans during Reconstruction," *Journal of Southern History* 40 (Aug. 1974):417-40; John P. Kellogg, "The Formation of Black Residential Areas in Lexington, Kentucky, 1865-1887," *Journal of Southern History* 48 (Feb. 1982):21-52; Pete Daniel, "The Metamorphosis of Slavery, 1865-1900," *Journal of American History* 66 (June 1979):88-99; Bobby L. Lovett, "Memphis Riots: White Reaction to Blacks in Memphis, May 1865-July 1868," *Tennessee Historical Quarterly* 38 (Spring 1979):9-33; George C. Wright, *Life behind a Veil: Blacks in Louisville, Kentucky* (Baton Rouge, 1985).

Many twentieth-century materials deal with the struggle for racial equality. Of special importance is Michael R. Belknap, *Federal Law and Southern Order: Racial Violence and Constitutional Conflict in the Post-Brown South* (Athens, Ga., 1987). See also Roger L. Rice, "Residential Segregation by Law, 1910-1917," *Journal of Southern History* 34 (May 1968):179-99; August Meier and Elliott Rudwick, "The Boycott Movement against Jim Crow Streetcars in the South, 1900-1906," *Journal of American History* 55 (March 1969):756-75; James W. Silver, *Mississippi: The Closed Society*, 3d ed. (New York, 1966); Gunnar Myrdal, *An American Dilemma: The Negro Problem and Modern Democracy*, 2d ed. (New York, 1962); Donald R. McCoy and Richard T. Ruetten, *Quest and Response: Minority Rights and the Truman Administration* (Lawrence, 1973); Numan V. Bartley, *The Rise of Massive Resistance: Race and Politics in the South during the 1950s* (Baton Rouge, 1969); Neil R. McMillen, *The Citizens' Council: Organized Resistance to the Second Reconstruction, 1954-1964* (Urbana, 1971); Philip B. Kurlarl, " '*Brown v. Board of Education* was the Beginning': The School Desegregation Cases in the United States Supreme Court: 1954-1979," *Washington University Law Quarterly* 1979 (Spring 1979):309-405; J.W. Peltason, *Fifty-eight Lonely Men: Southern Federal Judges and School Desegregation* (New York, 1961); David Alan Horowitz, "White Southerners' Alienation and Civil Rights: The Response to Corporate Liberalism, 1956-1965," *Journal of Southern History* 54 (May 1988):173-200; Richard A. Pride and J. David Woodward, *The Burden of Burning: The Politics of Desegregation in Nashville, Tennessee* (Knoxville, 1985); Carl V. Harris, "Stability and Change in Discriminating against Black Public Schools: Birmingham, Alabama, 1871-1931," *Journal of Southern History* 51 (Aug. 1985):375-416; Ronald H. Bayer, "Roads to Racial Segregation: Atlanta in the Twentieth Century," *Journal of Urban History* 15 (Nov. 1988):3-21.

Most immigration studies are quite general. Some of the general materials that contain data on the urban South are Stephen Byrne, *Irish Emigration to the United States: What It Has Been, and What It Is* (New York, 1873); Albert Faust, *The German Element in the United States*, 2 vols. (New York, 1912); Carl Wittke, *We Who Built America: The Saga of the Immigrant* (Cleveland, 1939); Stanley C. Johnson, *History of Emigration from the United Kingdom to North America, 1763-1912* (London, 1913). Excellent surveys of ethnic groups can be found in Stephen Thernstrom, ed., *Harvard Encyclopedia of American Ethnic Groups* (Cambridge, Mass., 1980). Of a more specific nature on the urban South are Dieter Cunz, *The Maryland Germans: A History* (1948; repr. Port Washington, N.Y., 1972); Robert T. Clark, "Reconstruction and the New Orleans German Colony," *Louisiana Historical Quarterly* 23 (April 1940):501-24; Bob Cyrus Rauchle, "The Political Life of the Germans in Memphis, 1848-1900," *Louisiana Historical Quarterly* 51 (Summer 1968):165-75; Earl Niehaus, *The Irish in New Orleans, 1800-1860* (Baton Rouge, 1965); Darrell Overdyke, *The Know-Nothing Party in the South* (Baton Rouge, 1950); Fredrick Marcel Spletstoser, "Back Door to the Land of Plenty: New Orleans as an Immigrant Port, 1820-1860," 2 vols. (Ph.D. diss., Louisiana State University, 1978).

Religion is a difficult subject with which to deal in a scholarly setting under any circumstances. Most studies make little distinction between rural and urban situations, further complicating any assessment of the impact of religious institutions on the southern city. In terms of both background and specific situations, works of value include Ray Allen Billington, *The Protestant Crusade, 1800-1860: A Study of the Origins of American Nativism* (New York, 1938); Hunter D. Farish, *The Circuit Rider Dismounts: A Social History of Southern Methodism, 1865-1900* (Richmond, 1938); Rufus B. Spain, *At Ease in Zion: Social History of the Southern Baptists, 1865-1900* (Nashville, 1967); Kenneth K. Bailey, "Southern White Protestantism at the

Turn of the Century," *American Historical Review* 68 (April 1963):618-35; Charles Reagan Wilson, "The Religion of the Lost Cause: Ritual and Organization of the Southern Civil Religion, 1865-1920," *Journal of Southern History* 46 (May 1980):219-38; W.W. Barnes, *The Southern Baptist Convention, 1845-1953* (Nashville, 1954); Paul N. Garber, *The Methodists Are One People* (Nashville, 1939); Carter Woodson, *The History of the Negro Church* (1921; repr. Washington, D.C., 1945); John M. Cromwell, "First Negro Churches in the District of Columbia," *Journal of Negro History* 7 (Jan. 1922):64-106; Kenneth K. Bailey, *Southern White Protestantism in the Twentieth Century* (New York, 1964); Wayne Flynt, "Religion in the Urban South: The Divided Mind of Birmingham, 1900-1930," *Alabama Review* 30 (April 1977):108-34; Kenneth T. Jackson, *The Ku Klux Klan and the City, 1915-1930* (New York, 1967). Studies pertaining to the Jewish community include Isaac Fein, *The Making of an American Jewish Community: The History of Baltimore Jewry from 1773 to 1920* (Philadelphia, 1971); Leonard Dinnerstein and Mawy Dale Palsson, *Jews in the South* (Baton Rouge, 1973); Eli N. Evans, *The Provincials: A Personal History of Jews in the South* (New York, 1973); Myron Berman, *Richmond's Jewry: Shabbat to Shookoe, 1796-1976* (Charlottesville, 1979); Steven Hertzberg, *Strangers within the Gate City: The Jews of Atlanta, 1845-1915* (Philadelphia, 1978).

Transportation development strategies, crucial to city building, are covered in such places as John F. Stover, *The Railroads of the South, 1805-1900: A Study in Finance and Control* (Chapel Hill, 1955); Eugene Alvarez, *Travel on Southern Antebellum Railroads, 1828-1866* (University, Ala., 1974); Edward Hungerford, *The Story of the Baltimore and Ohio Railroad, 1827-1927*, 2 vols. (New York, 1928); Maury Klein, *The Great Richmond Terminal: A Study in Businessmen and Railroad Strategy* (Charlottesville, 1970); Maury Klein, *History of the Louisville and Nashville Railroad* (New York, 1972); John L. Kers, *The Louisville and Nashville: An Outline History* (New York, 1933); Kincaid Herr, *The Louisville and Nashville Railroad, 1850-1963* (Louisville, 1963); Leonard P. Curry, *Rail Routes South: Louisville's Fight for the Southern Market, 1865-1872* (Lexington, Ky., 1969); Ulrich P. Phillips, *A History of Transportation in the Eastern Cotton Belt to 1860* (New York, 1913); Jesse C. Burt, Jr., "Four Decades of the Nashville, Chattanooga and St. Louis Railway, 1873-1916," *Tennessee Historical Quarterly* 9 (June 1950):99-130; Samuel Derrick, *Centennial History of South Carolina Railroads* (Columbia, 1930); Richard Price, *Georgia Railroads and the West Point Route* (Salt Lake City, 1962); John G. Clark, "New Orleans and the River: A Study in Attitudes and Responses," *Louisiana History* 8 (Spring 1967):117-36; R.B. Way, "The Commerce of the Lower Mississippi in the Period 1830-1860," *Mississippi Valley Historical Review* Extra Number (July 1920):57-68; Frank H. Dixon, *A Traffic History of the Mississippi River System*, National Waterways Commission, Doc. 11 (Washington, D.C., 1909); Merl E. Reed, *New Orleans and the Railroads: The Struggle for Commercial Empire, 1830-1860* (Baton Rouge, 1966); Lawrence H. Larsen, "New Orleans and the River Trade: Reinterpreting the Role of the Business Community," *Wisconsin Magazine of History* 61 (Winter 1977-

78]:112-24; Allan Pred, *Urban Growth and City-Systems in the United States, 1840-1860* (Cambridge, Mass., 1980).

A number of scholarly accounts concern the rise of industry in Dixie. They include Broadus Mitchell, *William Gregg: Factory Master of the Old South* (Chapel Hill, 1928); Fletcher M. Green, "Duff Green: Industrial Promoter," *Journal of Southern History* 2 (Feb. 1936):29-42; Herbert Collins, "The Idea of a Cotton Textile Industry in Ante-Bellum North Carolina, 1870-1900," *North Carolina Historical Quarterly* 34 (July 1927):358-92; Herbert Collins, "The Southern Industrial Gospel before 1860," *Journal of Southern History* 12 (Aug. 1946):383-402; Robert S. Cotterill, "The Old South to the New," *Journal of Southern History* 15 (Feb. 1949):3-8; Diffee W. Standard and Richard Griffin, "The Cotton Textile Industry in Ante-Bellum North Carolina," *North Carolina Historical Review* 34 (Jan. 1951):15-37; 34 (April 1957):131-66; Richard W. Griffin, "The Origins of the Industrial Revolution in Georgia: Cotton Textiles, 1810-1865," *Georgia Historical Quarterly* 42 (Dec. 1958):355-75. Weymouth T. Jordan, *Antebellum Alabama: Town and Country*, Florida State University Studies 27 (Tallahassee, 1957); Ernest M. Lander, Jr., "The Iron Industry in Ante-Bellum South Carolina," *Journal of Southern History* 20 (Aug. 1954):337-55; Carrol H. Quenzel, "The Manufacture of Locomotives and Cars in Alexandria in the 1850s," *Virginia Magazine of History and Biography* 62 (April 1954):181-89; Thomas S. Berry, "The Rise of Flour Milling in Richmond," *Virginia Magazine of History and Biography* 78 (Oct. 1970):388-408. Norris W. Preyer, "Why Did Industrialism Lag in the Old South?" *Georgia Historical Quarterly* 55 (Fall 1971):378-96; Raymond L. Cohn, "Local Manufacturing in the Ante-bellum South and Midwest," *Business History Review* 54 (Spring 1980):80-91; Charles D. Dew, *Ironmaker for the Confederacy: Joseph R. Anderson and the Tredegar Iron Works* (New York, 1966); Broadus Mitchell, *The Rise of Cotton Mills in the South*, Studies in Historical and Political Science, ser. 39, no. 2 (Baltimore, 1921); N.M. Tilley, *The Bright-Tobacco Industry, 1860-1929* (Chapel Hill, 1948); Jack Blicksilver, *Cotton Manufacturing in the Southeast: An Historical Analysis* (Atlanta, 1959); Ronald D. Eller, *Miners, Millhands, and Mountaineers: Industrialization of the Appalachian South, 1880-1920* (Knoxville, 1982); Mary J. Oates, *The Role of Cotton Textile Industry in the Economic Development of the Southeast, 1900-1940* (New York, 1975); Jonathan M. Wiener, *Social Origins of the New South: Alabama, 1860-1885* (Baton Rouge, 1978); Dwight B. Billings, Jr., *Planters and the Making of a "New South": Class, Politics, and Development in North Carolina, 1865-1900* (Chapel Hill, 1979); Bess Beatly, "Lowells of the South: Northern Influences on the Nineteenth-Century North Carolina Textile Industry," *Journal of Southern History* 53 (Feb. 1987):27-62; Roger L. Ransom and Richard Sutch, *One Kind of Freedom: The Economic Consequences of Emancipation* (Cambridge, England, 1977); Broadus Mitchell and George Mitchell, *The Industrial Revolution in the South* (Baltimore, 1930); Ethel M. Ames, *The Story of Coal and Iron in Alabama* (Birmingham, 1910); James C. Cobb, *Industrialization and Southern Society, 1877-1984* (Lexington, Ky., 1984); David L. Carlton, *Mill and*

Town in South Carolina, 1880-1920 (Baton Rouge, 1982); Ernest J. Hopkins, *Mississippi's BAWI Plan,* Federal Reserve Bank of Atlanta (Atlanta, 1944); James C. Cobb, "Beyond Planters and Industrialists: A New Perspective on the New South," *Journal of Southern History* 54 (Feb. 1988):45-68.

There are important works dealing with planning and architectural concerns. Those on national phases that relate to the South include John W. Reps, *The Making of Urban America* (Princeton, 1965); John W. Reps, *Town Planning in Frontier America* (Princeton, 1969); John W. Reps, *Monumental Washington: The Planning and Development of the Capital Center* (Princeton, 1967); Lewis Mumford, *The City in History: Its Origins, Its Transformations, and Its Prospects* (New York, 1961); James Marston Fitch, *American Building: The Forces That Shape It* (1948; repr. New York, 1977); Christopher Tunnard and Henry Hope Reed, *American Skyline: The Growth and Form of Our Cities and Towns* (New York, 1955); Vincent Scully, *American Architecture and Urbanism* (New York, 1969); Thomas A. Tallmadge, *The Story of Architecture in America* (New York, 1936); Talbert F. Hamlin, *Greek Revival Architecture in America* (New York, 1944). For trends in the South, see such studies as John W. Reps, *Tidewater Towns: City Planning in Colonial Virginia and Maryland* (Charlottesville, 1972); William Casey, *An Architectural Monograph: Charleston Doorways, Entrance Motives from a South Carolina City,* White Pine Series, vol. 14, monograph 81 (New York, 1928); Franklin Garrett, *Yesterday's Atlanta,* Seeman's Historic Cities Series, no. 8 (Miami, 1974); Everett B. Wilson, *Early Southern Towns* (South Brunswick, N.J., 1967); James Bonner, "Plantation Architecture of the Lower South on the Eve of the Civil War," *Journal of Southern History* 11 (Aug. 1945):370-88; Henry Forman, *Architecture of the Old South: The Medieval Style, 1585-1880* (Cambridge, Mass., 1948); David R. Goldfield, "Planning for Urban Growth in the Old South," *South Atlantic Urban Studies* 4 (1979):234-57; *An Omnibus of the Capitol,* House of Representatives, Doc. 412, 2d ed., 86th Cong., 2d sess. (Washington, D.C., 1959); Clayton B. Dekle, "The Tennessee State Capitol," *Tennessee Historical Quarterly* 25 (Fall 1966):213-38; Gilbert E. Govan, "The Chattanooga Union Station," *Tennessee Historical Quarterly* 29 (Winter 1970-71):372-78; Keith L. Bryant, "Cathedrals, Castles, and Roman Baths: Railroad Station Architecture in the Urban South," *Journal of Urban History* 2 (Feb. 1976):195-230; Frederick Gutheim, *Worthy of the Nation: The History of Planning for the National Capital* (Washington, D.C., 1979); Albert Fein, *Frederick Law Olmsted and the American Environmental Tradition* (New York, 1972). See also Margaret Ripley Wolfe, *Kingsport, Tennessee: A Planned American City* (Lexington, Ky., 1986).

The small body of literature on municipal affairs includes J. David Griffin, "Savannah's City Income Tax," *Georgia Historical Quarterly* 50 (Sept. 1969):173-76; John H. Ellis, "Memphis Sanitary Revolution, 1880-1890," *Tennessee Historical Quarterly* 23 (March 1964):59-72; Eugene J. Watts, *Social Bases of City Politics in Atlanta, 1865-1903* (Westport, Conn., 1978); E. Merton Coulter, "The Great Savannah Fire of 1820," *Georgia Historical Quarterly* 23 (March 1939):1-27; John B. Clark, Jr., "The Fire Problem in

Kentucky, 1778-1865: A Case History of the Ante-Bellum South," *Register of the Kentucky Historical Society* 51 (April 1953):92-122; Richard H. Haunton, "Law and Order in Savannah, 1850-1860," *Georgia Historical Quarterly* 56 (Spring 1972):1-24; Richard J. Hopkins, "Public Health in Atlanta: The Formative Years, 1865-1879," *Georgia Historical Quarterly* 3 (Sept. 1969):287-304; John H. Ellis, "Business and Public Health in the Urban South during the Nineteenth Century: New Orleans, Memphis, and Atlanta," *Bulletin of the History of Medicine* 44 (May-June 1970):197-212; David R. Goldfield, "The Business of Health Planning: Disease Prevention in the Old South," *Journal of Southern History* 42 (Nov. 1976):557-70; Joseph Ioor Waring, "The Yellow Fever Epidemic of Savannah in 1820, With a Sketch of William Coffee Daniell," *Georgia Historical Quarterly* 53 (Dec. 1968):398-404; John H. Ellis, "Memphis' Sanitary Revolution, 1880-1890," *Tennessee Historical Quarterly* 23 (March 1964):59-74; Donald Everett, "The New Orleans Yellow Fever Epidemic of 1853," *Louisiana Historical Quarterly* 33 (Oct. 1950):380-405; Jo Ann Carrigan, "Yellow Fever in New Orleans: Abstractions and Realities," *Journal of Southern History* 25 (Aug. 1959):339-55; Jo Ann Carrigan, "Privilege, Prejudice, and Strangers Disease in Nineteenth-Century New Orleans," *Journal of Southern History* 36 (Nov. 1970):568-78; John Duffy, "Nineteenth Century Public Health in New York and New Orleans: A Comparison," *Louisiana History* 15 (Fall 1974): 325-37; John Duffy, *Sword of Pestilence: The New Orleans Yellow Fever Epidemic of 1853* (Baton Rouge, 1966); M. Foster Farley, "The Mighty Monarch of the South: Yellow Fever in Charleston and Savannah," *Georgia Review* 27 (Spring 1973):56-70; Margaret Warner, "Local Control versus National Interest: The Debate over Southern Public Health, 1878-1884," *Journal of Southern History* 50 (Aug. 1984):407-28; Eugene Watts, "The Police in Atlanta, 1890-1905," *Journal of Southern History* 39 (May 1973): 165-82.

Few studies have been done on southern urban leaders. The subject is not an easy one to pursue, as indicated in David C. Hammack, "Problems in the Historical Study of Power in the Cities and Towns of the United States, 1800-1960," *American Historical Review* 83 (April 1978):323-49. Representative selections include Michael P. Johnson, "Planters and Patriarchy: Charleston, 1800-1860," *Journal of Southern History* 46 (Feb. 1980):45-72; John Radford, "The Charleston Planters in 1860," *South Carolina Historical Magazine* 77 (Oct. 1976):227-35; William Best Hesseltine, *Confederate Leaders in the New South* (1950; repr. Westport, Conn., 1970); Eugene J. Watts, *The Social Bases of City Politics: Atlanta, 1865-1903* (Westport, Conn., 1978); Carl V. Harris, *Political Power in Birmingham, 1871-1921* (Knoxville, 1977); Paul D. Escott, *Many Excellent People: Power and Privilege in North Carolina, 1850-1900* (Chapel Hill, 1985); Laurence Snare, *Southern Capitalists: The Ideological Leadership of an Elite, 1832-1885* (Chapel Hill, 1986); Robert J. Hopkins, "Status, Mobility, and Dimensions of Change in a Southern City: Atlanta, 1870-1910," in Kenneth T. Jackson and Stanley K. Schultz, eds., *Cities in American History* (New York, 1972); L. Tuffly Ellis, "The New Orleans Cotton Exchange: The Formative Years,

1871-1880," *Journal of Southern History* 38 (Nov. 1973):545-64; J.R. Killick, "The Transformation of Cotton Marketing in the Late Nineteenth Century: Alexander Sprunt and Son of Wilmington, N.C., 1866-1956," *Business History Review* 55 (Summer 1981):143-69; Otis C. Skipper, *J.D.B. De Bow: Magazinist of the Old South* (Athens, Ga., 1958); Samuel M. Kipp III, "Old Notables and Newcomers: The Economic and Political Elite of Greensboro, N.C., 1880-1920," *Journal of Southern History* 43 (Aug. 1977):373-94; William D. Miller, *Mr. Crump of Memphis* (Baton Rouge, 1964); Harold H. Martin, *William Berry Hartsfield,: Mayor of Atlanta* (Athens, Ga., 1978); Edward F. Haas, *DeLesseps S. Morrison and the Image of Reform: New Orleans Politics, 1946-1961* (Baton Rouge, 1974); Elizabeth Jacoway and David R. Colburn, eds., *Southern Businessmen and Desegregation* (Baton Rouge, 1982); J.K. Winkler, *Tobacco Tycoon: The Story of James Buchanan Duke* (New York, 1942).

Much froth has been written about the Sunbelt concept. Of special importance, in terms of providing both a historical perspective and a sweeping interpretation, is Carl Abbott, *The New Urban America: Growth and Politics in Sunbelt Cities* (Chapel Hill, 1981). For other representative accounts, see Kevin Phillips, *The Emerging Republican Majority* (New Rochelle, N.Y., 1969); Kirkpatrick Sale, *Power Shift: The Rise of the Southern Rim and Its Challenge to the Eastern Establishment* (New York, 1975); Richard M. Bernard and Bradley R. Rice, eds., *Sunbelt Cities: Politics and Growth since World War II* (Austin, 1983); Bernard L. Weinstein and Robert E. Firestine, *Regional Growth and Decline in the United States: The Rise of the Sunbelt and the Decline of the Northeast* (New York, 1978); Joel Garreau, *The Nine Nations of North America* (Boston, 1981); David C. Perry and Alfred J. Watkins, *The Rise of Sunbelt Cities* (Beverly Hills, 1977); Charles Pierce Roland, "The South, America's Will-O-the-Wisp Eden," *Louisiana History* 11 (Spring 1970):101-19. Atlanta is glorified in Erla Zwingle, "Atlanta: Energy and Optimism in the New South," *National Geographic* 174 (July 1988):2-29.

A number of other works, some old and some new, touch on aspects of the southern urban experience from the colonial period through the end of Reconstruction. Indispensable for the colonial period are Carl Bridenbaugh's *Cities in the Wilderness: The First Century of Urban Life in America, 1625-1742* (1938; repr. New York, 1970), and *Cities in Revolt: Urban Life in America, 1743-1776* (1955; repr. New York, 1955). Important agricultural change is discussed in Paul G.E. Clemens, *The Atlantic Economy and Colonial Maryland's Eastern Shore: From Tobacco to Grain* (Ithaca, 1980). See also John G. Clark, *New Orleans, 1718-1812: An Economic Study* (Baton Rouge, 1970), plus John P. Moore, *Revolt in Louisiana: The Spanish Occupation, 1776-1780* (Baton Rouge, 1976). Of help in studying the antebellum period are Leonard P. Curry, *Urban Life in the Old South* (St. Louis, 1976); Richard C. Wade, *The Urban Frontier: Pioneer Life in Early Pittsburgh, Cincinnati, Lexington, Louisville, and St. Louis* (Chicago, 1959); Julius Rubin, *Canal or Railroad? Imitation and Innovation in the Response to the Erie Canal in Philadelphia, Baltimore, and Boston,* Trans-

actions of the American Philosophical Society, n.s., vol. 51, pt. 3 (Philadelphia, 1961); David R. Goldfield, *Urban Growth in the Age of Sectionalism: Virginia, 1847-1861* (Baton Rouge, 1977). Valuable travel accounts include Basil Hall, *Travels in North America, in the Years 1827 and 1828,* 3 vols. (Edinburgh, 1829); Anne Royall, *Sketches of History, Life and Manners in the United States* (New Haven, 1826), and Joseph H. Ingraham, *The South-West. By a Yankee,* 2 vols. (1835; repr. New York, 1966). Useful studies for the middle period include Herbert Wender, *Southern Commercial Conventions, 1837-1859,* Studies in Historical and Political Science, series 48, no. 4 (Baltimore, 1930); Hinton Rowan Helper, *The Impending Crisis in the South: How To Meet It* (New York, 1857); Philip S. Foner, *Business and Slavery: The New York Merchants and the Irrepressible Conflict* (Chapel Hill, 1941); J.G. Randall, *The Civil War and Reconstruction,* (1937; repr. Boston, 1953); E. Merton Coulter, *The South during Reconstruction, 1865-1877,* A History of the South, vol. 8 (Baton Rouge, 1947); Frederick E. Siegel, *The Roots of Southern Distinctiveness: Tobacco and Society in Danville, Virginia, 1780-1865* (Chapel Hill, 1987). A very valuable urban biography is Harriet E. Amos, *Cotton City: Urban Development in Antebellum Mobile* (University, Ala., 1985).

Several books have material on the New South that extends to the present day. The New South section in this study is based on Lawrence H. Larsen, *The Rise of the Urban South* (Lexington, Ky., 1985). Valuable data can be found in Paul M. Gaston, *The New South Creed: A Study in Southern Mythmaking* (New York, 1970); Henry W. Grady, *The New South* (New York, 1890); C. Vann Woodward, *Origins of the New South, 1877-1913,* A History of the South, vol. 9 (Baton Rouge, 1951); Edgar Knight, *The Influence of Reconstruction on Education in the South* (1913; repr. New York, 1969); George A. Soper, *Modern Methods of Street Cleaning* (New York, 1909); Albert Bushnell Hart, *The Southern South* (New York, 1910); Gavin Wright, *Old South, New South: Revolutions in the Southern Economy since the Civil War* (New York, 1986); Gilbert C. Fite, *Cotton Fields No More: Southern Agriculture, 1865-1980* (Lexington, Ky., 1984). An important study on the early twentieth century is Blaine A. Brownell, *The Urban Ethos in the South, 1920-1930* (Baton Rouge, 1975). For suburban trends see Howard L. Preston, *Automobile Age Atlanta: The Making of a Southern Metropolis, 1900-1935* (Athens, Ga., 1979). Roger Biles, *Memphis in the Great Depression* (Knoxville, 1986), covers developments during the 1930s in a major city. See also Douglas L. Smith, *The New Deal in the Urban South* (Baton Rouge, 1988). Jo Anne E. Argesinger, *Toward a New Deal in Baltimore: People and Government in the Great Depression* (Chapel Hill, 1988). An extremely important and insightful study that contains valuable information on the urban South through World War II is George Brown Tindall, *The Emergence of the New South, 1913-1945,* A History of the South, vol. 10 (Baton Rouge, 1967). Basic for an understanding of the postwar period are Charles P. Roland, *The Improbable Era: The South since World War II* (Lexington, Ky., 1975); David R. Goldfield, *Promised Land: The South since 1945,* The American History Series (Arlington Heights, Ill., 1987); Pete Daniel, *Standing at the Crossroads: Southern Life since 1900*, American Century Series (New York, 1986). For promotional activities see James C. Cobb, *The Selling of the South: The Southern Crusade for Industrial Development, 1936-1980* (Baton Rouge, 1982).

A number of articles have dealt with specific topics in colonial and antebellum times. Selections on the colonial period include Edward M. Riley, "The Town Acts of Colonial Virginia," *Journal of Southern History* 16 (Aug. 1950):307-23; and John C. Rainbolt, "The Absence of Towns in Seventeenth-Century Virginia," *Journal of Southern History* 35 (Aug. 1969):343-60; John A. Ernst and H. Roy Merrens, " 'Camden's turrets pierce the Skies!': The Urban Process in the Southern Colonies during the Eighteen Century," *William and Mary Quarterly* 30 (Oct. 1973):549-74. Articles on the antebellum period include Lawrence H. Larsen, "Nineteenth-Century Street Sanitation: A Study of Filth and Frustration," *Wisconsin Magazine of History* 52 (Spring 1969):239-47.

The cities of the Civil War, Reconstruction, and New South eras have received some attention. Selections on the Civil War and Reconstruction include Jered W. Roberson, "The Memphis Commercial Convention of 1853: Southern Dreams and 'Young America,' " *Tennessee Historical Quarterly* 33 (Fall 1974):279-96. Some valuable articles on the New South are Howard N. Rabinowitz, "Half a Loaf: The Shift from White to Black Teachers in the Negro Schools of the Urban South, 1865-1890," *Journal of Southern History* 40 (Nov. 1974):565-94; Clay McShane, "Transforming the Use of Urban Space: A Look at the Revolution in Street Pavements, 1880-1924," *Journal of Urban History* 5 (May 1979):279-307; and Howard N. Rabinowitz, "The Conflict between Blacks and the Police in the Urban South," *Historian* 39 (Nov. 1976):62-76.

Helpful articles on the twentieth-century urban South include Blaine A. Brownell, "The Commercial-Civic Elite and City Planning in Atlanta, Memphis, and New Orleans in the 1920s," *Journal of Southern History* 16 (Aug. 1975):339-68; Steve Davis, "The South as 'The Nation's No. 1 Economic Problem': The NEC Report of 1938," *Georgia Historical Quarterly* 62 (Summer 1978):119-32; and James A. Burron, "The WPA in Nashville, 1935-1943," *Tennessee Historical Quarterly* 34 (Fall 1975):293-306; Charles Paul Garofalo, "The Sons of Henry Grady: Atlanta Boosters in the 1920s," *Journal of Southern History* 42 (May 1976):187-204; Raymond Arsenault, "The End of the Long Hot Summer: The Air Conditioner and Southern Culture," *Journal of Southern History* 50 (Nov. 1984):597-628. These and other accounts enrich the available sources for study of the urban South.

Many contemporary materials proved helpful in conceptualizing the rise of the urban South. These include a number of useful articles in *DeBow's Review:* William M. Burwell, "Virginia Commercial Convention," vol. 12 (Jan. 1853):30; J.D.B. DeBow, "Contests for the Trade of the Mississippi Valley," vol. 3 (Feb. 1847):98; Jesup W. Scott, "The Great West," vol. 15 (July 1853):51-3; "The Mouths of the Mississippi," vol. 17 (July 1854):15-25; "Competition of the Gulf and Atlantic Ports," vol. 24 (Jan. 1858):47-8; "The Banks and Insurance Companies of New Orleans," vol. 25 (Nov.

1858):561; George Fitzhugh, "Washington City and Its Characteristics," vol. 24 (June 1858):502-3; J. Childs, "Railroad Progress and the Mobile and Ohio Road," vol. 12 (Feb. 1852):203-4. See also "The Natural Laws of Commerce," *Western Journal* 1 (April 1848):137-77; "A System of Internal Improvement for the West," *Western Journal* 2 (Jan. 1849):1-8; "Mississippi Valley Railroad," *Western Journal and Civilian* 9 (Nov. 1852):14; "Commercial Delusions-Speculations," *American Review* 71 (Oct. 1845):341-57; Hinton Rowan Helper, *The Impending Crisis of the South: How to Meet It* (New York, 1857); Albion Winegard Tourgée, *A Fool's Errand* (New York, 1880); "First Report of the Committee on Public Hygiene of the American Medical Association," *Transactions of the American Medical Association*, vol. 2 (Philadelphia, 1849); M.B. Hillyard, *The New South: A Description of the Southern States: Noting Each State Separately, and Giving Their Distinctive Features and Most Salient Characteristics* (Baltimore, 1887); James Bryce, *The American Commonwealth* (New York, 1888); Edward King, *The Great South*, edited by W. Magruder Drake and Robert R. Jones (1879; repr. Baton Rouge, 1972); *Report of Israel D. Andrews on the Trade and Commerce of the British North American Colonies, and Upon the Trade of the Great Lakes and Rivers*, Senate Executive Document 112, 32d Cong., 1st sess., Serial 622 (Washington, D.C., 1854); Henry Grady, *The New South* (New York, 1890).

Many more documents deal with the rich urban experience in the South. The material cited above should be considered only a starting point for further investigation.

INDEX